TASCHEN
est. 1980

Japanese Prints

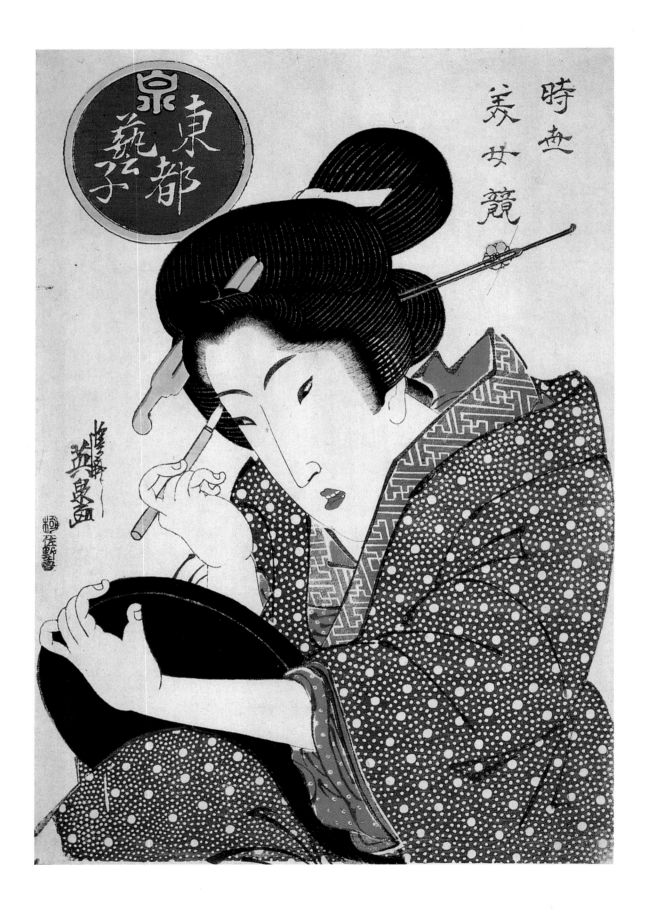

JAPANESE PRINTS

edited by
Gabriele Fahr-Becker

TASCHEN

HONG KONG KÖLN LONDON LOS ANGELES MADRID PARIS TOKYO

ILLUSTRATION PAGE 2:
Keisai Eisen
Contest of Beauties:
A Geisha from the Eastern Capital
Oban 37.2 x 25.6
Nishiki-e
Published by Sanoya Kihei
mid Bunsei era (1818–1830)
(for commentary, see p. 144)

To stay informed about upcoming TASCHEN titles, please request our magazine at
www.taschen.com/magazine or write to TASCHEN America, 6671 Sunset Boulevard,
Suite 1508, USA-Los Angeles, CA 90028, contact-us@taschen.com, Fax: +1-323-
463.4442. We will be happy to send you a free copy of our magazine which is filled with
information about all of our books.

© 2007 TASCHEN GmbH
Hohenzollernring 53, D–50672 Köln
www.taschen.com
and Gabriele Fahr-Becker, Munich

Original edition: © 1994 Benedikt Taschen Verlag GmbH
© Illustrations: Riccar Art Museum, Tokyo
Picture commentaries: Mitsunobu Satō, Yoshino
Moriyama, Hideko Yamaguchi, Yuriko Iwakiri
English translation: Michael Scuffil, Leverkusen
Artists' biographies: Ingo F. Walther, Alling
Cover design: Sense/Net, Andy Disl and Birgit Reber, Cologne

Printed in South Korea
ISBN 978-3-8228-3509-8

Contents

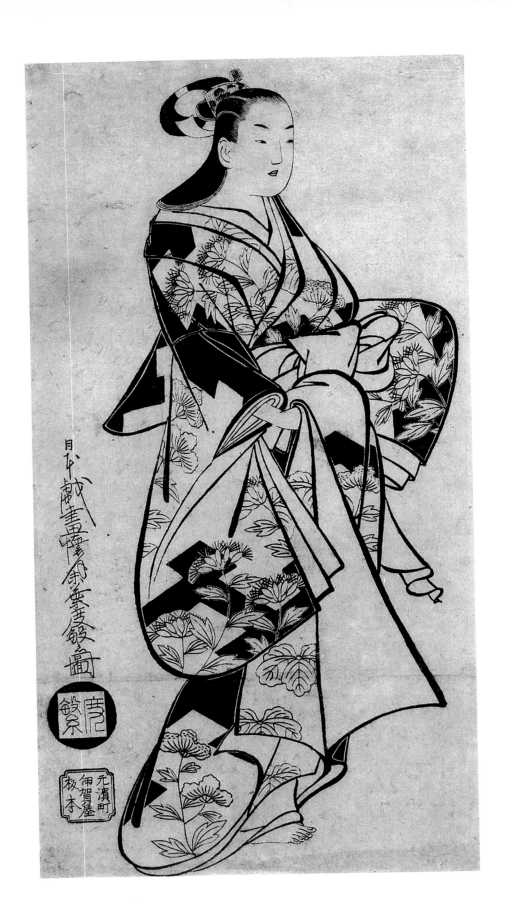

Kaigetsudō Dohan
Standing Woman★
Oōban 56.3 x 29.6
Sumizuri-hissai
Published by Igaya Kanbei
Shōtoku era (1711–16) – Kyōhō era (1716–36)

Ukiyo-e
Origins and History

The first *ukiyo-e* [1] appeared in 17th-century Japan in Edo, present-day Tokyo, in which, as the largest city of its day, a bourgeois culture of considerable originality had emerged. These pictures depict in vivid fashion the pleasurable side of life at that period, and for this reason they are known as *ukiyo-e*, "pictures of the floating world".

They are in most cases woodblock prints, in other words pictures produced by craftsmen from woodcuts on the basis of originals painted by artists. Woodblock prints are inexpensive, and can thus be reproduced in large quantities. In order to appeal to the largest possible number of buyers, these prints depicted a very broad variety of motifs: scenes from the everyday life of Edo, different views of famous places, historical pictures, landscapes, pictures of animals and flowers at different seasons of the year or times of the day, erotic pictures — no subject was left uncovered. There was a particularly heavy demand for scenes of brothels and theatres, where the people of Edo would seek pleasure and distraction. Such pictures of courtesans, *geishas* and tea-house waitresses formed a category of *ukiyo-e* in their own right, and were generically termed *bijin-ga* ("pictures of beautiful women"). Also in great demand were the *yakusha-e*, pictures of actors in popular *kabuki* roles.

In order to be able to answer the question of when and how these specifically Japanese *ukiyo-e* "pictures of the floating world" appeared, one must first go back to the landscape paintings which originated at the start of the Japanese Middle Ages during the "Period of the Warring Provinces".

The "Period of the Warring Provinces" had begun with the Onin War (1466–1467). This was followed by a series of civil wars in which the city of Kyoto, which had blossomed during its long period as capital, was destroyed, along with the social order in the whole country. During the 16th century, a historically new order, ushering in the Early Modern Age in Japan, was created by the two unifiers of the country, Oda Nobunaga (1534–1582) and Toyotomi Hideyoshi (1536–1598). In art history, this period, during which power was exercised first by Nobunaga and then by Hideyoshi, is known as the Momoyama period.

In accordance with the spirit of the *bushi*, or warriors, who had gained one victory after another over the rival local lords, the art of this period was shaped by the notion of a robust warrior culture with its overtones of masculinity. The castles they erected and the paintings with which they decorated them bear witness to this warrior culture. In the 16th century, simple hilltop castles were superseded by castles on the plains designed to manifest the power of their masters. Turreted castles of many storeys were put up, from which the *jōkamachi* ("town under the castle") could be kept under surveillance. Their interiors were decorated with sumptuous paintings of flowers and birds with magnificent golden colours, reflecting the authority of the lord. Nobunaga's

[1] italicized expressions are explained in the "Glossary of Technical Terms" on pages 191–194

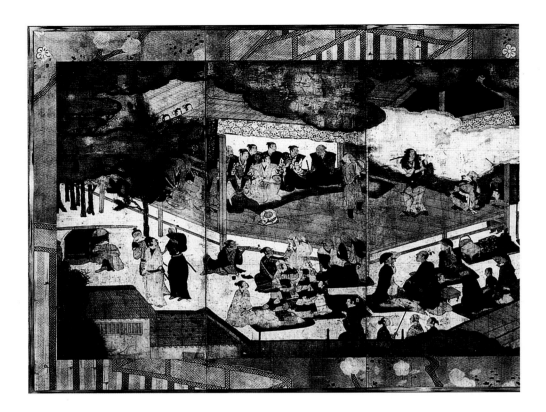

Ill. 1
Screen depicting Okuni *Kabuki*.
National Museum, Kyoto

Azuchi Castle is reputed to have been the most splendid of all. It was burnt down in the year Tenshō 10 (1582) during the rebellion led by General Akechi Mitsuhide. This castle was home to the lavish gold paintings by Kanō Eitoku (1543–1590) and his pupils. Few of the works of this most prestigious master of the Momoyama period, who served both Nobunaga and Hideyoshi, are still extant. One of his masterpieces, a screen with large lions, is today in the Imperial Palace collection. It is two metres tall by four broad, and depicts two gigantic lions strolling majestically around. It was with such imposing pictures that the rulers of the time wished to demonstrate their power over their subjects.

For the rest, the magnificence of the Momoyama style comes across in the florescence of its landscape paintings, which make up their own category within the genre of *yamato-e.*. They depict pleasure trips to the immediate surroundings and show predominantly scenes from the lives of ordinary people, documenting their changing lives and lifestyles over the years.

This period, during which the lords were busy proclaiming their own *de facto* power in this peaceably pompous manner, also allowed the middle classes certain freedoms, within the framework of which they were able to develop fashions and pleasures of their own. Kyoto, the capital, which had been rebuilt by the citizens after the turmoil of the wars, raised its Gion quarter once more to a centre of bustling life, illustrated in Kanō Eitoku's "Views of Kyoto and its Surroundings". These pictures portray vividly and in some detail the everyday lives of the people and give us an overview of the life of the city and of the famous places in the vicinity, including the seasonal festivals, the pleasures and the everyday doings of the inhabitants. These are all motifs which were later to reappear in the *ukiyo-e*. However, these pictures were still being commissioned by the powerful, who were enabled as a result to inform themselves about the lives of the town-dwellers. Indeed, that was their purpose: the pictures were instruments of surveillance.

Eitoku's "Views of Kyoto and its Surroundings" stimulated new developments in landscape painting. Attention now focussed upon individual aspects of everyday city life: pictures of entertainments, of festivals, of *kabuki* performances, of brothels etc. Painters taking their commissions from the ruling class followed the style of the Kanō school, depicting their motifs from above, in a bird's eye perspective. However, there were other painters from an urban background who compromised with other styles of painting, producing numerous works depicting urban scenes and views. The Kanō school had interested itself primarily in landscape painting, but its expressivity was limited to the extent that these painters took their commissions – and hence their prescribed motifs – from the ruling class, and thus did not portray things from the point of view of the bourgeoisie. As a result, the urban painters increasingly turned their attention to the life of the streets and the inhabitants of the towns and cities. Although the age was glorified as one in which a new social order had been inaugurated, in the patriarchal hierarchy which characterized the next two centuries a firm distinction continued to be made between rulers and ruled. Since the middle classes wanted to liberate themselves from this system, they demanded a place where they could be themselves, away from the everyday pressures of feudal life, where rulers and ruled were kept strictly apart. These places may have been little short of dens, but they reflected the innermost desires of the urban population. Later they were to crystallize as the most important motifs of *ukiyo-e*. The Shijōgawara and Rokujōmisujimachi districts of Kyoto developed during this period into centres of *kabuki* and prostitution.

It was the year Keichō 8 (1603) which saw the rise to fashion of *kabuki*, the "song-dance-art" founded by Izumo no Okuni. It arose from a desire to entertain the souls of those who had been killed during the late wars with dances in which all could take part. Gradually, however, it developed into an art form, in which performers were separate from spectators.

Ill. 1 depicts "Okuni kabukizu byōbu", in which Okuni, dressed in male attire, appears as a dancer in the centre of the stage, a sword over her shoulder, playing the role of the "*kabuki*-mono". She thus caricatures the men who could be seen going along the streets of the city in this comical manner. It was the fashion at the time to go from tea-house to tea-house with street-musicians and actors and act out this scene of the "*kabuki*-mono". In this way the dances came to enjoy such great popularity that prostitutes also started setting up stages in their brothels, where they performed the "*kabuki*-mono" to the musical accompaniment of a *shamisen*. In the course of time, the dances became increasingly lively. From them there emerged a particular courtesan's dance whose express purpose was to attract clients; this, however, was regarded as a violation of the principles of good conduct, and led to a ban on the performance of *kabuki* dance by prostitutes. At the same time, teenage actors were also forbidden to perform *kabuki* drama. Performances were restricted to men whose shaven foreheads were the sign that they had reached manhood.

Ill. 2
Screen depicting fan dance

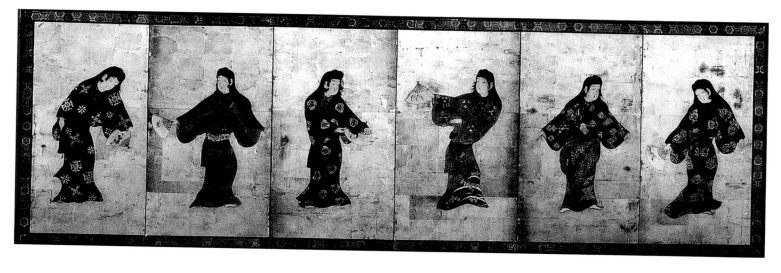

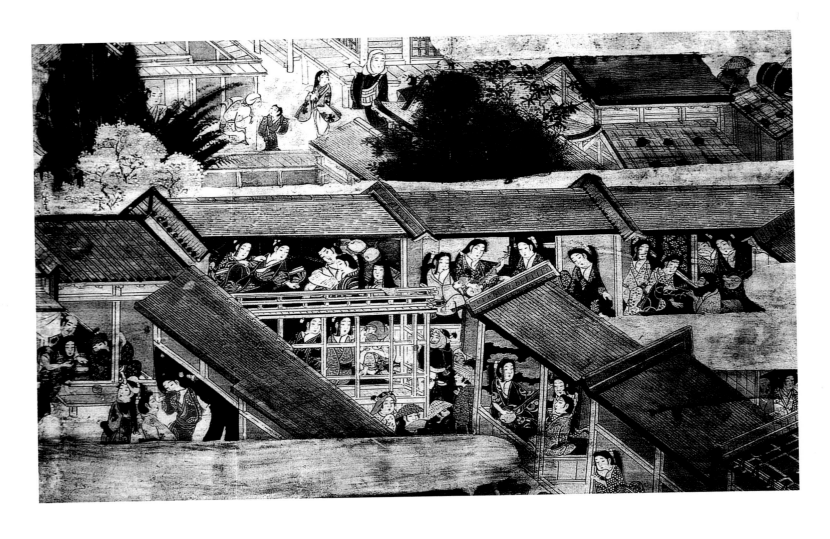

Ill. 3
Screen of "Views of Famous Places in Edo"
(left-hand section, detail)
Idemitsu Museum of Arts, Tokyo

Once the liberal theatre, with its dances, songs and musical performances by prostitutes and male *geishas*, had been put under strict control, *kabuki* changed to become a portrayal of actual situations. Looking at pictures of *kabuki* scenes in the following years, there is a clear trend away from depictions of lively Shijōgawara street scenes. Instead, artists increasingly focus their interest on the people inside and outside the theatres, and on the stage on which the drama is unfolding in all its magnificence.

The pleasure quarter, where the *kabuki* underwent its development at the hands of the prostitutes, was transferred from Nijōyanagimachi to Rokujōmisu-jimachi, where it continued with undiminished vigour. Whereas Eitoku's "Views of Kyoto and its Surroundings" depicted relationships between pros-titutes and clients, interest gradually shifted to scenes within the pleasure quarter. More and more pictures were painted of the entertainments offered in the rooms of the brothels, depicting *maiko* against a simple golden background, attending to the entertainment of the guests (Ill. 2). Finally, individual portrayals of stand-ing prostitutes also appeared. In general, portrayals of the beauties of the Kanbun era (1661–1673) are referred to as "Kanbun bijin zu". These include, however, not only representations of courtesans in portrait format, but also pictures of actors. In the succeeding period, these gave rise to the independent genres known as *bijin-ga* and *yakusha-e*.

Depictions of general street scenes thus developed into interior views of theatres and brothels, until these eventually came to be restricted to portraits of individuals. It was no longer very far to the motifs of the *ukiyo-e*. The works produced in Kyoto and Osaka, however, were still reserved for the eyes of the well-to-do. This was slowly to change with the advent of the Tokugawa period.

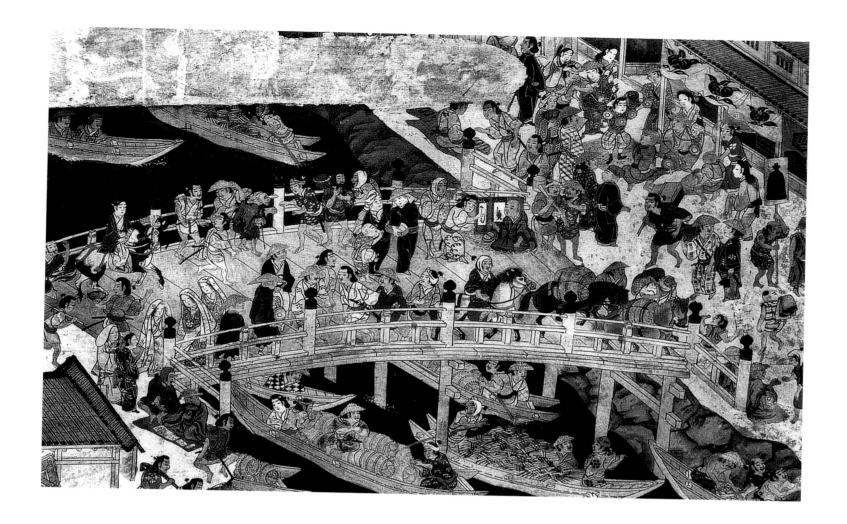

Hideyoshi was succeeded as ruler by Tokugawa Ieyasu (1542–1616). The year Keichō 8 (1603) saw the establishment of the shogunate in Edo, and with it the transfer of the country's policital centre from the Kyoto/Osaka region to the east coast. Measures to build up the city quickly followed: in the centre, Edo Castle was erected, while land was reclaimed in the Tsukiji area, which saw the establishment of residences for *daimyō* and *bushi*, as well as temples and housing developments. This construction boom attracted numerous craftsmen to Edo both from the immediate surroundings and indeed from the whole country. They in turn were followed by an influx of merchants to supply their needs. There was a rapid increase in population, but it was a purely male society. The residential districts were occupied first of all by the craftsmen and artisans. Here there grew up – in contrast to those districts where the *daimyō* lived – a non-aristocratic society. The atmosphere in these new residential districts was perhaps somewhat coarse, but it was informal, cheerful and full of life. It is an atmosphere clearly reflected in the *ukiyo-e*, to which we are about to turn.

A screen entitled "Views of Famous Places in Edo" depicts the life of that city in the first half of the Kan'ei period (1624–1644). The right-hand side of this eight-section screen consists of views of various well-known sights: Sensōji and Kaneiji temples, Kandamyōjin and Motoyoshiwara shrines (ill. 3) and Nihonbashi (ill. 4). To the left can be seen Edo Castle, Kyōbashi, Shinbashi, Atagoyama, Shibazōjōji temple and Shibaura. This picture does not take the bird's eye view of "Views of Kyoto and its Surroundings", however, but is painted from a lower standpoint, thus giving the beholder a feeling of nearness to the people of Edo.

As the city of Edo had been newly built, it had no culture of its own; for its cultural life it was indebted to the region around Kyoto and Osaka. In the year

Ill. 4
Screen of "Views of Famous Places in Edo"
(left-hand section, detail)
Idemitsu Museum of Arts, Tokyo

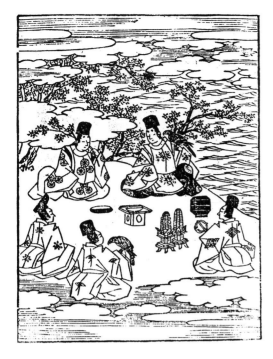

Ill. 5
Ise monogatari

Meireki 3 (1657), Edo Castle was razed to the ground in a fire which also consumed the residences of the *daimyō* and the *bushi* and the houses of the local population. The virtually new city was almost entirely destroyed, along with much of the cultural heritage from the Kyoto/Osaka region. As a result, bourgeois culture had a unique chance to develop anew.

The ground was thus prepared for the birth of *ukiyo-e*. The woodblock print arose as the new form of expression of bourgeois art, whose technique made it possible to produce large editions at an affordable price.

The technique of woodblock printing had already been in use in Japan before the Edo period. It initially served chiefly religions (Bhuddist) ends; in the Kyoto/Osaka region, for example, Buddhist sutras and representations of Buddhist deities were reproduced on paper in this way. In the 16th century, the technique was further developed with the publication of Chinese texts and books. The greatest advantage of woodblock printing was that it enabled pictures to be reproduced in large numbers.

The most important work of this kind was "Ise monogatari", a book in which the luxurious amusements of the aristocracy were depicted in gratifying detail (ill. 5). This is the best-preserved work of the period, dating from the year Keichō 13 (1608), and represents a valuable piece of evidence on the origin of the woodblock printing technique.

The technique of book-printing was also brought to Edo from its original home in Kyoto and Osaka. The new capital saw a gradually increasing demand for books, which were not however delivered to Edo as finished products, but rather printed there from plates produced in Osaka. It was not long before the plates, too, began to be manufactured in Edo.

It was during this period that Tsuruya, Masuya, Yamagataya and Urokogataya – book wholesalers from Kyoto and Osaka – set up branches in Edo's commercial districts of Odenmachō and Aburachō, where they gave employment to the draughtsmen, woodblock cutters and printers already settled there. The woodblocks of the period were being produced by little-known artists, and were used to illustrate simple books intended for entertainment or as teaching materials. At first the ink pictures were coloured in yellow, green or vermilion. Over the course of time, the orginial motifs gradually evolved into an individual, informal style of painting, which in turn led to the emergence of a specific artistic style for the illustration of books.

The increase in the output of illustrated literature was fed by numbers of books on customs and festivals illustrated by artists of some renown. There was a particularly heavy demand for pictures of the red-light district of Yoshiwara and of the world of the theatre. Urokogataya, the first bookseller to settle in Edo, led the way by publishing two books, "Yoshiwaramakura" and "Yoshiwaraka-gami", with erotic illustrations [Manji 3 (1660)]. Among the books on the theatre were "Haginooi", published by Masuya in the year Kanbun 2 (1662) and "Tsurezuregusa", published by Urokogataya in Kanbun 11 (1671). Yoshiwara's courtesans and *kabuki* actors were the subject of published critiques, while pictures of high-class prostitutes and their clients appeared in so-called *ehon* ("picture books").

At first these books were unsigned, but the quality of their woodblock prints was of a high order. It may therefore be assumed that the artists involved included Moronobu and Jihei, who went on to become masters of the art of woodblock illustration. The *ehon* found a ready market among the book-buying public of Edo, and they made a major contribution to the development of realistic portrayals and techniques in woodblock printing. The genre gave birth in the Enpō era (1673–1681) to a particular type of individual picture, from which the *ukiyo-e* developed.

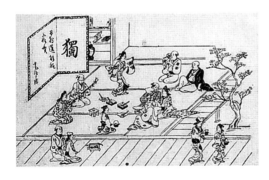

Ill. 6
Hishikawa Moronobu: People from Yoshiwara: Young Pair of Lovers
Riccar Art Museum, Tokyo

The Beginnings of Ukiyo-e

Hishikawa Moronobu (1618 or 1625–1694) is regarded as the inaugurator of *ukiyo-e*. He came from a family of embroiderers in Awanokuni Yasudamura (in the present-day prefecture of Chiba), but moved to Edo, where book-printing was just becoming established. He learnt painting in the Kanō and Tosa schools, but went on to develop a style of his own. He cut his own woodblocks of scenes from the pleasure districts and of the courtesans, and gave free rein to his brush when depicting the everyday life of Edo. Moronobu thereby established a specifically Edo style of painting, which he called *yamato-ukiyo-e*. Moronobu and his pupils Morofusa and Moroshige were active from the Enpō era (1673–1681) to the Genroku era (1688–1704). At this time the technique of woodblook printing was still relatively unsophisticated; the resulting prints, called *sumizuri-e*, were monochrome, and had to be coloured in by hand as required. Despite their simple, unpolished, even coarse impression, they provide a vivid reflection of the everyday life of the middle classes in Edo as the city was taking shape.

In the year Genna 3 (1617), the Yoshiwara pleasure quarter was established in Nihonbashi-Fukiyamachi in the centre of Edo. Considerations of public morality led, however, to a decree ordering its transfer to Asakusa in the year Manji 2 (1659). To distinguish it from the old, the new district in Asakusa was called Shin-Yoshiwara (New Yoshiwara). Almost all *ukiyo-e* depict the life of this new quarter. As a guide to the "red light district" of Yoshiwara, Moronobu produced the twelve-part series "Yoshiwara no karada". Ill. 6 shows one of the scenes; this is a monochrome *sumizuri-e*, showing in detail the entertainments available in the brothels. The series thus offers an important historical insight into life in Yoshiwara. Furthermore, it includes Moronobu's best works. As he was working on the model of the *ehon*, most of his works took the form of twelve-part series. While conceived as a set, each picture can be viewed in its own right as an individual work. It was only in later years that individual prints became more common; Jihei, a contemporary of Moronobu, is generally seen as the father of the single print.

The Kaigetsudō school also chose the life of the courtesans and their sumptuous costumes in the officially approved pleasure quarter of Yoshiwara as the themes of their work. The school was founded by Kaigetsudō Yasunori (dates unknown); its painters did not at first produce pictures for reproduction, but they did paint numerous pictures with the same motifs, in order to be able to sell them in large numbers. Kaigetsudō's pupils Yasutomo, Norishige and Noritatsu produced pictures of attractive courtesans in almost identical standing poses. At first these were almost exclusively brush-and-ink drawings; towards the end of the Genroku era, however, in order to liven up the monochrome monotony of the final print, they began to colour them in with green, yellow and vermilion. The invention of these *tan-e* represented a further step forward in the gradual advance of colour.

Against the background of life in the expanding city of Edo, the *kabuki* of the Genroku era saw the appearance of the specific role of the *aragoto* as the antithesis of the elegant courtly culture of Kyoto. The *aragoto*, a lead player bursting with energy, was in tune with the effervescent spirit of the population of Edo, and soon came to enjoy great popularity. The "Kabukizu byōbu" (ill. 9) is attributed to Moronobu's studio; on the curtain are written the words "Nakamura Kanzaburō during a performance of a *kyōgen*", thus indicating a scene in the Nakamura theatre. Along with the Ichimura and Morita theatres, the Nakamura-*za* was one of the three officially licensed playhouses in Edo, and it was also the oldest. A comparison with "Okuni kabukizu byōbu" (ill. 1) shows how stage design had developed over the years.

The Torii school, centring on Torii Kiyonobu (1664–1729), formed close links with Edo's *kabuki* theatres. The members of the school painted not only posters

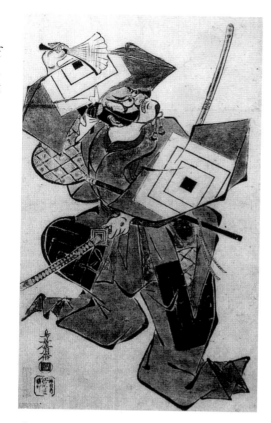

Ill. 7
Torii Kiyomasu: Shibaraku ("halt!") pose, adopted by Ichikawa Danjūrō I
Riccar Art Museum, Tokyo

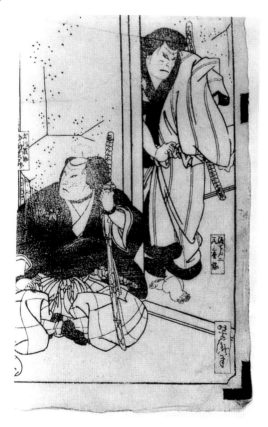

Ill. 8
Register marks (*Kentō*)

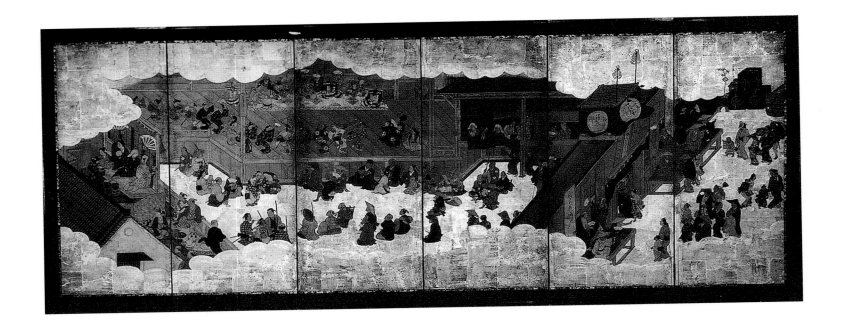

Ill. 9
Screen showing *kabuki* scene
Suntory Museum of Art, Tokyo

and programmes, but also portraits of individual actors on stage. In the succeeding period, the development of *ukiyo-e* ran parallel with that of *kabuki*. In the case of theatre posters, in particular, a new style of painting was developed, emphasizing the role of the *aragoto* with his bulging muscles. The screen reproduced in ill. 10 depicts Ichikawa Danjūrō, the creator of the *aragoto* role. The atmosphere of the Edo *kabuki* at this period comes across very clearly. In accordance with the tastes and inclinations of the citizens, a contemporary of Danjūrō's by the name of Torii Kiyomasu (dates unknown) developed a style of his own under the label of "*yakusha*-e no Torii" ("Torii of the actor-portraits", ill. 7) and introduced it as an independent genre.

As though to break the monopoly of *yakusha* portraiture, Okumura Masanobu (1686—1764), who had had the advantage of training in the Hishikawa and Torii schools, introduced a new stylistic trend. In addition, he managed a bookshop named "Akabyōtan". On the basis of his experience of both sides of the business, he made a valuable contribution to both the qualitative and quantitative development of *ukiyo-e*. It was he who was responsible for the extension of the particular character of the *yakusha-e* to the *bijin-ga*, or pictures of beautiful women. As models he used not just courtesans, but bourgeois women too. The more elegant the ladies became, the more he adapted his technique. Instead of vermilion, he made increasing use of crimson *(beni)*, in some cases mixed with indigo and yellow. Thus arose the *beni-e*. Masanobu was also the originator of the *urushi-e*, or lacquer picture, in which the ink was mixed with bone-glue, which produced a shimmering effect in the costumes of the actors thus depicted. If copper-dust was sprinkled on it, then the picture took on a golden sheen. Masanobu also experimented with very hard paper, in order to be able to hang individual figures as "post pictures" *(hashira-e)*, and in addition he introduced a further innovation by arranging three pictures in the *hosoban* format. His new ideas very soon made him popular. One of his pupils, Toshinobu, was active during his master's *urushi-e* period, and went on to surpass him in elegance and colourful expressivity.

Masanobu's *uki-e* of the interiors of theatres and other rooms are mostly symmetrical in their construction, which also creates a sense of spatial depth. He thus made an early, if imperfect, attempt to absorb Western art, and thereby prepared the ground for the adoption of linear perspective by the landscape painters of a later period. Alongside Masanobu's output, works by Nishimura Shigenaga and Torii Kiyotada (ill. 11) have also been preserved.

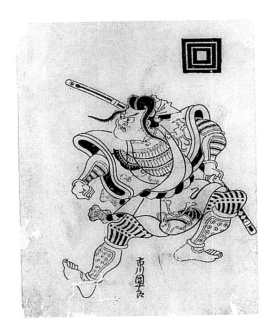

Ill. 10
Torii Kiyonobu: Elegant four-section screen depicting Ichikawa Danjūrō II
Riccar Art Museum, Tokyo

Under the influence of polychromatic printing from China, a new technique developed in the Enkyō era (1744–1748). After being printed in black-and-white, the sheet was printed once more in a second colour, usually red or green. As crimson was most commonly employed, this technique came to be known as *benizuri-e*. In order to ensure precise alignment of the two printings, it was necessary to introduce *kentō* or register marks; these marks were made in the corners of the plate and indicated the angle at which the paper was to be laid against it. Mostly these register marks left an impression on the paper, visible at the edge of the print (ill. 8). The *benizuri-e* technique made it possible to produce prints in splendid colour, a major advance in the development of *ukiyo-e*. Simple as it was, it endured through the Hōreki era (1751–1764) to the start of the Meiwa era (1764–1772).

The *bijin-ga* produced using the *benizuri-e* technique by Ishikawa Toyonobu (1711–1785) were in a style of his own. His female figures have supple faces and bodies (ill. 12); it was with him that *bijin-ga* achieved the status of an independent genre, exercising an enormous influence on subsequent artists. Coloration came to be increasingly differentiated. "Since I have not spent my whole life hanging around the pleasure districts, I was able to depict conditions there very well," we are told in the book "Ukiyo-e ruikō". Torii Kiyomitsu (1735–1785) was one of the third generation of the Torii school. He and Toyonobu mark the end of the initial period of *ukiyo-e*. Kiyomitsu left numerous masterpieces in the *benizuri* style, but he liberated himself from the robust images of the Torii school, introducing a much more delicate and refined technique. His pupils Kiyoshige, Kiyotsune and Kiyohiro also painted predominantly *yakusha-e*.

Ill. 11
Torii Kiyotada: *Uki-e*, theatre scene
Riccar Art Museum, Tokyo

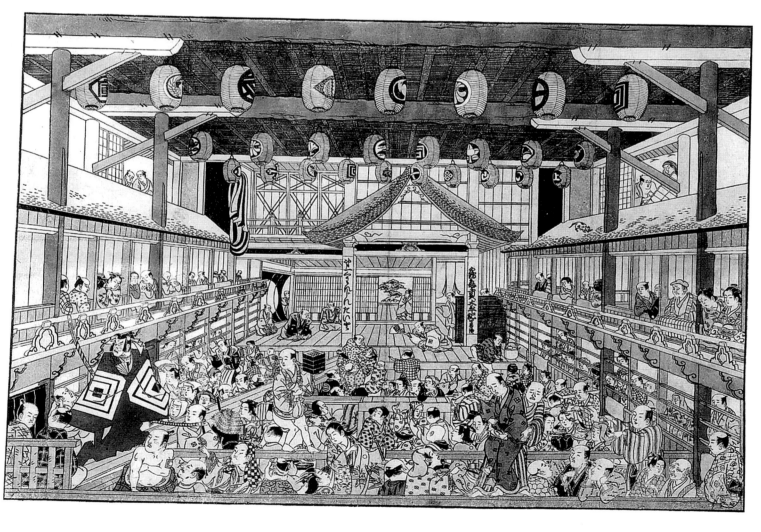

The Development of Nishiki-e

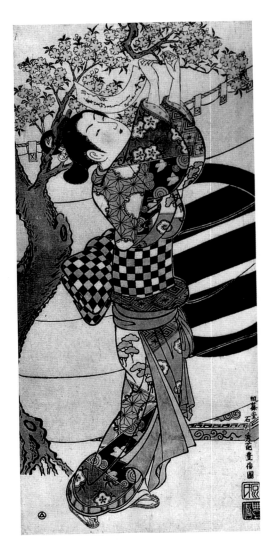

Ill. 12
Ishikawa Toyonobu: Beauty beneath Flowers
Riccar Art Museum, Tokyo

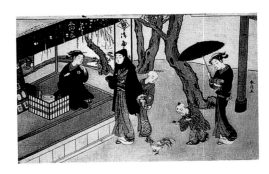

Ill. 13
Suzuki Harunobu: Yanagiya Ofuji
Riccar Art Museum, Tokyo

The beginnings of the monochrome ink picture (sumi-e) now lay about 100 years in the past. The intervening period had witnessed the development of polychrome woodblock prints. The year Meiwa 1 (1764) saw the adoption by the affluent *bushi* and burghers of Edo of a fashion by which a new calendar picture was displayed each month. These pictures were exchanged one for another, thus broadening the market for extravagant woodblock prints considerably. The initiators of the fashion were a *bushi*, Okubo Jishirō Tadanobu, who had adopted the literary pseudonym of Kyogawa, and Abe Hachinojō Masahiro, whose pseudonym was Sakei. Not only were they connoisseurs of woodblock prints, they also encouraged co-operation between famous painters and woodblock cutters and printers, in order to ensure a source of the finest possible prints for their collections. One result of this patronage of art and craft was the appearance of the *nishiki-e*, in which a number of colours were freely combined.

Among those who produced and exchanged these calendar pictures was Suzuki Harunobu (1725–1770), who thereby made a major contribution to the development of *nishiki-e*. He is said to have been a pupil of Nishimura Shigenaga, but he was also heavily influenced by Nishikawa Sukenobu – who came from the Osaka/Kyoto region – as well as by the Chinese painter Kyūei. With great imaginative flair, he transposed classical novels into a modern setting, illustrating them with colourful pictures of elegant beauties. These novels enjoyed a very broad readership (ill. 14). Harunobu is also well-known through his portrayal of bourgeois beauties in the *nishiki-e* style. Typical are his Osen of the Teashop in front of the Kasamori Inari Shrine, and his Ofuji of the Haberdashery in front of the Temple of Asakusa Kannon (ill. 13). In view of his high reputation, his style was widely imitated. The works of Suzuki Harushige (1747–1818), in particular, are virtually only distinguishable from those of Harunobu by their signatures. Harushige later assumed the name of Shiba Kōkan, and adapted European painting for the Japanese market.

Isoda Koryūsai (*fl. c.* 1765–1788), a contemporary of Harunobu's, adhered at the start of his career, under the name of Haruhiro, closely to the style of Harunobu. However, from the beginning of the An'ei era (1772–1781), he developed his own form of expression, based on sensuous and realistic pictures of beautiful women. His most important works include the series "Hinagata wakana no hatsumoyō", pictures of courtesans dressed in the latest fashion (pp. 74 and 75). The series has gone down in the history of woodblock printing as the first from which more than 100 prints were made from each block. In addition, by incorporating not just one figure but several, cleverly arranged in a confined space, Koryūsai continued and developed the *hashira-e* style initiated by Masanobu (ill. 16).

A further development of *nishiki-e* made it possible to use several blocks and to apply different colours, thus enabling artists to achieve ever more realistic images. *Yakusha-e* grew more and more popular, as many of the actors' followers showed ever-increasing interest in acquiring portraits of their idols. Especially popular were the works of Ippitsusai Bunchō (*fl. c.* 1764–1790) and Katsukawa Shunshō (1726–1792). The masterpieces of both in the actor-portrait genre appeared in book form under the title "Ehon butai ōgi" [Meiwa 7 (1770)]. Bunchō was another of those influenced by Harunobu, and many of his works testify to his acuity of observation and delicacy of touch. Shunshō did not hold with the stereotype *yakusha-e* of the Torii school, and for his part portrayed the actors as they appeared during stage performances, thus capturing their characteristic poses. This style of representation appealed very much to the public, so that from now on, actors were only depicted in portrait form. Shunshō's pupils Shunkō (1743–1812), Shūn'ei (1762–1819), Shunchō (*fl. c.* 1780–1795) and Shunrō (1760–1849, later to achieve fame under the name of Hokusai) were the leading representatives of the Katsukawa school.

The *nishiki-e* technique enormously extended the scope of carving and printing, resulting in the development of a very much finer and more detailed manner of composition.

The Golden Age of Ukiyo-e

It was during the Genroku era (1688–1704) that Edo's home-grown culture enjoyed its first flowering, and in the Tenmei era (1781–1789) that it experienced its second. It was during this time that an independent bourgeois culture took shape, in which both the theatre and the pleasure-houses flourished. The people of Edo led a free and easy life. Great value was attached to entertainments of all kinds, for example excursions to the surrounding countryside as appropriate to the season. The middle classes came to enjoy a moderate affluence, and for the *ukiyo-e*, too, it was the dawn of a golden age.

There were by now an increasing number of print artists. The first of this new era was Kitao Shigemasa (1739–1820), who had concentrated in particular upon book illustrations since the An'ei era, but had also painted *bijin-ga*. His preference, however, was not for the delicate ladies of Harunobu or Bunchō, but for rather more stately figures (ill. 15). His pupils were highly talented: Masanobu (1761–1816), for example, later wrote books under the name of Santō Kyōden. Masayoshi (1764–1824) also changed his name, and as the court painter Sukigata Keisai bequeathed many works from this period.

A list of masters of the Tenmei era would not be complete without Torii Kiyonaga (1752–1815), one of the fourth generation of the Torii school of *yakusha-e*, though he was in fact better known for his *bijin-ga*. His delicate brush-strokes and clear coloration when depicting his well-proportioned, healthy-looking women earned him the highest praise. One of his masterpieces is entitled "Okawabata Yūsuzumi" (ill. 17): it is a perfect example of the precision which he had acquired during his apprenticeship as an illustrator. Against the background of the Sumidagawa river, three women are depicted, one wearing the broad apron of a tea-shop waitress. The finely-patterned kimonos suit them well; the garments are Kiyonaga's way of underlining the beauty of the women themselves. In order to achieve a maximum of naturalness, Kiyonaga would extend his compositions to two or three sheets. In this picture, all three figures are looking in the same direction; to the right, therefore, another picture was intended. The views of Edo which form the background to his *bijin-ga* are typical of his landscape style. He can be considered in this regard as the precursor of Hokusai and Hiroshige. Shunchō and Toshimitsu (1757–1820) imitated the style of Kiyonaga, and themselves left a number of *bijin-ga* masterpieces.

The Kansei era (1789–1801), which followed the Tenmei, is regarded as the period when the art of woodblock printing reached its zenith. It witnessed the creation by Kitagawa Utamaro (1753–1806) of his masterpieces, mostly seated female figures. During the Tenmei era, Utamaro had met the publisher Tsutaya Jūzaburō, who had made his own debut with Toriyama Sekien. In his early days as an illustrator, Utamaro worked under the name of Kitagawa Toyoaki. Later he extended his activities to the production of *ukiyo-e*, and assumed the name of Utamaro. The way his *bijin-ga* were composed brought him rapid popularity: he made the faces of his models the focal point of his pictures *(okubi-e)*. No longer were the garments and the externals the most important feature, but rather the ideal beauty that lay concealed within his sitters' inner being (ill. 18). The invention of the mica-dust print *(kira-e)* also goes back to Utamaro. At that time, Yoshiwara was the most popular and the most populous pleasure quarter in Edo, and not surprisingly, Utamaro used its courtesans as his models. But prostitutes

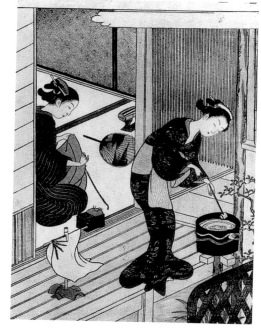

Ill. 14
Suzuki Harunobu: 8 Views:
Fluttering Cloth
Riccar Art Museum, Tokyo

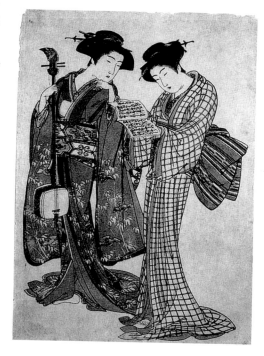

Ill. 15
Kitao Shigemasa: Geisha
Riccar Art Museum, Tokyo

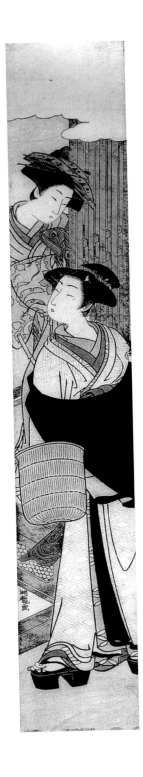

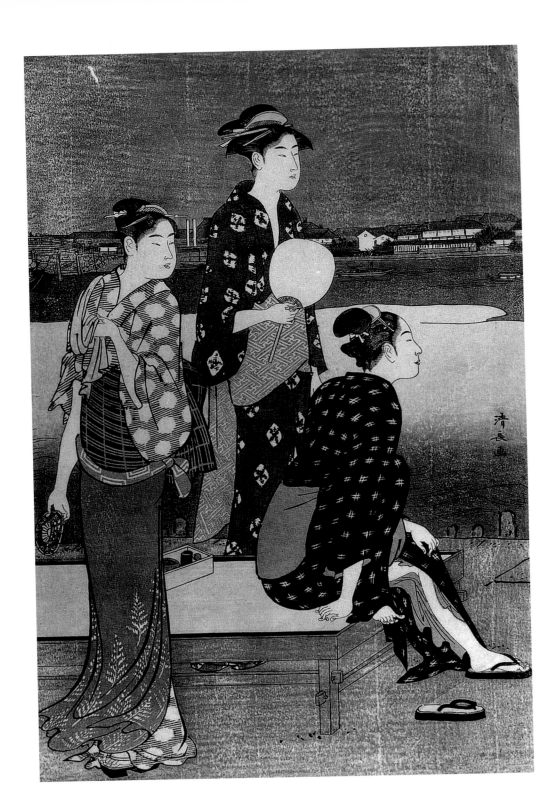

Ill. 16
Isoda Koryūsai: Wandering Priest
Riccar Art Museum, Tokyo

Ill. 17
Torii Kiyonaga: The Evening of the Star Festival
Riccar Art Museum, Tokyo

from unlicensed red light districts, as well as quite ordinary women, also figure in his woodblock prints. He was so popular that not only was he fêted as the master of *bijin-ga*, but the whole concept of *ukiyo-e* became synonymous with his name. His reputation attracted numerous artists, who attached themselves to him and became his pupils. The most important of these was Eishōsai Chōki (*fl. c.* 1780–after 1800). One man to rival Utamaro was Chōbunsai Eishi (1756–1829), who hailed from a *samurai* family. As the eldest son of one Tokiyuki, he was destined to assume responsibility as head of the family, but he preferred to become an artist, and renounced his birthright in favour of his next-of-kin. Eishi was influenced by Kiyonaga and Shunchō, and he drew inspiration from Utamaro too. His works display a peculiar elegance and nobility. His pupils Chōkōsai Eishō, Ichirakutei Eisui and Chōensai Eishin – whose dates are unknown – likewise produced primarily *bijin-ga*. The late period of Utamaro and his successors can justifiably be called the "golden age of *bijin-ga*".

It was at this time that Japanese artists first encountered Western painting. Utagawa Toyoharu (1735–1814) was the founder of the Utagawa school, whose creativity flowered towards the end of the Edo period. He is also noteworthy for his development of the *uki-e* form initiated by Masanobu and Shigenaga. Toyoharu introduced the linear perspective of Western painting into his Japanese landscapes, thus creating a new form of *uki-e*. In so doing, he gave a new impetus to *ukiyo-e* landscapes. At this time, Harushige changed his name to Shiba Kōkan, and together with his friend Hiraga Gennai developed a new technique: the copperplate engraving, which was much used for landscapes (ill. 19). The new technique also influenced the work of Hokusai and Hiroshige.

In concentrating upon the *bijin-ga* masters of the Kansei era such as Utamaro, we should not overlook another master, in this case of *yakusha-e*, Tōshūsai Sharaku. His creative period began in the year Kansei 6 (1794) and lasted only eleven months. In this short time, he produced the incredible number of 134 actor portraits, and 9 pictures of sūmo wrestlers. His *yakusha-e* mostly took the form of *ōkubi-e*, in other words, portraits of actors whose characteristic facial and personality features he gently exaggerated. Their artistic talents also come across well in these pictures. Sharaku's perspicuity is unmatched by any other master of *ukiyo-e* (ill. 20). Little is known of his life: he appeared from nowhere, and

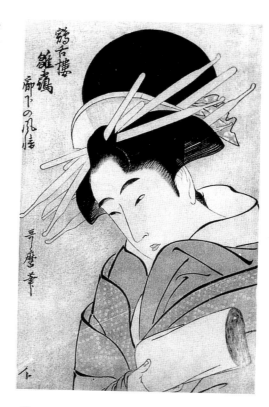

Ill. 18
Kitagawa Utamaro: Keizetsurō Hinazuru in the Corridor
Riccar Art Museum, Tokyo

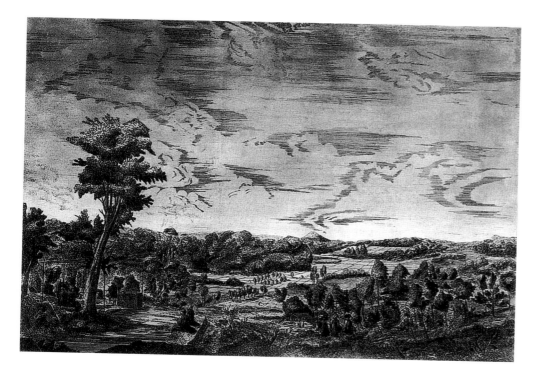

Ill. 19
Shiba Kōkan: Copperplate engraving
Riccar Art Museum, Tokyo

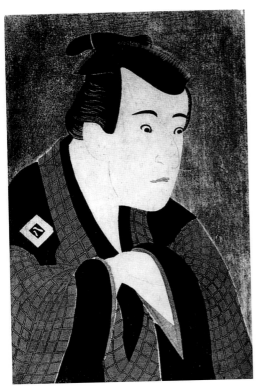

Ill. 20
Tōshūsai Sharaku: Ichikawa Yaozō III
as Tanabe Bunzō
Riccar Art Museum, Tokyo

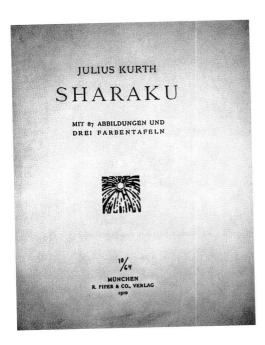

JULIUS KURTH

SHARAKU

MIT 87 ABBILDUNGEN UND
DREI FARBENTAFELN

10/64
MÜNCHEN
R. PIPER & CO. VERLAG
1910

Ill. 21
Julius Kurth: Sharaku

disappeared again soon after, but his great talent has assured him of an enduring reputation. Both in Japan and abroad, Sharaku's life and work became a topic of research in view of the desire to discover more about his life and career. The year 1910 saw the publication by the German scholar Julius Kurth of a book entitled simply "Sharaku" (ill. 21), which gave an impetus to further studies.

At the same time, Utagawa Toyokuni (1769–1825), a pupil of Toyoharu, was also active; indeed, he was so successful that his impact on *ukiyo-e* endured until the end of the Edo period. Actors from Kansei 6 (1794) onwards form the subject of his series "Yakusha butai no sugatae". His works were extremely popular, and he may be said to have been the leading exponent of actor–portraiture of his day. The people of Edo took his elegant lines, flowing style and clear coloration to their hearts, thereby determining the course to be taken by *yakusha-e* until the close of the Edo period. Toyokuni's book "Yakusha nigao hayageiko" (ill. 22), dating from Bunka 14 (1817), demonstrates the typical features and modern techniques of the Utagawa school. The people of Edo were extremely enthusiastic about his works, so it may be assumed that he captured the artistic taste of the contemporary bourgeoisie. Toyokuni did not confine himself to *yakusha-e*, however, but left many *bijin-ga* too. Many of his pupils were extremely talented, and the Utagawa school became the largest *ukiyo-e* school of the Bunka and Bunsei eras. Among its most important members were Kunimasa, Kunisada, Kuniyasu, Munimaru and Kuniyoshi.

Ukiyo-e towards the End of the Edo Period

The Tenmei and Kansei eras were the heyday of bourgeois culture; under the influence of the Kansei reforms, however, decay began to set in. The priority of the shogunate was how to react to the demands of foreign powers for the country to be opened up; in consequence, domestic politics were neglected. The arts, too, received no new impulses. They lost their naturalness. Exaggeration and caricature were all that people could now expect.

This is the background against which the work of the Utagawa school must be judged. Utagawa Kunisada (1786–1864), the most talented among them, produced numerous *yakusha-e*, such as the "Oatari kyōgen no uchi", along with scenes of everyday life. Of all *ukiyo-e* artists, he has left the largest number of *ukiyo-e*, depicting a wide variety of motifs. Under the name of Utagawa Toyokuni III, he became the leading figure in the Utagawa school, and from the Tenpō era onwards was the most important exponent of *ukiyo-e*.

Another tendency within the Utagawa school was initiated by Utagawa Kuniyoshi (1797–1861) with his warrior pictures (*musha-e*). At first he also produced *yakusha-e* and *bijin-ga*, but the major corpus of his œuvre consists of historical pictures. On account of his vivid depiction of heroes, he was known as "Musha-e no Kuniyoshi" (Kuniyoshi, the warrior painter). Among his published work was a series of pictures illustrating the novel "Suikoden" by Kyokutei Bakin, dating from the year Bunsei 8 (1825) (ill. 23), which achieved great popularity. The publisher, Kagaya Kichiemon, had been previously little known, but this series brought him instant celebrity. Kuniyoshi also painted landscapes and pictures of fishes in the Western style. For a master to be active across so broad a spectrum was very uncommon. He became extremely popular: his school continues to this day. Its leading representatives include Tsukioka Yoshitoshi, Mizuno Toshikata, Kaburagi Kiyokata and Itō Shinsui.

Towards the end of the Edo period, Kikukawa Eizan (1787–1867) and Keisai Eisen (1791–1848) were also producing *bijin-ga*. Eizan followed the later style of Utamaro (ill. 24), and supplied evidence of his talents in many fields. From the type of strong-willed woman with evident *joie de vivre* portrayed by Utamaro, Kunisada took over the finely drawn eyes and projecting lower lip.

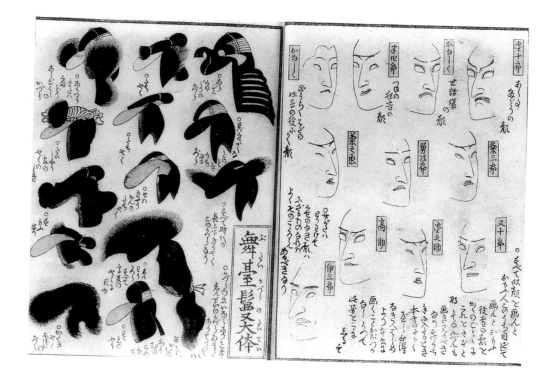

Katsushika Hokusai (1760–1849) took up painting in or around the year An'ei 8 (1779) under the name of Katsukawa Shunrō. Strictly speaking, Hokusai should already have been mentioned in connection with the emergence of *nishiki-e*; since his characteristic pictures are landscapes, however, and since his masterpiece, the series "36 Views of Mount Fuji" (Fugaku sanjūrokkei) was published in the Tenpō era, he is discussed here. Hokusai was a pupil of Shunshō, but studied the techniques of numerous schools and continually tried out new styles, among them those of the Kanō, Tosa and Kōrin schools, in addition to deriving inspiration from Chinese and Western painting. Later he found a style all of his own, adopting the name by which he is now known. Devoting himself to landscape painting, he attracted the attention of all his contemporaries. He painted a whole variety of motifs, did illustrating work, designed ink prints, and carved woodblocks himself, yet few individual pictures by him survive. His name is inseparable from the "36 Views of Mount Fuji", which dates from the first half of the Tenpō era. The depictions of the sacred mountain from a variety of viewpoints using highly individual compositional techniques constitute his most important *ukiyo-e* in the field of landscape.

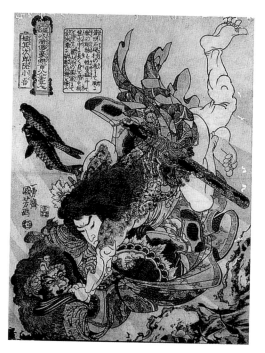

Utagawa Hiroshige (1797–1858) was a pupil of Utagawa Toyohiro (1773–1829), who had studied together with Utagawa Toyokuni (1769–1825). In the history of landscape prints, Hiroshige is no less important than Hokusai, but in comparison with his older colleague, Hiroshige lived a relatively sedate life. He, too, was active at first in the genres of *yakusha-e* and *bijin-ga*. In the year Tenpō 1 (1830), he caused a stir with his series of "Famous Places in the Eastern Capital" (Tōtōmeisho), which appeared under the signature "Ichiyūsai" through the Kawaguchi Shōzō publishing house. It was not until two years later, in Tenpō 3 (1832), that he accompanied the *Tokugawa* government on a journey to Kyoto. On the way, he made a number of sketches, which were brought out on his return to Edo by the publishing house of Hōeidō under the title "Tōkaidō gojūsan tsugi no uchi" (53 Stations on the *Tōkaidō*). The series was typical of his romantic landscape style. It deals with the four seasons and the everyday lives of the people of Japan, and it made him and his works well-known throughout the country. Hiroshige depicted other famous locations, for example the *Kisokaidō*, but his work concentrates largely on Edo and its environs, where he lived. One of his masterpieces is an eight-part series featuring famous sights of Edo, "Edokinkō hakkei". He gives expression to their beauty through great precision of line, sophisticated composition and a romantic feeling for nature. In his work "Tamagawa shūgetsu", he depicts a scene on the banks of the Tamagawa on a moonlit autumn evening in such a way that the viewer really feels the chill in the air. Here, as in many of his works, he included a poem, an indication of his literary upbringing. It is above all his highly personal sensitivity to nature, based upon his feeling for lyrical effect, which conveys the impression that we, the viewers, are really present at the place depicted, a statement which is no less valid now than it was in his day.

During the Kaei era (1848–1854), many foreign ships came to Japan. It was a period of unrest, a state of affairs reflected in the *ukiyo-e* of the time. Numerous pictures and caricatures were produced which alluded to the current situation in the country. Following the Meiji restoration in 1868, all kinds of cultural imports came to Japan from the West, photography and printing techniques being received with particular enthusiasm. As a result, the art of *ukiyo-e* went into decline.

Ukiyo-e is an art form with a history spanning more than three centuries. It developed as the bourgeoisie's own form of cultural expression, and is unique in the world. In the course of time, the style of *ukiyo-e* naturally underwent changes, as did the lives of the people with which these woodblock prints were closely linked. But from Japan they have travelled the world; unbeknown to their creators, *ukiyo-e* have had a profound influence on modern Western painting. With this in mind, we can still appreciate their great vitality today.

Mitsunobu Satō

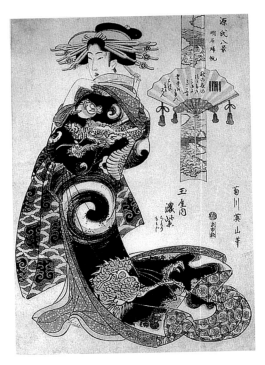

Ill. 24
Kikukawa Eizan: 8 Views from
the Tale of Prince Genji:
Return of the Ships to Akashi
Riccar Art Museum, Tokyo

Cherry · Wood · Blossom

1

"We live only for the moment, in which we admire the splendour of the moonlight, the snow, the cherry blossom and the colours of the maple-leaves. We enjoy the day, warmed by wine, without allowing the poverty which stares us in the face to restore our sobriety. In this drifting – like a pumpkin carried along by the current of the river – we do not allow ourselves to be discouraged for a moment. This is what is called the floating, fleeting world."[1]

This "New Age" text is taken from a story written in 1661. Not long before, in the year 1638, the young Tokugawa regime had sealed Japan off from all communication with the outside world. In 1657 Edo, modern-day Tokyo, was ravaged by fire.

In the course of the subsequent construction boom, the pleasure quarter of Yoshiwara was rebuilt on a new site: it took the form of a rectangular grid of streets of green houses, surrounded by walls and ditches. Only with a special pass were the ladies of this earthly paradise allowed to leave its confines.

In this sophisticated, neatly-painted pleasure city, as in the Kabuki theatre, social distinctions were blurred. It worked its attractions on the new bourgeoisie no less than on the old nobility. Artists familiar with the old traditions found in this milieu new motifs and a new form of mass-reproducible art for a new market.

Although "nature" – landscape, flora and fauna – continued to have its place in the popular views of festive existence painted over the following two centuries, and in particualr in the 19th century, the heart of this festive existence beat in the contemplative side-views of everyday life, and above all, for the courtesans and actors, the goddesses of Yoshiwara and the idols of the *Kabuki* theatre. Through their art the lowest on the social ladder came to be the highest on the Olympus of *joie de vivre* and fantasy, and colour prints bestowed immortality upon them.

And it was this world which brought forth the very embodiment of the Japanese print: *ukiyo-e*, pictures of the floating, fleeting world.

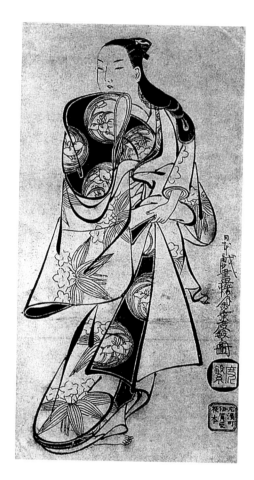

Kaigetsudō Norishige: Standing Woman, *c.* 1725. Riccar Art Museum, Tokyo

2

The floating world is thus also, and firstly, the rapid but precise passage of the ink-brush over the paper. The virtuoso command of this skill formed the basis of both calligraphy and painting. Meticulously, the woodblock carver rendered the brush-stroke on the printing block. The floating world is the drama of lines: their currents, their sweeps, their curves, their loops, their zigzags, their thrusts. It is the rhythm of directions, as they run with and against each other, as they diverge and snap together again. It is the interplay of line and plane, of figure and background, of printed and unprinted paper, of passion and tranquility. It is the maze of patterns and folds which draws the eye to the erotic force-field of

[1] Asai Ryoi: Tales from the Floating World of Pleasure, Kyoto 1661.
Quoted from: Franz Winzinger, Shunga, Exhib. Cat. Nuremberg 1975

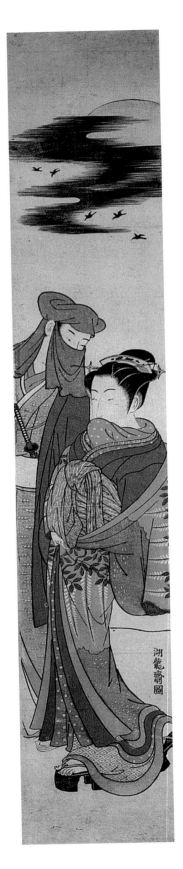

Isoda Koryūsai
The Morning After★
Hashira-e 69.5 x 12.9
Nishiki-e
Publisher unknown
early An'ei era
(1772–1781)
(for commentary, see p. 68)

garments which enshroud the bodies; it is the fashionable display of costly fabrics and mannered coiffures.

Bodies? Between the silhouetted heads of hair – sweeping into elaborate curves before being tied back again – and the vertical play of clothes, there appears a mask-like face captured in just a few fine strokes, demarcated from the surrounding emptiness by no more than a tender, gently curving outline. Otherwise just a tiny hand in the middle, and a foot below. Let us cast our eyes over an early work by Norishige (p. 23): it is only the position of head, hand and foot in the rapid sweep of the whole which even suggests a figure in an elegant pose. The movement moves the eye and the imagination of the beholder. Nothing is more than hinted at; everything hinted at is ambiguous, but nothing is blurred. The body disappears behind the folds; it has no volume, no shadow, no weight. There is no floor, no depth.

Any emotion lacking in the unmoving face appears all the more vehemently in the restlessness of the garments. The cascade of hair responds to the curves of the puffed sleeve; this in turn to the similarly-patterned wedge of fabric with its unpatterned counterpart – and together they nudge at the fingers from below. The raised sleeve conceals the other hand; it reveals only the opening, on which a ball seems to hang like the inside of a butterfly net in which an iris is seen to blossom. Above and around the visible hand, by contrast, directions accumulate into folds resembling a pointed fan, a stout hose, a long-nosed mask. This centre of energy gives rise to whirlpools from which straight jets radiate far into a bizarre outline, only to turn about, some rounded, some angular.

"Remember," said Henri Matisse to his pupils in 1908, "that the character of the curved line is easier to comprehend if, as often the case, it is contrasted with a straight line. The converse is also true."

The more one immerses oneself in these clear, well-defined lines, the more their wealth of association unfolds. The folds brace themselves against the large floral patterns. We have once more an interplay of contrasts: the irises, bent to fit into closed, white discs on a black ground, like moons half covered by the clouds; the Paulownias, open against a white background, like stars radiating in all directions. Some of the blossoms and leaves straddle the force-lines of the folds unhindered, while others are cut off by them.

This print by Norishige is a "primitive" in the history of Japanese woodblock printing, one of the direct descendants of the pioneering works of Moronobu which were appearings full of archaic strength and freshness, in the years around 1700. The prints were in black-and-white, until the introduction of hand-colouring in about 1710. Not until the mid-18th century did the classical age of polychrome printing begin.

3

What manner of sovereign figure is this, in her decorative pose and dynamically interwoven composition? She would tower above the average Japanese woman by two heads, as though the picture were scaling down the real world to the format sometimes assigned by the classical masters of the woodblock print to a maid in the presence of a lady. And thus the dependency relationship between art and reality is reversed. The lady, as Art, does not imitate Reality, but formulates perceptions to enhance Reality.

These extravagantly-garbed figures were an advertisement for the latest designs in hairstyles and clothes. The parades of the leading courtesans in Yoshiwara were events with a capital E. Norishige's print may be seen in this context: behind the austerity of the design one can sense the rustle of the embroidered silk, and the unapproachable pose before the eyes of the public.

This idealization of a culturally up-market Miss World makes no distinction between prostitute and princess. Only initiates know: the former knotted their *kimono* sashes in front. What Western morality has wrenched apart and driven into painful contradictions – heavenly and earthly love, the Madonna and the whore – are shown in the non-naturalistic female figures of the Japanese wood-block masters as aspects of a holistic human nature. And that alone is real. The only Reality is life in the harmony of opposing forces, even though it may only be realized fleetingly or vicariously or in the contenplation of living, painted or printed images. Thus say the artists, with a wink and a nudge; meanwhile they work hard, and "savour the moment".

Even men and women are often difficult to tell apart in the woodblock prints. Both sexes wear long flowing garments, both wear their hair done up in a sophisticated bun. The delicate, motionless doll-like faces are interchangeable. In one of Koryūsai's prints the end of the standing woman's sash – knotted in front – touches the shoulder of the recumbent man, while the latter's coiffure nudges against the woman's hip. This sort of thing is one of the fine distinctions within this feminine aesthetic with its flattering hues, which adapts the outward aspect of the male to that of the female.

On the *kabuki* stage, female roles were played by men. The corresponding actor portraits achieve perfect mimesis: their exterior beauty represents a mani-fold reflection of so-called reality: the portrait of a man impersonating a woman in a role created by show-business according to prespecified rules. Only the legend identifies the actor, the role and the play from the transient world of the performance, captured by a painter and distributed by a publisher, whose names are likewise mentioned.

At most the actor portraits by Sharaku – with their craggy, dry facial features – hint at the man behind the female mask (pp. 121–130). The passionate *kabuki* audiences knew everything there was to know about the theatre: the plots, the personal details of the stars, and the particular roles in which they excelled. They wanted to recognize them in these colour prints, as well as enjoy the charm of their graphic transfiguration.

It would appear that the ancient oriental wisdom of yin and yang, of the balance between the male and female principles, had appeared in the form of the easy muse of the tea-house and the stage, and perfumed the cast of the *ukiyo-e* with sweet androgynous scents.

4

With bulging muscles, grimaces, spits and hisses, strutting like a turkey with bristling feathers, bursting with strength: in the pictures of the heroes of melo-dramatic stories, of wrestlers and of artistes, masculinity is glorified by a genre of its own.

The rough and ready pictorial language of the "primitives" could have been made to order for these musclemen; the images endure to this day in contem-porary comic-strip magazines. As though he had discharged his energy in a flash as he sprang into the picture, the corpulent fighter dominates the lower half of a print by Kiyonobu (p. 40). He extends not lengthways but sideways, filling out the square in which he is placed right up to the sides of the picture. Were he to summon his reserves of strength, stretch out his bent left arm and kick out with his bent left leg, the written characters would be sent flying off the edge of the paper.

The fellow is half naked. The nakedness is characterized by a wavy outline filled in with brilliant orange, and is concentrated in the bloated belly, which nevertheless seems capable of exerting further fearsome pressure. Centring on this belly, the garment bursts out in three directions. It too is hand-coloured, but in light ochre, only slightly deeper in hue than the paper itself. The stronger and more thrusting the orange, the sharper and harsher is the effect of the black of

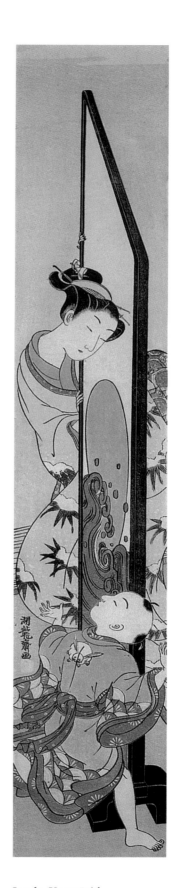

Isoda Koryūsăi
Tag★
Hashira-e 70.4 x 12.4
Nishiki-e
Publisher unknown
early An'ei era
(1772–1781)
(for commentary, see p. 70)

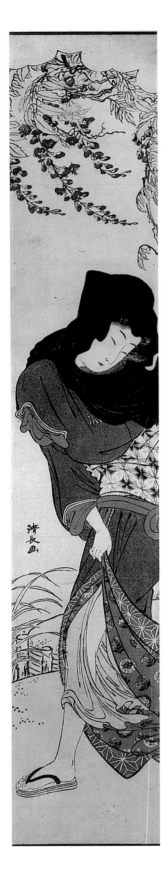

Torii Kiyonaga
Figure of a Woman beneath
Wistaria★
Hashira-e 67.4 x 12.2
Nishiki-e
Publisher unknown
c. Tenmei 1 (1781)
(for commentary, see p. 90)

the pattern elements, which are carrying on a struggle with the lines of the folds. Both qualities – the rigid geometry and the dynamic stroke – are mutually intertwined.

The grey rival in the top half of the picture – perhaps a demon, certainly the villain of the piece – while moving threateningly above the back of the hero's neck, is not characterized by anything like the latter's potency. True, a pointed black form is bearing down upon the hero's bald head, but the orange of the villain's garment is reduced to narrow stripes, so that its importance is visually reversed: paths of energy, flowing from the muscleman, seem to break up the more meagre figure of the villain and displace his presence from a position of superiority into the background.

The feminine portraits of anonymous grace differ from the masculine images of courage, aggression and intrigue also in respect of their facial expression. The former are characterized by a tranquil, light-hued oval (rarely in profile) their almond eyes almost closed, their mouth a mere dot, and their lips sometimes like tiny wings trying to open. The latter by contrast are marked by rolling eye-balls, maybe with a squint, and a grim mouth with its corners pulled outwards and downwards; these features are often further enhanced by war-paint covering the face like some unleashed arabesque.

With his body and his physiognomy, his movement, his garb and his warrior's accessories, the hero comes supplied with the whole arsenal of macho gestures designed to intimidate his opponent by the mere sight of him, while transfixing with a thrill of horror theatregoer and picture-beholder alike.

5

In our attic there hung colour reproductions of Franz Marc and Vincent van Gogh, a Chrysanthemum from the Mustard-seed Garden, the Wave and the View of Mount Fuji by Hokusai (pp. 149, 150). They channelled the longings of an adolescence plagued by Latin vocabulary away from the misery of the post-war years on to a mental image of Nature – wide, pure and unspoilt. Into this idyll there came one day a head by Sharaku. From that day on, the sound of the name alone took on a magical charisma which acted upon the same nerves as give rise to goose pimples.

The actor and the role: "Ichikawa Komazō III as Shigano Daishichi" (p. 127). Whoever the two-in-one-person may be, the *kabuki* theatregoers in May 1794, like today's connoisseurs, knew who it was, just as today's film buffs know who is meant when they see a still captioned "Humphrey Bogart as Rick". The legend is dispensable; the picture itself suggests all that is needed. Alongside Shakaru's shady character, Kiyonobu's hero comes across as hyperactive, slightly ludicrous windbag, and the scene as if taken from a village barn theatre or an African war-dance, a rustic knees-up, full of vitality, rich in associations, but lacking in deeper intent.

The picture by Sharaku, by contrast, confronts us with an overpowering apparition which conceals more than it reveals. The figure creeps up from the side, silent as a cat, and is suddenly there, right next to us, in black and white. Suddenly the dark space is illuminated by a palely-gleaming head, from which in place of a neck, a no less bright banana grows. With a razor-sharp edge, the black coiffure sits upon the long mask of the face with its long nose. Beneath this nose, the mouth appears in the shape of a thin bone, an illusion created by the tightly pressed lips. The action would seem to have reached its climax. All is quite silent. We hardly dare breathe. Something is about to happen – or has just happened. Now the hero has appeared – or is about to withdraw. He is pulling something from his garment – or else he is just replacing it. The hand and hilt are clearly discernible, but are subsumed in the harsh contrast between the white neckline and the black cloak, like a whisper lost in a hubbub of shouting. I am face to face with the intruder, who rolls his eyes till almost nothing but the whites can be seen.

Murderer or lover? Rescuer or sleepwalker?

This print requires an aesthetically demanding, practised viewer with a predilection for the sinister, someone who loves indirect associations which can stimulate his fantasy to psychological games.

There are just a few large fields in this picture, accompanied by just a few thin lines; unambiguous decisions, yet accompanied by delicacy and finesse. And there is only black, white and grey, with barely noticeable nuances of hue to give some colour to the dramatic chiaroscuro.

Mysterious, outwardly at least, is also how best to describe Sharaku's artistic career; almost all biographical details are lacking, leaving us to supply the deficit from our imagination. A former *Nō* dancer creates 144 actor portraits in nine months; after that, nothing. Their effect transcends the work of all other masters of woodblock printing – at least for the Europe of Goya and Dostoevsky.

6

From overtly or subliminally violent masculinity, let us return once more to the intimate serenity of the green houses.

The lady steps inside from the garden. Within, it is no less airy than outside. A little servant girl hands her a cup. A kimono is carelessly wrapped around the naked body of the young mistress. She looks back to the garden, where a jetty leads across the water, drawing out the line of our vision. Has someone just departed? Or is someone expected? From the garden, one could see her bare shoulders, otherwise only the kimono. We, by contrast, as beholders of the picture, get to see far more. If she would just open her delicate hand, the fabric would fall open, and we should see everything.

This early three-colour print by Toyonobu offers us a story for the spinning (p. 53). It depicts an everyday toilette tantalizingly on the verge of becoming a strip-tease. Immediately before the climax, the scene stops where it is, as a *tableau vivant*. Presented as a maidservant, the diminutive figure at the side arouses no suspicion. But her eager profile betrays the voyeur and his desires. The role of the miniature domestic in her simple floral garment with its enormous bow behind is offered to the beholder as camouflage. The beauty herself has in her something of the spoilt daughter of the *grande dame* on the Norishige print which we considered earlier (p. 23). There is less power and pride, but to make up for that, more tenderness and seductive sophistication. The same is true of the style of the print as a whole.

The point at which these discreet allusions end, where, at the top of the leg where the open kimono is just held together, we are given a glimpse of public hair – this is the point where the so-called *shunga* begin, where nothing is hidden. These *shunga*, either on single sheets or in albums, were evidently very widespread. The genre continues the ordinary print, as it were, behind the screen, from where it retrospectively enables the customer to place a more informed interpretation on the hints imparted this side of the screen.

The interplay between body and garment sets the standing or seated single figure vibrating, with minimal involvement of hands or feet: when it comes to the floor routine of sexual athletics, it treats the four-hand, four-foot entanglement with great tenderness. The recurrent schema of elegantly curvilinear poses, as maintained for the public outside, here within brings forth an endless variety of positions where inventiveness is given a free rein. The lines and patterns are as precisely delimited and as clean as those we have already met, but the precision knows no bounds, while cleanliness is ensured on occasion by a small kerchief in

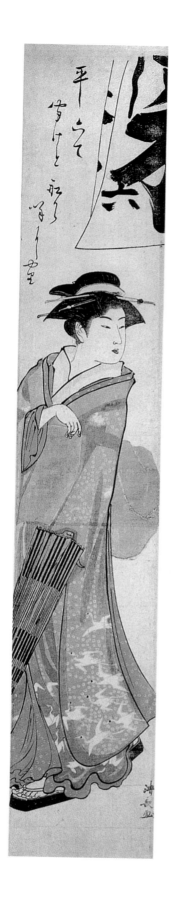

Torii Kiyonaga
Geisha Leaving Heiroku's Shop★
Hashira-e 70.3 x 12.3
Nishiki-e
Publisher unknown
early Tenmei era (1781–1789)
(for commentary, see p. 90)

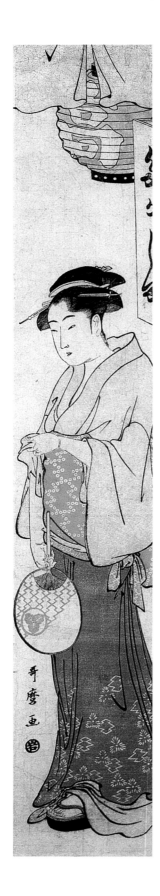

Kitagawa Utamaro
Takashimaya Ohisa★
Hashira-e 70.7 x 12.0
Nishiki-e
Published by Tsutaya Jūzaburō
c. Kansei 5 (1793)
(for commentary, see p. 98)

a delicate hand. No matter how entangled the entanglement, no matter how vehemently intrusive or subtly clothed the nakedness, the elaborate coiffures never have a hair out of place. If the figures are totally naked, then their bodies and limbs, uncoloured, come across like those of rubber dolls. Except for one thing: it is at this point that we discover what it is that the tiny white hands in the clothed pictures are capable of – namely, an enormous contrast. An occasional tree stump then awakens further associations. For all their hypertrophia, the *shungas* maintain a sense of proportion; for all their violence, they maintain their grace; for all their indiscretion, they maintain their subtlety; for all their matter-of-factness, they maintain their poetry; for all their didacticism, they maintain their sense of fun.

Often, a male or female spectator turns up in the picture, less as a voyeur, more as an attentively sensitive observer. He or she follows the act from close proximity without embarrassment. If he or she conceals him or herself behind a screen or in a niche, then it is, if anything, in order not to disturb the rhythm of the couple during their lesson. The observer *in* the picture excuses the observer *of* the picture. And yet this is not the right way to put it: the intimate glimpse is not so burdened by guilt that, for all its sophistication, it could give rise to any embarrassment that would need to be excused.

Back in front of the screen, on the way out, so to speak, we cast our eyes once more upon a bust by Utamaro. A lady gazes into a hand-held mirror, to examine the teeth she has just blackened (p. 105). The warm grey background is just a hint darker than the natural colour of the paper, as evidenced by the untinted face and arms. The greater, then, is the contrast created by the light and dark areas, accompanied by a delicate duet of light orange and dark green. The black tower of hair gives emphasis to the orientation of the head as it leans forward – its impetus absorbed by the oval mirror. Between hair and mirror is the three-quarter profile with the incredibly fine sweep of its outline. How eagerly she leans forward out of the blackness to look into the blackness which she holds so closely to her face, in order to examine in the reflection (hidden to us) the blackness in her mouth! And how, on the back of the mirror, the yellowish petals of the stylized flower are beginning to wilt before our eyes!

7

The apprentice painter underwent a strict process of instruction during which he learnt the repertoire of signs and the skills of brush-handling through continual practice, just as one learns vocabulary, grammar and pronunciation until fluency is achieved.

Academic art theory in the West had established a study of nature which, with the help of classical schemata, sought to render the world as a body in a space by means of light and shade. The naked human body stood as anthropocentric model. In the East, by contrast, the eye and hand were schooled by copying models in which the pictorial experience of centuries was distilled to an extreme level of concentration. The rules, however, aimed not at the external imitation of stereotypes, but at developing a feeling for the animated brush-stroke, which, in its organically controlled progress, was required to reflect the original being copied. In the process, the eye inspects not only the shape of the lines which together go to make up a blossom, a wave, a fold or a hand, but also, and with the same attention, the intervening spaces, or rather, the emptiness in between. It is this emptiness which determines the rhythm of the drawing and the tension in the pictorial plane. The lines are drawn briskly. As there is no way of correcting an ink-drawing, the pupil had to learn to master his repertoire of brush-strokes so that the result was right first time.

The totality of motifs and stylistic devices is what defines a particular school. Its collective experience was passed on – with a greater or lesser degree of

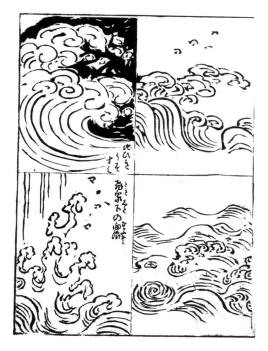
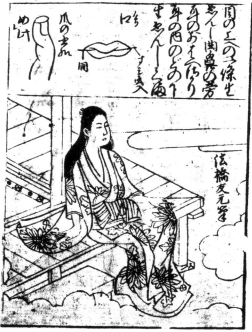
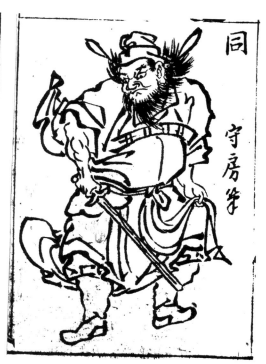

variation – by the masters, and often preserved in albums of woodblock prints running to serveral volumes. The examples illustrated here are taken from a copybook produced by the Kanō school in the 18th century, a six-volume work containing a wealth of models in sketch form. There were various such schools, all of them part of a development which led from the "primitives", via the classical masters, to the late masters of the 19th century, whose works reveal the increasing influence of the geometric perspective of Western painting. On the whole, though, the era of the Japanese print presents a homogeneous picture, by virtue both of the tradition of the schools and of the restrictions imposed by the woodblock printing technique itself.

Illustrations from an artist's teaching manual, Kanō school, 18th century

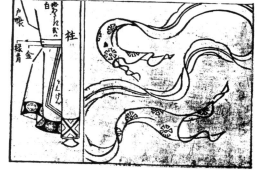

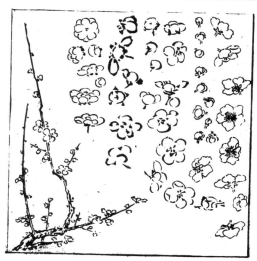

This technique was based on the precision and strictly linear character of the drawing, which excluded any painterly dissolution of the brush-stroke. The key block – the first step in the printing process – was characterized by a framework of open and closed outlines alongside areas destined to be black in the final print. Within this network of lines, the empty fields could then take up the interplay between untinted areas (i.e. the original colour of the paper) and tinted areas (whether uniform, shaded or patterned). Each new colour was inked into this linear skeleton with a separate printing block, or was created as a secondary hue from the overprinting of several colours. The tradition of an iconic language, the conditions imposed by the technique and the studio process by which the work was divided into various phases, together guaranteed the fixed pictorial logic of the elements of line, field and ornament. Like individual musical instruments, they maintain their intrinsic value while allowing the most astounding contrasts and modulations, and playing in concert produce the decorative overall effect. By contrast, contemporary European painting, from Tiepolo to Turner, achieved its dynamic quality through the fusion of pictorial elements.

As a rule, the artist would use a brush to draw a line or fill in an area in black on thin, transparent paper. He had to be able to move the brush across the paper so surely as to be able to create not only crescendos and diminuendos, but also lines of even fineness and fields with exact contours. This drawing was then stuck face down onto a block of cherry or box wood, so that the ink drawing adhered, easily visible but laterally reversed, to the surface of the wood. The next stage – the carving of the key block – was left to the woodblock cutter. He would isolate the black areas with a contour knife by cutting along the edges of the drawing with extreme precision. The areas to be left untinted, or to be printed with colour, were then scraped away with a chisel. Black-and-white proofs were then pulled from this key block; on these proofs, the artist would indicate the colours to be employed in the various areas of the picture. On the basis of these instructions, the individual colour blocks were then prepared. A fine line and an angular register mark at the bottom edge ensured the exact superimposition of successive colour impressions. Finally, the set of completed blocks would be passed on to the printer, who would use a brush to apply a watercolour mixed with ricepaste to the surface of each block, and press the paper against it by hand or with a brayer. In overall charge of the whole process, from the design stage via production to sales and distribution, was the publisher.

8

In 1853 Japan's ports were opened up to trade with the West. This marked the start of a period during which the influence of Japanese aesthetics on the modern movement in Europe, up to and beyond Art Nouveau, can hardly be overestimated. It encompassed every field of craft and design, encouraged tendencies in modern architecture, and above all came as a revelation to the first modern painters, from Degas, van Gogh, Gauguin and Toulouse-Lautrec to Schiele and Klimt.

The feeling for the arabesque in place of volume, for pictorial surface *per se* in place of illusionistic depth, for the intrinsic value of point and line, of colour and rhythm in place of their representational value, and above all a sense of expressive emotion in place of naturalistic imitation: the European avant-garde recognized that all these things which had been agitating them so greatly were already present as a mature art form in the Japanese prints that had been arriving in Europe, and especially in Paris, since the 1860s.

Influences now began to flow in both directions between East and West. But whereas the arrival of Japanese art in Europe brought positive results, the converse was hardly true. During the period of Japanese isolation, the Dutch were the only nation to be allowed a trading post in Japan, and even that was a sealed-off island in Nagasaki harbour. From there, European etchings filtered into Japan, where individual artists borrowed certain aspects of their exotic perspective for use in their own graphic art. No doubt it held the same curiosity as did their own art for their counterparts in the West, and through the closer observation of nature which it engendered, it may have contributed to the enrichment of their pictorial language. Prints by Hokusai, Hiroshige, Toyokuni, Kunisada and Kuniyoshi demonstrate a knowledge of the rules of Western art going back well before the mid-1800s – a knowledge which subsequently contributed to the end of *ukiyo-e*. Conversely, it was in particular the prints by masters already influenced by European traditions which first helped Western artists to liberate themselves from those very same rules.

Some outstanding graphic works in the Staatliche Graphische Sammlung in Munich and a painting in Amsterdam, seen side by side with the works of Japanese masters, provide a more or less indirect reflection of this Eastern influence.

Take a great landscape drawing from van Gogh's late period, for example (p. 31): the movement of the short lines in black chalk and red ink proceeds in waves upwards from the lower edge of the picture. This wave movement is then cut off by a horizontal bar, above which it continues in part horizontal and in part vertical. In the uppermost section is a large disc, surrounded by concentric lines. Bottom to top at the same time represents near to far. While there is a vanishing point in the form of a clump of trees, the rhythm of the almost evenly heavy strokes emphasises the pictorial surface and sets it vibrating. The breadth of the landscape leads to emotional depth, not to spatial depth. On the subject

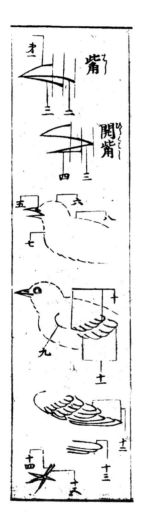

Artist's teaching manual,
Kanō school,
18th century

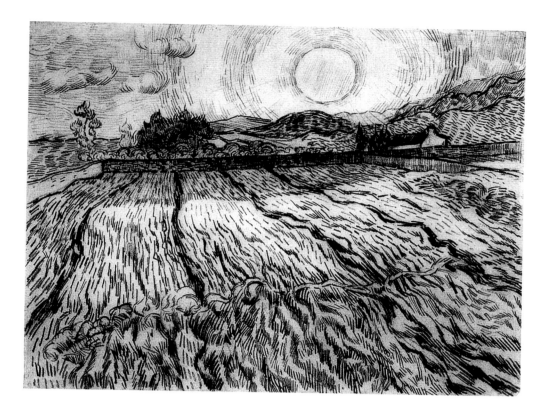

Vincent van Gogh:
Field with Rising Sun, 1889
Chalk and reed pen
Staatliche Graphische Sammlung, Munich

of two comparable, albeit more detailed, differentiated drawings of a broad landscape constructed with even greater physical depth, which van Gogh executed
in Montmajour a good year earlier, the artist wrote to fellow-painter Emile
Bernard: "They do not look Japanese, and yet they are the most Japanese thing
I have done" (letter no. 501, dated 18 July 1888).

We are not concerned with value-judgements when we consider alongside
this drawing a little print by Hokusai, the master of the views of Mount Fuji –
the busiest, most versatile, most productive, and in Europe initially the most
admired of Japanese artists (p. 31). The landscape looks at first somewhat didactic:
indeed, that was how it was intended. All the better, then, to demonstrate the

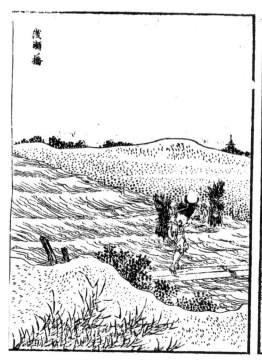
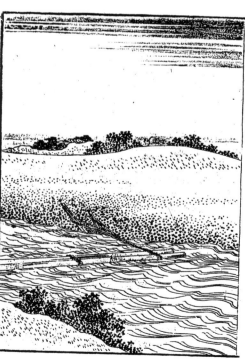

Katsushika Hokusai:
Landscape from the artist's "Manga"
sketchbooks, published in 15 volumes from
1814

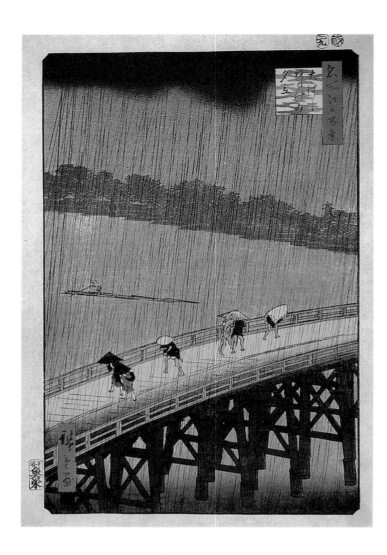

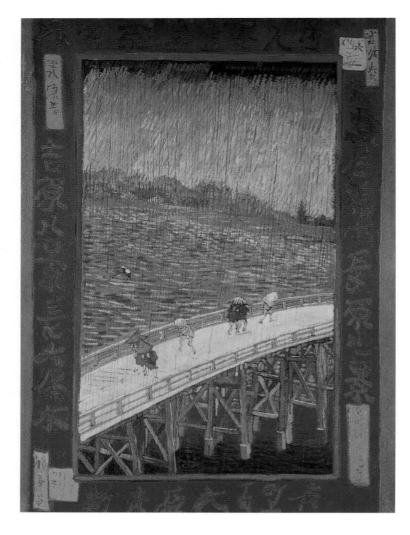

Left:
Utagawa Hiroshige:
100 Views of Famous Places in and around
Edo: Ōhashi Bridge, Sudden Shower near
Atake, 1857
(for commentary, see p. 185)

Right:
Vincent van Gogh:
Japonaiserie: Bridge in Rain, 1887
(after a print by Hiroshige)
Oil on canvas, 73 x 54 cm
Rijksmuseum Vincent van Gogh, Vincent
van Gogh Foundation, Amsterdam

stylistic means employed: the layering of the landscape from bottom to top; the evenly sustained strength of the drawing, the way the surface takes on a rhythm through undulating lines and dotted fields, and the characterization of ground, plants, foliage and water by means of graphic abbreviations.

The lithograph "Woman in Bed, Profile, Awakening", part of the series "Elles" by Toulouse-Lautrec dating from 1896 (p. 33), offers another starting-point for comparison. As a colour print, as an everyday brothel scene, and in the consistent intermeshing of patterned and plain, coloured and uncoloured areas, this picture has many similarities with an *ukiyo-e*. Before the blanket becomes a blanket, lying on top and hanging down, it is and remains a double-printed cold pink, which has to be seen in relation to the bright orange head of hair sported by the otherwise totally uncoloured figure of the madam. This pink nudges against the thin open arms of the girl, making her pallor appear yet more consumptive, and indeed causing everything else in the picture to pale into relative insignificance. Just a few casual strokes separate the white upper body of the girl from the white bedlinen, making it possible for her to get out of bed, and turning the pillows into a monstrous growth, a silent cry, pushed into the background by the submissive gesture of the arms. Contrasts like these, creating ambiguous relationships between the different areas of the picture, over and above the representational meaning of the outline, are found again and again in Japanese woodblock prints. The lithograph also contains highly pertinent lines of great economy – not as calligraphy, but as psychic seismography. Here, everything is direct; nothing is stylized. The patterns on the blanket were daubed on with a brush, while

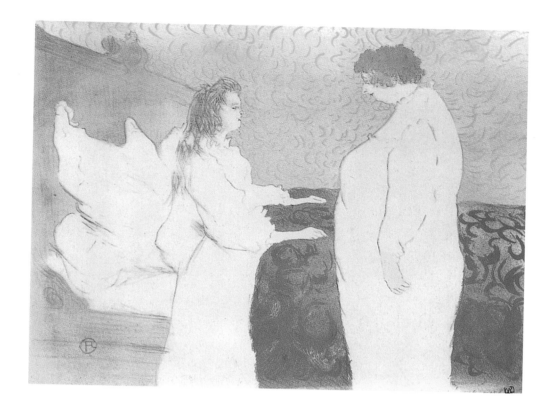

Henri de Toulouse-Lautrec:
Woman in Bed, Profile, Awakening
from "Elles", 1896
Colour lithograph
Staatliche Graphische Sammlung, Munich

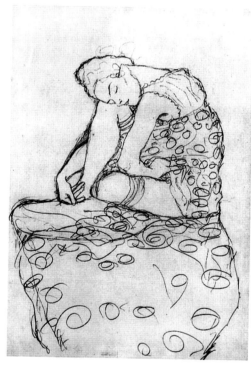

Gustav Klimt:
Seated Woman, Huddled 1908/09
Pencil
Staatliche Graphische Sammlung, Munich

those on the wallpaper do not serve to decorate the wall, but encircle the two women's heads like restless, compulsive ideas. The contours of the various fields are fixed, block-like; there is no curvaceous sophistication. The garments of the two figures are devoid of colour or decoration; there is no elaborate fabric to act as an arena for the interplay of patterns and folds. We are looking into the plain interior of an establishment, not into the elegant interior of one of Yoshiwara's green houses. It is not the stylistic means that are realistic, but the circumstances of those depicted. The poetry lies in the very personal sensitivity and its powerful expression, not in the transfiguration of beautiful appearances.

A drawing by Klimt (p. 33) also demonstrates extreme economy and sensibility, with the body devoid of all volume and shade. Yet in the peaceful mood of the girl, sunk in her own thoughts, and in the interplay of limbs and fabric, she bears an affinity with the Japanese ladies. She occupies a large area of the picture, sitting on the spread of the cloth as upon a plinth, ensconced within a closed outline. On the right, the line feels its way up from below, over the back to the shoulder, from there making almost a right angle at the nape of the neck and the head, and then dropping on the left-hand side in a series of almost straight lines, heavily reinforced like a barrier protecting the more exposed side of the body. All the movement is within this outline: the arms and the legs are curled up, the thigh juts out conspicuously from the garment, while the agitated curls in the pattern of the cloth take up the motif of the curled-up body in a fleeting shorthand within a sparkling current. As in a Japanese clothed figure, the ornamentation spreads out across the picture in an autonomous rhythm which responds to the rhythm of the delicate fold-lines. But in place of the technical precision and geometric order of the Japanese print, the pencil here dances freely across the paper, its strokes representing not the splendour of the costume, but fundamental symbolic gestures, which – at the highest artistic level – rediscover the spontaneity of childhood.

The pictures of the fleeting, floating world derive from two different worlds, which meet in poetic inspiration.

Thomas Zacharias

Colour Plates and Commentaries

Dates are given in accordance with the Japanese calendar, with the corresponding year(s) of the Gregorian calendar in parentheses. As the months in the Japanese calendar follow the lunar cycle and have alternately 30 and 29 days, they do not always correspond with those of the Gregorian calendar, in particular in view of the fact that intercalary months are occasionally inserted. For this reason, only the relevant Japanese month is indicated, without Gregorian equivalent; e.g. 5th month of Ansei 4 (1859).

An asterisk ★ placed after the title of a picture indicates that the work in question is classified as a "Japanese National Treasure" or as a "Major National Cultural Heritage Item". The details of the illustrations are presented as follows:
Name of the artist
Title; for series: series and individual titles, where known
Format; dimensions (height x width) in cm
Technique
Publisher (where uncertain, in parentheses)
Date

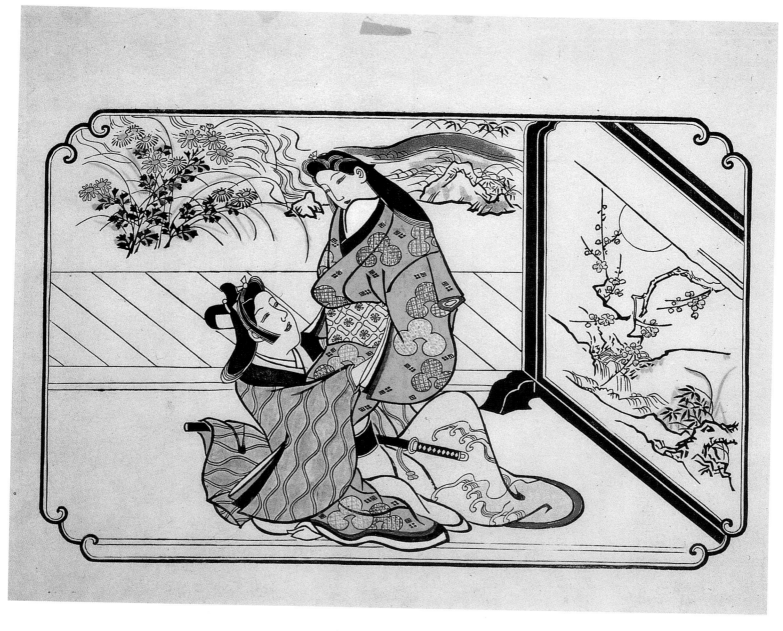

Moronubu's individual prints, where not of the frankly erotic genre known as *shunga*, frequently depict lovers. Such pictures, dating from the early part of his career, include numerous motifs which in the normal run of things would not be exposed to public gaze. This picture is one of a 12-part series. It is not certain which number in the series it is, but a comparison with other works known to form part of the same series makes it fairly clear that it must belong to the opening scenes. What we see is a young warrior flirting with a beauty behind a single-section screen, which serves to partition the *tatami* room. The couple are clearly enjoying themselves. The focus of the picture is the figure of the woman as she nestles up to the recumbent man. Beyond the verandah can be seen a stone-rimmed pool and flowering chrysanthemums, symbolizing an autumnal garden.

Similar landscape-format pictures are to be found in Moronobu's erotic album "Shinban Yamato no kuni bijinasobi". The economic coloration has been applied by hand to the monochrome ink print. This picture differs from those in other collections, suggesting that it was not coloured by the master himself. It may be that the colours were added later by a pupil or even a collector; possibly the picture was only intended as a study or working sketch, for the purpose of trying out certain techniques.

Hishikawa Moronobu
Young Couple
Yoko-ōban 30.4 x 37.1
Sumizuri-hissai
Publisher unkonwn
Enpō era (1673–1681)

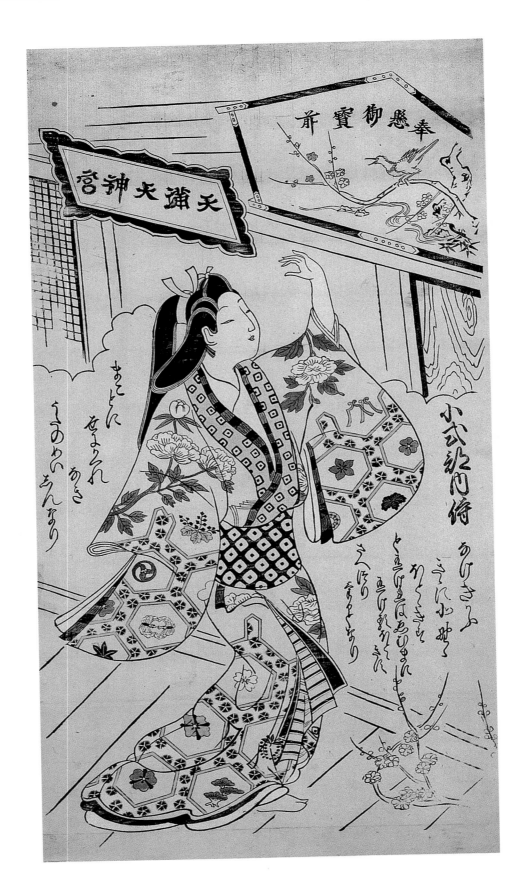

Sugimura Jihei
The Court Lady Sho-Shikibu★
Oōban 58.9 x 32.5
Sumizuri-hissai
Publisher unknown
late Enpō era (1673–1681) – late Genroku era (1688–1704)

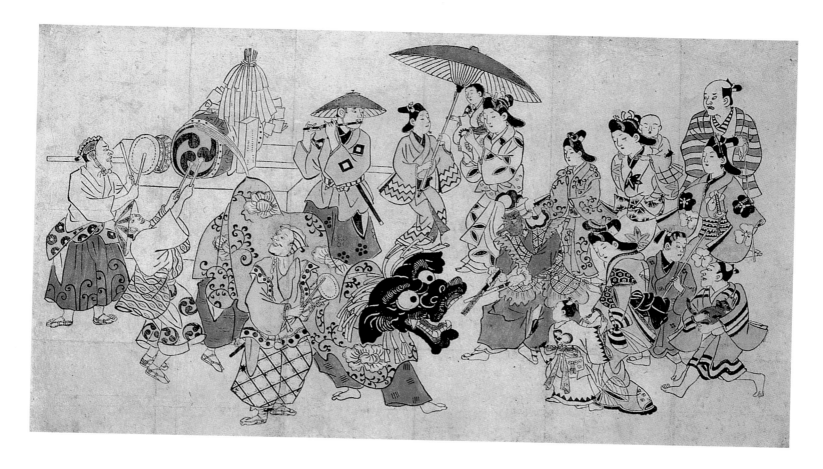

Although this picture is unsigned, the manner in which figures fill the pictorial ground is typical of the work of Jihei. The Lion Dance is being danced in supplication for fertility and a rich harvest and to dispel evil spirits. It is part of the *daikagura* shrine dance, and was also performed at weddings.

At New Year, scenes such as this were general throughout Edo. The dance is still performed in many places today, but only at shrine festivals or at New Year, and then as a tourist attraction. To the right of centre, a horse-boy is depicted wearing the long-nosed mask of Tengu, the Spirit of the Mountains. The Lion Dance itself is being performed by two young men in mask and costume. Musical accompaniment is provided by flute and drums, with the attitudes of the musicians expressive of movement and rhythm. The spectators on the right of the picture, dressed in their New Year finery, are enjoying the Lion Dance and the accompanying fun and games. A young girl is supervising a small child who is clearly nervous of the lion. On the far right, a youth is carrying a dog in one arm, while another runs past with a stick over his shoulder. The group of spectators also includes a mother carrying a baby on her back. In the middle of the picture at the top can be seen ladies of the aristocracy, who have a parasol to protect them from the sun. Top right is a samurai, with shaven forehead and the typical coiffure of a plait bent double to point forwards. This print is highly interesting insofar as it gives a picture of the everyday lives of young and old at the time.

The court lady Sho-Shikibu was a *waka* poetess, who was active in the middle of the Heian era (999–1025). Her mother Izumi Shikibu was also a *waka* poetess, whose works were selected for inclusion in the famous collection entitled "Ogura hyakunin isshū". The picture depicts the Kitanotenmangu shrine, where Sho-Shikibu read a *waka* which was so beautiful that even a nightingale carved on a votive tablet began to sing, or so legend has it. The picture is unsigned, but its style points to Jihei. He produced many such unsigned ink drawings, although in many cases the characters of his name can be found concealed in the picture.

Sugimura Jihei
Lion Dance★
Yoko-ōōban 32.2 x 57.4
Tan-e
Publisher unknown
late Enpō era (1673–1681) –
late Genroku era (1688–1704)

Sugimura Jihei
The Court Lady Sho-Shikibu
(p. 36)

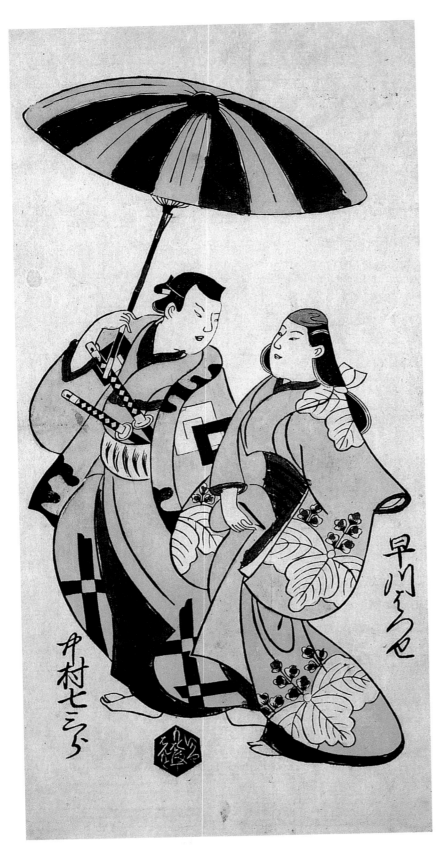

The play "Michiyuki", which portrays lovers out walking, has as its central theme the mutual attraction of young couples. However, there are also scenes with only one person, or with parents and children. This picture depicts the actors Shichisaburō and Hatsuse playing a scene from the drama "Shinoda atonoyama". The performance took place in the middle of the 8th month of Genroku 15 (1702) in the Yamamura theatre. These two performers were regarded as the leading actors and *onnagata* in Edo during the Genroku era (1688–1704). Hatsuse came from Kyoto to Edo in the 11th month of Genroku 13 (1700), and found an ideal partner in Shichisaburō. They appeared together in numerous plays, and were enormously popular with the audiences of the time. The costume displaying Hatsuse's family arms is typical of the sumptuous fashions of the Genroku era: one half of the garment is coloured differently from the other, but the colour combination is extremely tasteful. Together the two figures pace across the picture beneath a parasol, held by Shichisaburō; the particular charisma of his part is thereby given splendid expression. The superimposed squares are Shichisaburō's family emblem. He was particularly famous for his portrayal of celebrated roles in traditional Japanese drama, and in a sense was the counterweight of Danjūrō I, whose thespian achievements were likewise highly regarded. Shichisaburō used his own good looks to considerable effect; he had made his name with his renditions of love-scenes. It is thanks to Kiyonobu's skill that the memory of these outstanding actors has been preserved in such a striking visual fashion.

Torii Kiyonobu
Hayakawa Hatsuse and Nakamura Shichisaburō★
Hosoban 32.5 x 15.8
Tan-e
Published by Igaya Kanbei
Genroku 15 (1702)

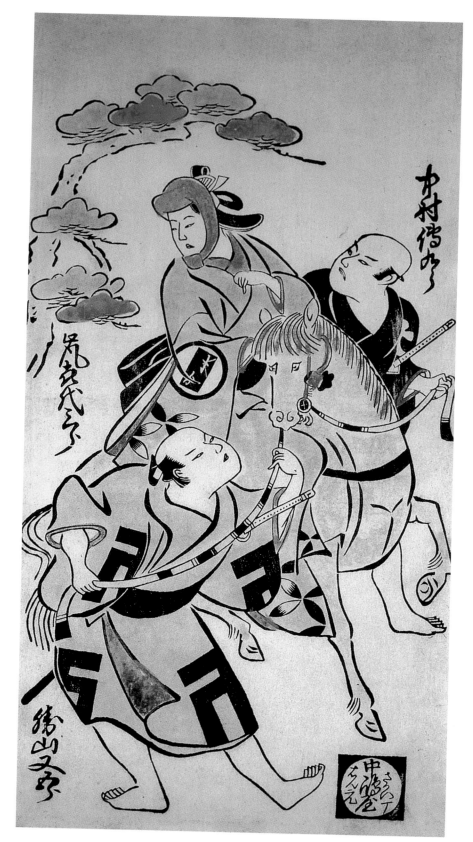

This picture is said to have been based on the play "Miyasudokoro Monomi Guruma", performed in the Nakamura theatre in the year Hōei 5 (1708); it is not altogether certain, however, that this is the case. It depicts the actors Kiyosaburō, Denkurō and Matagorō. From the 11th month of Hōei 5 (1708) until the autumn of the following year, and from the years Shōtoku 1 to 3 (1711–1713), the three actors appeared together. There are some ten different prints of them dating from this period. In the present case, the colouring was added later. The total composition is very rhythmic. The horse is trying to press onwards, but is being restrained. The force with which it wants to break free is almost tangible. Matagorō's grasp on the rein is no less energetic. Each kimono bears the family emblem of the respective actor. During the early phase of *yakusha-e*, costumes were almost always depicted with family crests. This particular print is unsigned; it is attributed to Kiyonobu on stylistic grounds, although some consider it an early work by Kiyomasu.

Kaigetsudō Dohan:
Standing Woman
(page 6)

Kaigetsudō Yasunori's followers founded the Kaigetsudō school, from which we have numerous hand-painted pictures of women dating from the Shōtoku era (1711–1716) and Kyōhō era (1716–1736). Alongside the school of Miyakawa Chōshun, the Kaigetsudō school was the only one in the history of woodblock printing to devote itself to this particular genre. They produced their own inexpensive, popular prints of women, without availing themselves of the services of a publisher. The pose was usually the same, the only variation being in the patterning of the kimono. The whole picture, with its fine and broad lines, was drawn in a single movement.

These pictures of proud and energetic women were especially popular among the inhabitants of Edo at that time. The Kaigetsudō school eviced a certain arrogance, in that they advertised their works by claiming to be the successors of the painters of *yamato-e*, and signing their works with the words "Nippon giga" ("caricatures"). No works by Yasunori himself are extant, but his followers Norishige, Yasutomo and Noritatsu have left us various works produced in cheap editions, for example that by Norishige reproduced here. The school's policy of keeping all stages of production in its own hands, though, has resulted in few of its works being extant today.

Torii Kiyonobu
Nakamura Denkurō,
Katsuyama Matagorō and Arashi Kiyosaburō★
Hosoban 30.4 x 15.5
Tan-e
Published by Nakajimaya Isaemon
c. Hōei 5–6 (1708– 1709)

Kiyonobu, who achieved fame through his theatrical posters and his book illustrations, was also the initiator of the "single-sheet" *yakusha-e*, in which actors were depicted in theatrical roles. His initiative led to *bijin-ga* and *yakusha-e* becoming pivotal genres in woodblock printing. At first, most such portrayals were unsigned, as is the case with this print too; it is, however, generally attributed to Kiyonobu. It depicts Heikurō in the role of Rōba Kurozuka and Danjūrō II in that of Kengorō Kagemasa in the play "Banmin ōfukusode", which was performed in the Nakamura theatre in the 11th month of Shōtoku 4 (1714). Heikurō specialized in playing the part of the villain, while Danjūrō II played the courageous hero, or *aragoto*, who saw to it that the villain received his just deserts. Both were among the most popular and most talented character actors of the time. The blue-painted face of Kurozuka could not be anything but evil, while not only the face, but the whole body of the hero is depicted in a reddish-orange symbolic of strength and vitality, combined with honesty and courage. In this, Kiyonobu is exploiting one of the stylistic devices of *kabuki*, which used colour to give powerful visual expression to the character of the part. This particular picture has a typical Torii-school feature, introduced by Kiyonobu and Kiyomasa, namely the representation of extreme muscularity in the limbs, achieved by the use of thick and thin strokes; the stormy action on stage is thereby brought to life on paper.

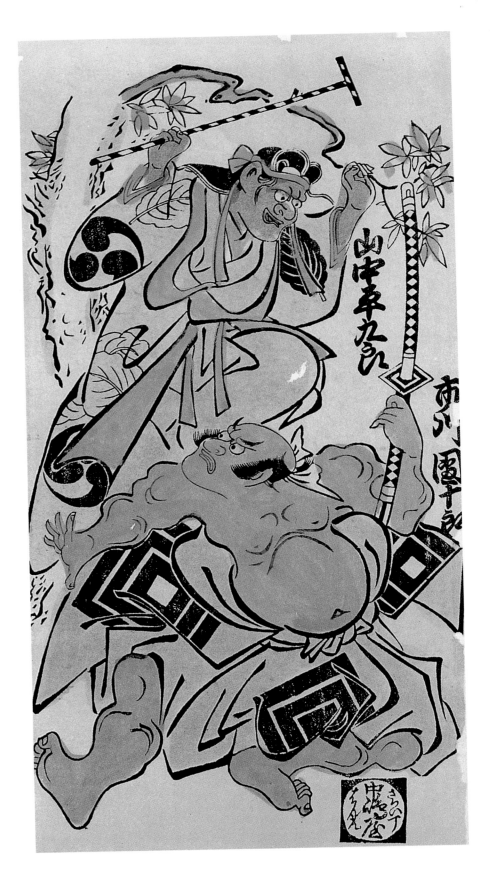

Torii Kiyonobu
Yamanaka Heikurō and Ichikawa Danjūrō II★
Hosoban 30.1 x 15.4
Tan-e
Published by Nakajimaya Isaemon
Shōtoku 4 (1714)

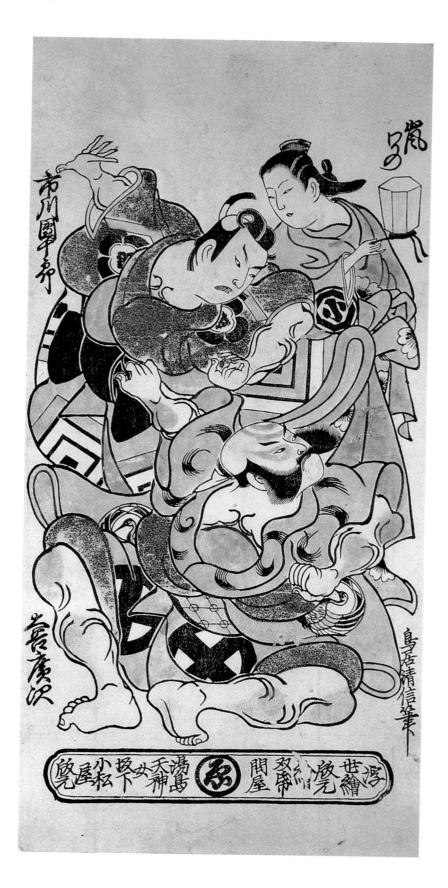

The *kabuki* play "The Tale of Soga" has been variously treated in Japanese art over the years and was highly popular with the Edo public. The story revolves around the brothers Jūrō and Gorō, whose father had been killed and who, after 18 years of hard but patient waiting, were finally able to avenge the murder. They learn that the traitor is called Kudō, and they take his ally Asahina prisoner. A similar scene is found in the play "Zori-hiki". At the première in the Nakamura theatre in Edo in the 11th month of Kyōhō 8 (1723), the last part of the story of "Soga koyomibiraki" was performed, entitled "Suijōchō no hanetsugai"; in which Danjūrō played Gorō, Otani Hiroji played Asahina, and Arashi Wakano played an officer disguised as Gorō's mistress.

This print depicts the scene in which Gorō, in his youthful rage and full of fiery courage, holds Asahina by his belt, pulls off his false beard, and rips his coat with its crane emblem from his body. The muscularity of the figures – a hallmark of the Torii school – gives vivid and dynamic effect to the trial of strength between the two. No less effective is the contrast with the seemingly powerless mistress, revealing the true strength of Kiyonobu, who established a new direction with his portraits of women.

Torii Kiyonobu
Arashi Wakano as Soga no Obihiki,
Ichikawa Danjūrō II as Gorō together with Otani Hiroji★
Hosoban 34.3. x 16.4
Tan-e
Published by Komatsuya
Kyōhō 8 (1723)

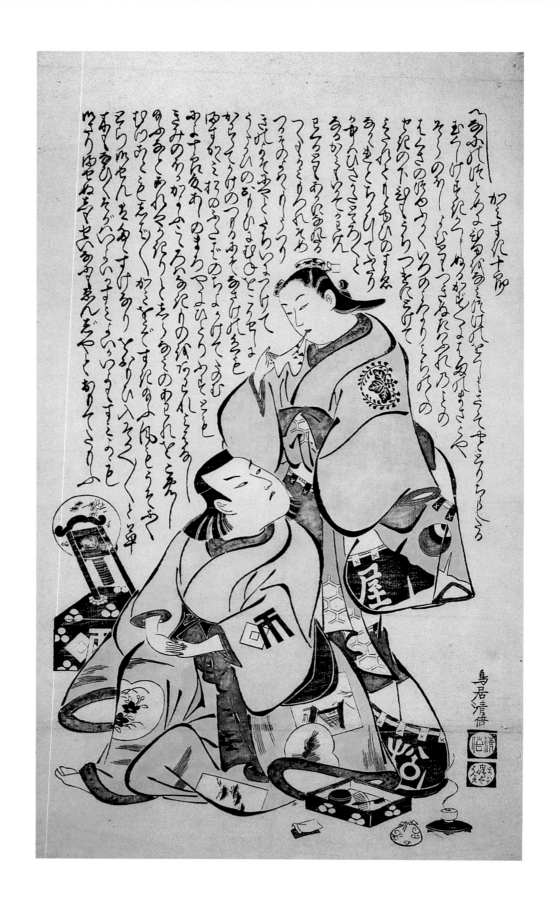

Torii Kiyomasu
Kamisuki Jūrō★
Oōban 56.4 x 33.2
Sumizuri-hissai
Published by Nakajimaya Isaemon
Shōtoku 5 (1715)

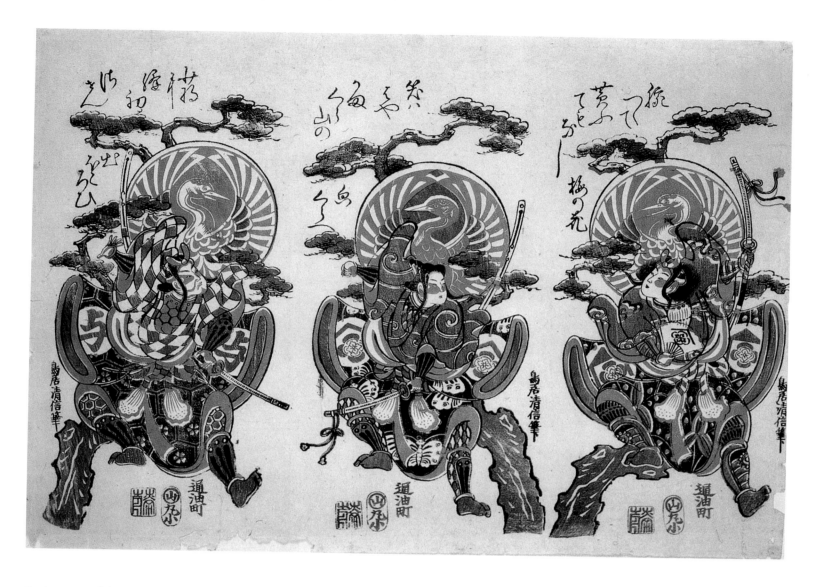

In the story of the Soga brothers Jūrō and Gorō, they fulfil their mission to avenge their father's death. This story forms the basis for *Nō* dramas as well as an accompaniment to puppet-theatre and *kabuki* pieces. From the Kyōhō era (1716–1736) onwards, a Soga *kyōgen* was performed in Edo at every New Year, and thus the spring performances of the Soga *kyōgen* took on a formal function as a New Year celebration.

From the background here, which hints at a stage set, a New Year celebration can be inferred. For the rest, the personnages depicted are the chief characters in the Soga saga. The kimonos, however, do not bear the family emblems of the actors, so that we cannot identify them. What we do have beneath the figures, however, are the names of the painter, the publisher, and the "colour master".

Torii Kiyonobu II
Mitate no Soga: Jūrō, Gorō, Yoshihide★
Yoko-ōban 31.5 x 44.1
Benizuri-e
Published by Maruya Kohei
Enkyō era (1744–1748) – Kan'en era (1748–1751)

Since the Kyōhō era, the custom had grown up of performing the Soga *kyōgen*, so beloved of Edo audiences, each year at the beginning of spring. This play tells of the deep attachment between the elder of the Soga brothers, Jūrō, and his lover Oisono Toragozen. The themes are loyalty, good deeds, communication between lovers, and separation, as well as relations between parents and children, husbands and wives, and superiors and subordinates. Audiences liked the play to have a musical accompaniment. To judge by the emblem on the kimono, Jūrō is being played by Tōsan Sōgorō and Oisō by Fujiura Hadayū. The performance took place in the Nakamura theatre in the 5th month of Shōtoku 5 (1715). Hadayū's dramatic art was extremely popular, and the mutual attachment of the couple comes across well in the picture. The round hand-bell on the table bears the emblem of Sōgorō, while in the drawer, make-up equipment can be seen. The design of the kimono pattern was a novelty for the time.

Torii Kiyomasu
Kamisuki Jūrō
(p. 42)

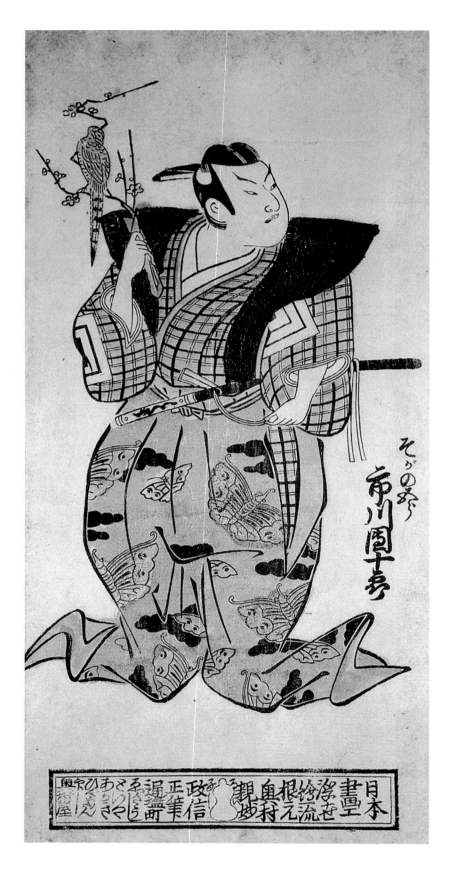

This print depicts Danjūrō II in the role of Soga no Gorō in the *kyōgen* "Yuzuriha nemoto Soga", performed in the Naka-mura theatre in the year Kyōhō 12 (1727). In the year Kenkyū 4 (1193), the Soga brothers Jūrō and Gorō succeeded after 18 long years of waiting in avenging the wrong done to their father. This true story was the basis of "The Tale of Soga" (Soga monogatari), a story of revenge. It provided the subject matter for numerous genres, not least in the *kabuki* theatre, where various versions were regularly staged.

Danjūrō II, who took the role of the *aragoto* in many per-formances, is depicted here about to chastise Gōyūmusō for his misdeeds. It was a moment of considerable tension on the stage. The role re-inforced the great renown in which Danjūrō was held among the theatregoers of Edo. His stature and his accoutrements radiate masculine strength. The *hakama* with the butterfly pattern, and the black stole worn over Danjūrō's typical kimono, were both stock garments belonging to the character of Gorō. Danjūrō's hair is tied up in the kakumae style; in one hand he holds a plum-blossom twig, with its promise of spring, on which is perched a pheasant, while the other hand grasps the sling of his sword. The black gleam of the stole was achieved with an admixture of bone-glue, the gold effect in the butterflies by the application of copper filings. No previous artist had ever succeeded in producing such a handsome portrayal of Gorō, the archetypal *aragoto*.

Okumura Masanobu
Ichikawa Danjūrō II as Soga no Gorō
Hosoban 31.5 x 14.0
Urushi-e
Published by Okumura Genroku
Kyōhō 12 (1727)

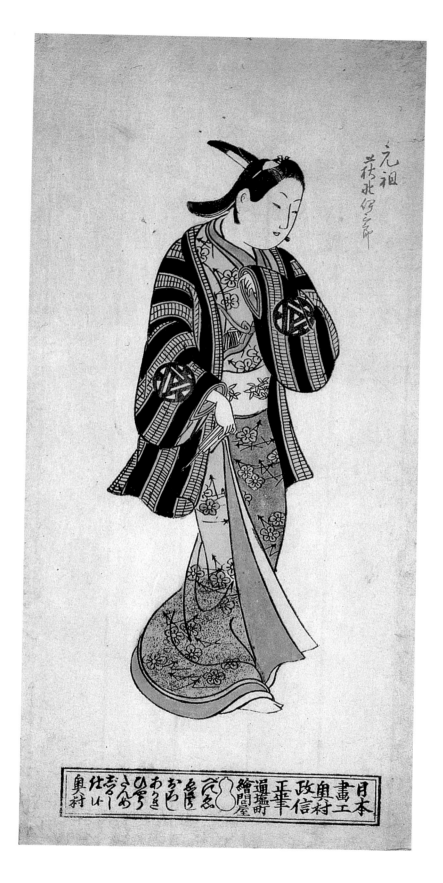

Before the development of the polychrome print, or *nishiki-e*, in the year Meiwa 2 (1765), there existed the *sumizuri-e*, the "ni-e", in which brick-red was used, the *beni-e*, using crimson, and, developed at the same time as the *beni-e*, the *urushi-e*, in which a glossy effect was achieved by the use of an admixture of bone-glue. Over the years, techniques developed to such an extent that simple polychrome prints, or *benizuri-e*, also became possible. Masanobu was active for a long period, from the year Genroku 14 (1701) until well into the Hōreki era (1751–1864), and his many works employed a number of different techniques.

The picture reproduced here is a polychrome print in the *urushi* manner: the black folds of the *haori* shine as though they were lacquered. Masanobu used in addition yellow and *beni* red; for the *kimono*, he added copper filings to the yellow. As a result, the figure has a certain splendour in spite of the few colours actually used. The emblem on the sleeve indicates that the actor in question is one Isaburō, who came to Edo from Kyoto in Tenpō 8 (1723) and there achieved a certain popularity as a player of young male roles *(wakashūgata)*. The particular play involved here is unclear, but to judge by Isaburō's hair-style and attitude, as well as by the manner in which the picture is composed, it must be one dating from the middle of the Tenpō era. That this handsome youth is a *wakashūgata* is evident from the fact that the forehead is unshaven – a sign that the age of majority had not been reached. Isaburō was of a delicate build, and his acting skills were widely recognized. He was also an actor of female roles, or *onnagata*. In Genbun 3 (1738) he graduated to leading parts, and achieved yet more fame thanks to his versatility and artistry. In this print, his youthful charisma finds its expression in the modest spread of the *kimono* and his artistic gestures.

Okumura Masanobu
Ogino Isaburō★
Hosoban 33.7 x 15.7
Urushi-e
Published by Okumura Genroku
mid Kyōhō era (1716–1736)

The 3rd month of Kyōhō 16 (1731) saw Kikunojō I playing the beautiful courtesan Kazuragi in the Nakamura theatre. The figure of Kikunojō, hair all dishevelled, trying to catch a chicken in front of a storeroom bearing the inscription "treasure chamber", is depicted with great vivacity. During this scene, the audience would cry "ōatari" in their enthusiasm. The characters in the centre of the picture give the name of the play, "Tsumamukae niwatori Soga", of the scene, "Oatari", and of the actor, "Segawa Kikunojō". This is evidence that prints were also used as a direct means of presenting information. According to the "Kabuki Chronicle", the play was the second kyōgen from "Keisei fukubiki Nagoya", which was performed from the 1st month onwards. The dance of the first day of the 2nd month, in which he beat a washing basin instead of the traditional silent bell, made Kikunojō so famous that the production was extended until the end of the 5th month. This second kyōgen was still being played in the 3rd month, although by then the dances with the bell, which hitherto had been performed as "nagauta" (ballad with dance accompaniment) in the story of the Dōjōji temple, had been collected and performed for the first time under the title "Bumakane shindōjōji". This in essence created a new play, albeit one based on the original Dōjōji form. Kikunojō only came to Edo from Kyoto in the 11th month of Kyōhō 15 (1730), but was already entrancing audiences with his performances within a very short time, so that he was soon being fêted as the best onnagata in Edo, Kyoto and Osaka.

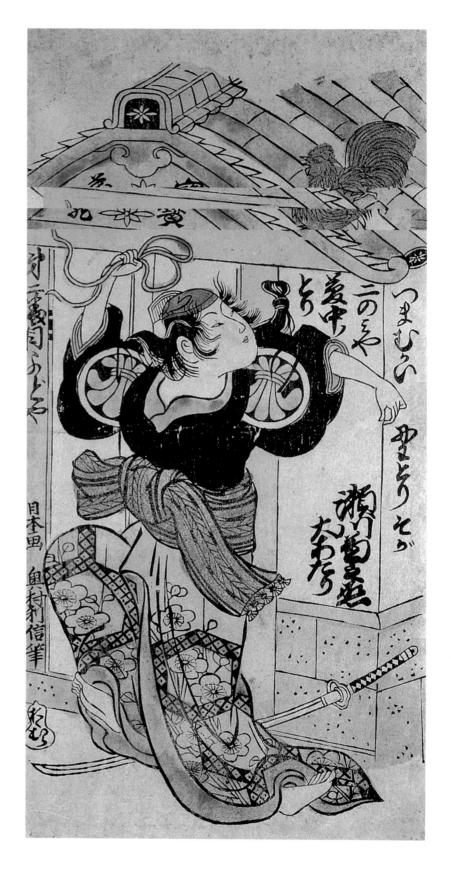

Okumura Toshinobu
Segawa Kikunojō I in a Successful Role
Hosoban 33.2 x 15.7
Urushi-e
Published by Okumura Genroku
Kyōhō 16 (1731)

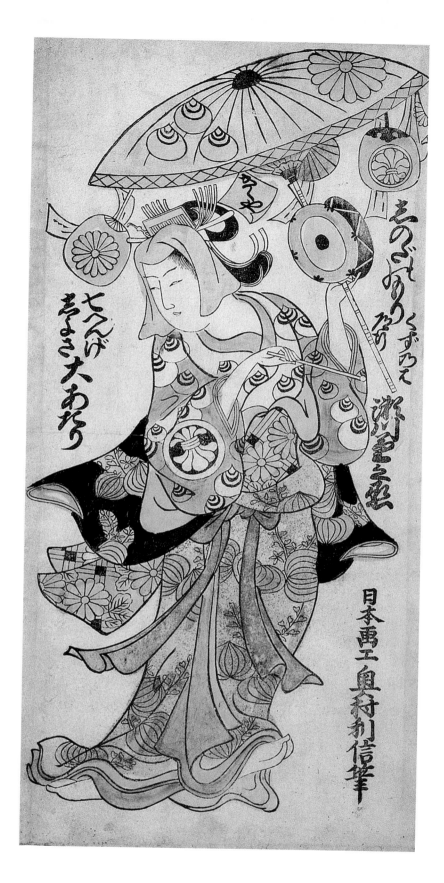

The "Tale of Shinoda's Wife" has been known for centuries under the alternative title of the "Tale of Kuu no Hagitsune and his Unusual Fiancée". It was continually being revived in various forms both in the puppet theatre and on the *kabuki* stage. This print depicts a performance in the year Genbun 2 (1737), in which Kikunojō I played the part of the wife. Kikunojō had been born in Osaka, and appeared on the stage both there and in Kyoto, before moving to Edo in Kyōhō 15 (1730). There he enjoyed major successes with "Buma no kane", "Ishibashi" and "Kono-kimi hodo no ningyō ha arimajiki" ("There is no better *onnagata* than he"). The inscriptions in the picture read: "The successful role of Shinoda no Mori, in which he changed his costume seven times". This part brought Kikunojō acclaim after his return to Kyoto, as did the play, "Ashiya Michimitsu ōuchi kagami". From the 3rd to the 9th month, the *kyōgen* "Gomei-zan" from "Shinoda's Wife" was performed. Kikunojō took this part immediately upon his return to Kyoto. Although it was a long time before he appeared on the stage in the capital again, when he did so, he was received by the audience with rapturous applause.

Okumura Toshinobu
Segawa Kikunojō I as Shinoda no Mori★
Hosoban 32.3 x 15.3
Urushi-e
Publisher unknown
Genbun 2 (1737)

Kiyoshige is assumed to have entered the school of Torii Kiyonobu and there to have produced *benizuri-e* and *urushi-e* of women and actors. His portrayals of women *(bijin-ga)* reflect the style of that school: the figures are on the squat side; his actor-portraits *(yakusha-e)*, by contrast, represent an attempt to introduce a new style to the Torii school.

The *benizuri-e* reproduced here, coloured in red, green, indigo and violet (the last being a superimposition of red and indigo), is an outstanding work, whose colours are in an unusually good state of preservation for a print of this period. The basic hue of the kimono is red changing to blue; the pattern includes the Hikosaburō family emblem, a crane within a circle, which also appears on the sleeve. Alongside the crane emblem is a cucumber emblem, indicating that the role in question is a character in "Soga monogatari", perhaps that of Saburō in the play "Kyūjūsannori ooyose Soga", which was performed in the Ichimura theatre in the 1st month of Hōreki 8 (1758). The final year of the Hōreki era saw the appearance of numerous prints of actors in their star roles, often incorporating *haiku* by the actors themselves or by famous poets. The name "Shinsui" in the middle of the picture is the pseudonym of *haiku* poet Hikosaburō II. The accompanying poem reads: "This is no young nightingale, but a young cuckoo." Young and bold, Hikosaburō II was highly popular with the women and girls of the time. He died at the early age of 27.

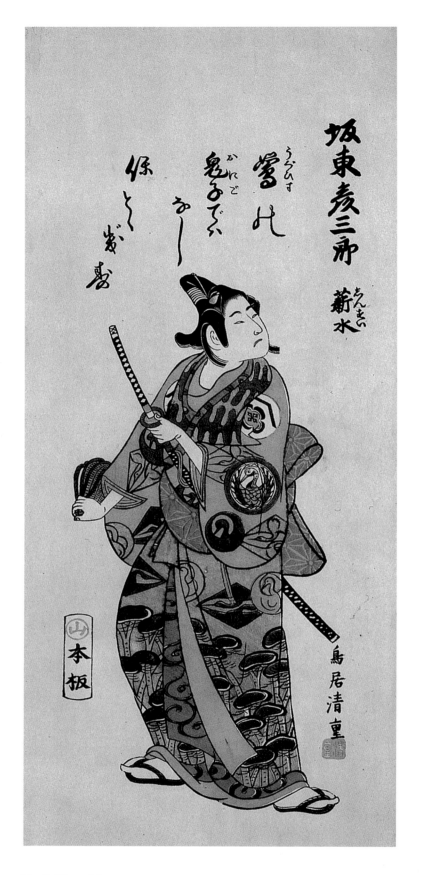

Torii Kiyoshige
Bandō Hikosaburō II★
Hosoban 39.7 x 17.8
Benizuri-e
Published by Maruya Kuzaemon
c. Hōreki 8 (1758)

The *benizuri-e* of the Kyōhō era (1716–1736) frequently feature street-traders, dealers in such commodities as kimono fabrics, haberdashery items, fans, needles and the like. However, the pictures of these traders were usually based more on their portrayal in the *kabuki* theatre than on their appearance in reality. Sometimes the wheel turned full circle, though, with street-traders imitating the portrayals of themselves in the *kabuki*, in particular in terms of their dress. The street-trader Uiro Uri achieved considerable celebrity in this manner.

This print depicts Sanjō Kantarō II as a street-trader carrying a case full of books. The kimono displays the actor's family emblem. Kantarō II's fame originally rested on his playing of female roles, and many *ukiyo-e* depict him thus. In his younger days, he played the parts of young men, graduating to leading male roles in the year Kyōhō 20 (1736).

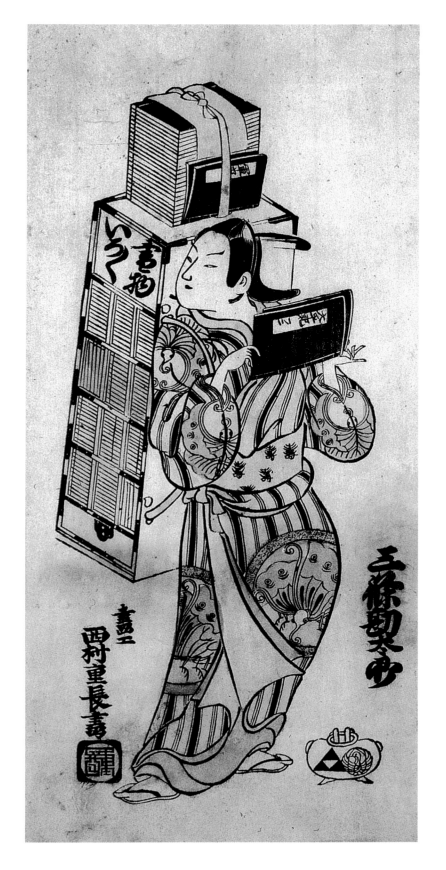

Nishimura Shigenaga
Sanjō Kantarō II★
Hosoban 31.8 x 14.6
Urushi-e
Published by Tsuruya Kiemon, Magobei
Kyōhō era (1716–1736)

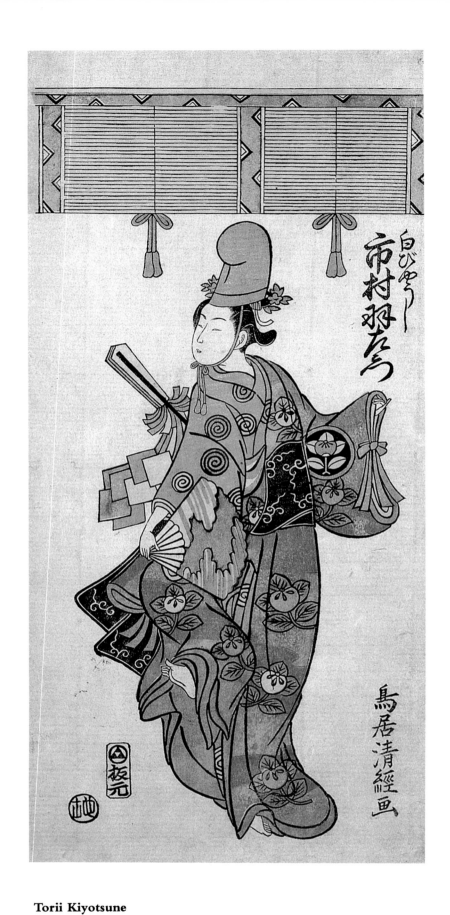

Torii Kiyotsune
Ichimura Uzaemon IX as Shirabyōshi★
Hosoban 30.8 x 14.5
Benizuri-e
Published by Magobei
c. Hōreki 13 (1763)

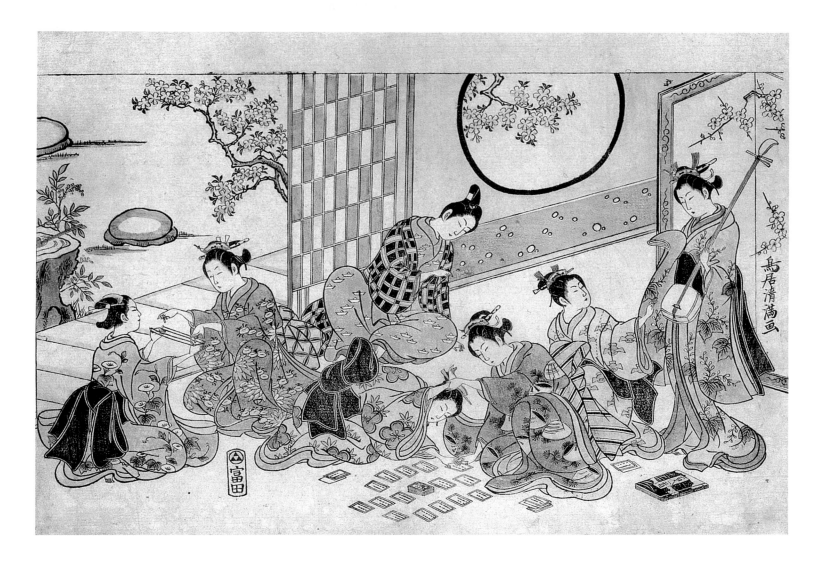

Behind the round windows and the *shōji* sliding doors, the cherry-trees are in full blossom. On this peaceful spring day, a group of girls are playing games indoors. In the middle of the picture, one girl is gracefully extending her arm, dreamily reaching for the card which another girl is showing her. A card-game with famous verses by 100 poets was very widespread at the beginning of the Edo period. The cards each had half a *waka* written on them; the aim of the game was to match the first half of the poem, which was read out, with the second half, which had to be found among the cards laid out on the floor. In the picture, the pile of cards in the middle are those from which the verse was read out, while the cards spread out around them contain the respective second halves. In this scene, the presumably eldest girl is reading the beginnings of the poems, while the others have to find the endings. The whole poems can be looked up in a book which can be seen lying in the bottom right-hand corner.

Shirabyōshi was a *geisha*, who was popular at the end of the Heian period (794–1185) and the beginning of the Kamakura period (1185–1392). Dressed as a man, wearing a ceremonial cap and carrying a water-pot and a long sword, she would perform songs and dances. She was a prostitute, and in great demand in the warrior and noble houses of Taira Kiyomori and Mina-moto Gikei. Actors portraying her on stage would also wear a ceremonial cap, as shown in this picture. Here we have a double transvestite act: the male actor Uzaemon is depicted playing the part of a female *geisha* who herself is impersonating a man. He is wearing a kimono, off the shoulder, decorated with the family emblem of a wild mandarin orange. The undergarment displays a spiral pattern. The actor is performing a lively dance in front of a raised curtain. It is not known what the play in question is, but the fan which Uzaemon holds in his hand, together with the ceremonial shintō wand or *(gohei)*, on which zigzag paper strips are fastened, which is tucked into the back of his *obi*, suggest a religious dance. Uzaemon IX was an outstanding actor, who specialized in *kabuki* dances; he was known as Japan's leading *kabuki* dancer.

Torii Kiyomitsu
Indoor Games★
Yoko-ōban 30.7 x 43.6
Benizuri-e
Published by Tomitaya
Hōreki era (1751–1764)

Torii Kiyotsune
Ichimura Uzaemon IX as Shirabyōshi
(p. 50)

Kiyomitsu was one of the third generation of the Torii school, which was celebrated for its *yakusha-e* tradition. During the Hōreki era, he numbered amongst the leading exponents of *yakusha-e* . It was during his period of artistic activity that the transition was made, in the Meiwa era (1764– 1772), from *benizuri-e* to the true polychrome print, although most of his works were still produced in the *benizuri* style. This particular print is coloured in green, *beni* red, and indigo. With its fine colour composition, it is one of the earliest prints in the *nikishi* style. The very constraints imposed by the limited number of colours lend great expressivity to the vigour of the character of Kagekiyo, whose indefatigable strength enabled him to tear down even the most solid prison walls with his bare hands. Albeit only a subsidiary figure in the 13th-century warrior novel "Heike monogatari", his outstanding dramatic portrayal by Ichikawa Danjūrō IV made him so popular a character in the *kabuki* theatre that Kagekiyo plays with various plots were specially written to accommodate him. Danjūrō IV had made his name with *aragato* parts in the Soga stories. In this print, we see his face made up in the characteristic *kabuki* fashion. The written character on his chest signifies the part being played. In later life, Danjūrō IV went on the play villains, and refined the art of *aragato* portrayal to a hitherto undreamt-of degree. Thanks to his imposing figure and mellifluous voice, he became known as "Kiba no Suyadama", or the "Jewel of Kiba". Kagekiyo was one of his star roles.

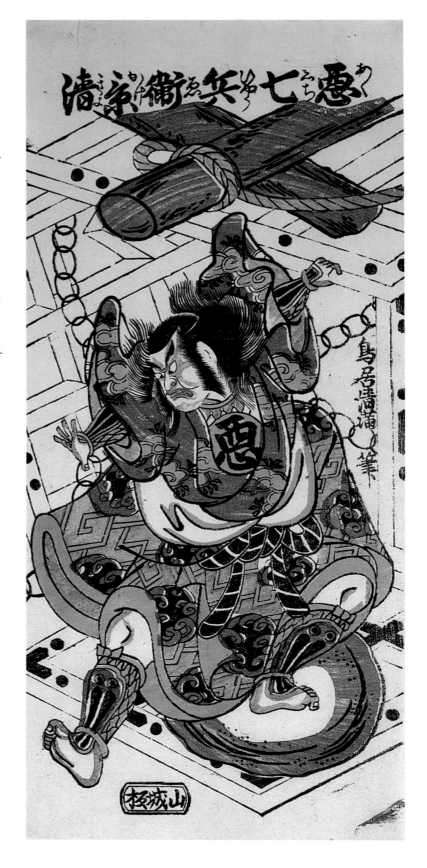

Torii Kiyomitsu
Ichikawa Danjūrō IV as the Villain Kagekiyo★
Hosoban 31.5 x 14.2
Benizuri-e
Published by Yamashiroya
late Hōreki era (1751– 1764)

Toyonobu specialized in portraits of women in the *benizuri* style, the precursor of the polychrome print. His fame rested on his portrayal of elegant beauties with a certain softness of figure. The print reproduced here belongs to the genre of *abuna-e*, or erotic pictures, on account of the degree of nakedness of the woman's body. Having just emerged from her bath and wrapped a cotton kimono (yukata) loosely about her, the lady is being handed tea by a young maidservant. Her eyes are following the glimmer of the glow-worms dancing in the summer night. She appears to be oblivious of her own appearance and dress. The *waka* poem in the background reads: "Thoughts flare up noiselessly, even the glow-worm appears without a sound", presumably a reference to her own thoughts with respect to a man unknown to the beholder of the picture. Toyonobu, who managed a boarding house, has little in common with the image of the pleasure-seeking town-dweller of that period. He was well-versed in ancient Japanese literature and *haiku* poetry, doubtless thanks to the education he received at the hands of his father Masamochi, who introduced him to numerous *kyōgen* when he was young. With its simple colours of red, yellow and green, Toyonobu has conceived a picture of harmonious beauty, whose attractions are quite different from the polychrome prints of the subsequent era.

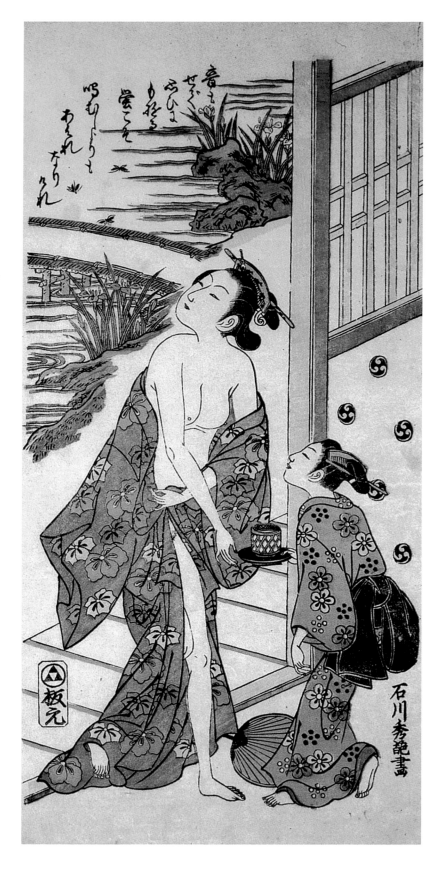

Ishikawa Toyonobu
After the Bath★
Hosoban 31.4 x 14.7
Benizuri-e
Published by Magobei
Kanpō era (1741–1744) – Enkyō era (1744–1748)

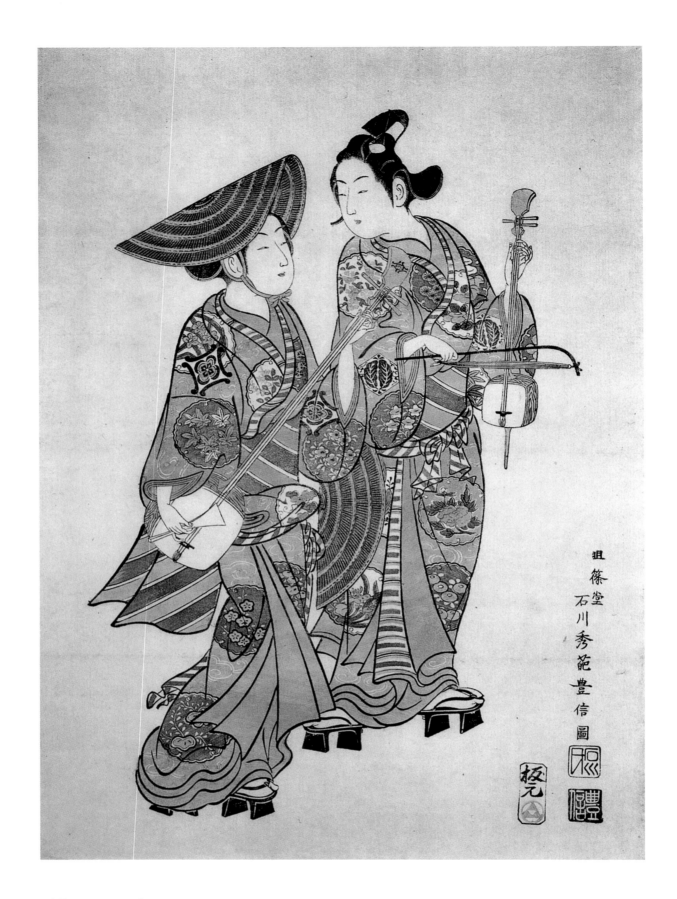

Ishikawa Toyonobu
Nakamura Kiyosaburō III and Onoe Kikugorō
as Wandering Musicians★
Oōban 44.8 x 32.6
Benizuri-e
Published by Magobei
Kan'en 2 (1749) – Hōreki 2 (1752)

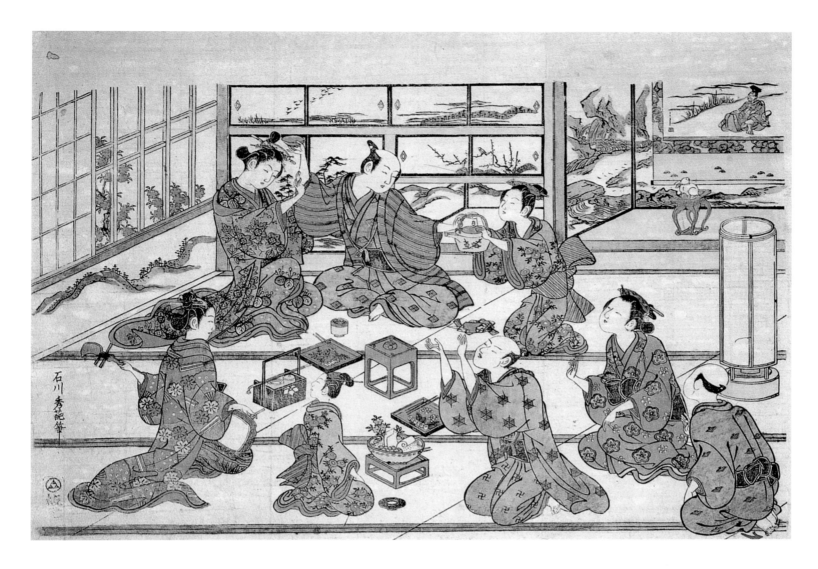

A *tatami* room in a high-class brothel in Yoshiwara is here the scene of merrymaking. In a *tokonoma* (alcove) at the back of the room is a splendid scroll bearing the portrait of a famous poet, while a rabbit is sitting on a red-lacquered stool. The whole room is richly ornamented, and the supporting posts of the *tokonoma* and the doors are hung with landscapes. The guest, wearing a red *haori*, has already indulged in a quantity of sake (rice wine). The courtesan to the left of him as we look at the picture has just offered him another dish of sake; this he has firmly refused, and he turns instead to the *kamuro*, the courtesan's maid, on the other side. The mood is cheerful and relaxed: an entertainer is on hand to see that the guests are amused. An older woman with shaven eyebrows attends to the needs of courtesans and guest alike. A higher-ranking courtesan, on the left of the picture, is playing on the three-stringed *shamisen*.

The two actors can be identified by the emblems on their sleeves: the one with the *shamisen* and the broad-brimmed hat is Kiyosaburō III, and the other, with a smaller stringed instrument, is Onoe Kikugorō. In order to drive away the birds and animals which were causing havoc in the fields, wandering musicians would roam the countryside once a year; at the same time, the peasants would pray for a rich harvest. In Edo, this custom underwent a modification: the musicians would visit all the towns and villages in the vicinity in spring, and religious songs were sung. The Lion Dance and the Mikawa Bansai formed part of the same festivities. This print, however, does not represent a scene from a spring festival; it depicts two well-known *kabuki* actors who have used the occasion of the festival to dress up as young wandering musicians. Kiyosaburō III came to Edo from the Kyoto/Osaka region, and was considered one of the "prettiest" *onnagata*; Kikugorō was also an *onnagata* during his time in Osaka and Kyoto but from the 11th month of Hōreki 2 (1752) he specialized in lead roles, through which he attained great popularity. This picture of the two beauties – with just a hint of soft plumpness – is regarded as one of Toyonobu's masterpieces in the *benizuri* style.

Ishikawa Toyonobu
Drinking Bout in a Brothel★
Yoko-ōban 31.4 x 44.8
Benizuri-e
Published by Magobei
mid Hōreki era (1751–1764)

Ishikawa Toyonobu
Nakamura Kiyosaburō III and Onoe Kikugorō as Wandering Musicians
(p. 54)

Suzuki Harunobu

8 Views: Early Morning Mist in Ogi

(p. 57)

The "8 Views" have their origin in the calendar illustrations first commissioned by Jinshirō. Later they were published by Shōkakudō. The series is one of Harunobu's major works, and the one which is said to have represented the breakthrough of the polychrome technique in woodblock printmaking. Like the Chinese pictures on which it is based, the series depicts scenes from everyday life. The stories behind the Chinese originals are from the pen of the *haiku* poet Teiryū.

Early morning mist, the haze in the air of what will turn out to be a sunny day, covers the sun like a fan. The kimono of the girl with the fan has the shape of a cloud seemingly concealing a willow. In the background there is just the corner of a house with its barred window. Everything else is reduced to near monochrome. Not even a horizon is visible. Such an abstract depiction of space is quite frequent in Harunobu's work.

Suzuki Harunobu

8 Views: The Evening Bell

(p. 58)

This picture shows a woman freshening herself up on the verandah after taking a bath. The small clock in the background is reminiscent of the temple bells which used to chime the hours in Edo in the days before clocks were widespread. During the Edo period, clocks were indeed made, but they were valuable objects and by no means every household possessed one. Nevertheless, in spite of their relative rarity in real life, they put in an appearance in a number of pictures.

This particular lady is based on a work by Nishikawa Sukenobu entitled "Ehon Tamakazura". The works of Kōryūsai likewise have a great similarity with this and other prints by Harunobu. Harunobu himself attached great importance to the composition of his pictures. The vertical, horizontal and diagonal lines of the verandah boards, the *tatami*, the screen and the *shōji* frame are precisely attuned to one to another.

Suzuki Harunobu

8 Views: Flight of the Wild Geese

(p. 59)

The two girls depicted here may be based on the "Catalogue of 100 Courtesans" illustrated by Sukenobu. The bridges supporting the strings of the *koto* are reminiscent of the formation of wild geese in flight. The girl in front is leafing through a collection of songs for *koto* accompaniment, which she has just taken out of a box. The other girl is putting the plectrum on her finger. The atmosphere of a quiet autumn day is conveyed by the blossoms of the hagi bush in the garden.

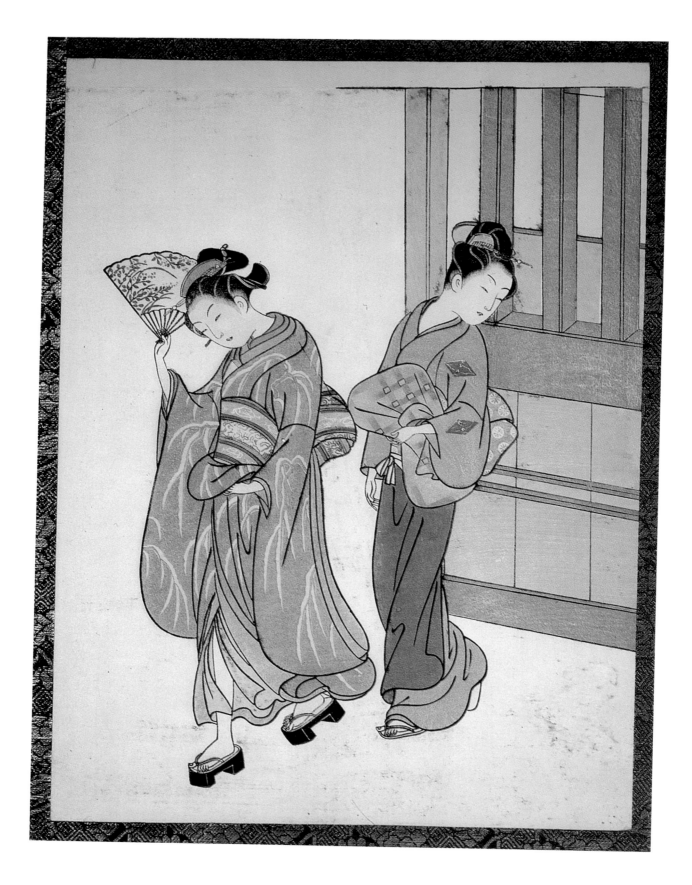

Suzuki Harunobu
8 Views: Early Morning Mist in Ogi★
Chūban 28.6 x 20.9
Nishiki-e
Published by (Shōkakudō)
c. Meiwa 3 (1766)

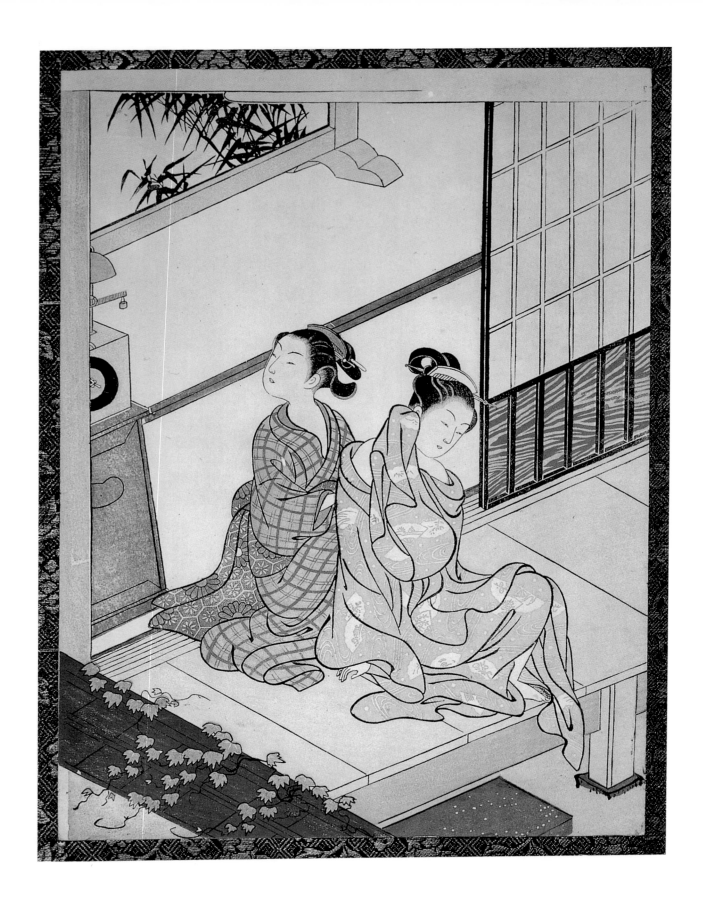

Suzuki Harunobu
8 Views: The Evening Bell★
Chūban 28.6 x 21.0
Nishiki-e
Published by (Shōkakudō)
c. Meiwa 3 (1766)

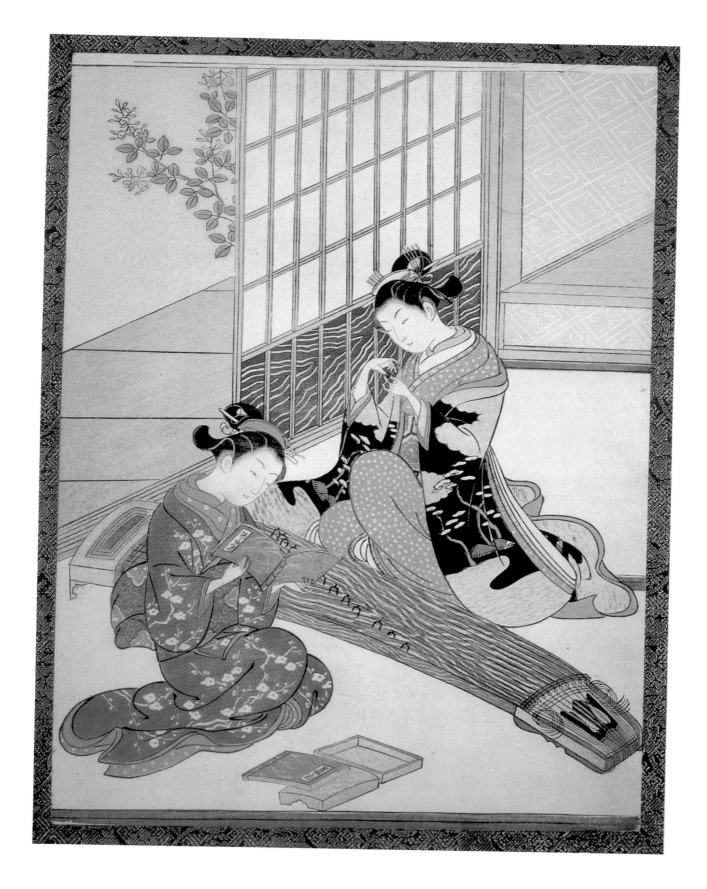

Suzuki Harunobu
8 Views: Flight of the Wild Geese★
Chūban 28.6 x 21.0
Nishiki-e
Published by (Shōkakudō)
c. Meiwa 3 (1766)

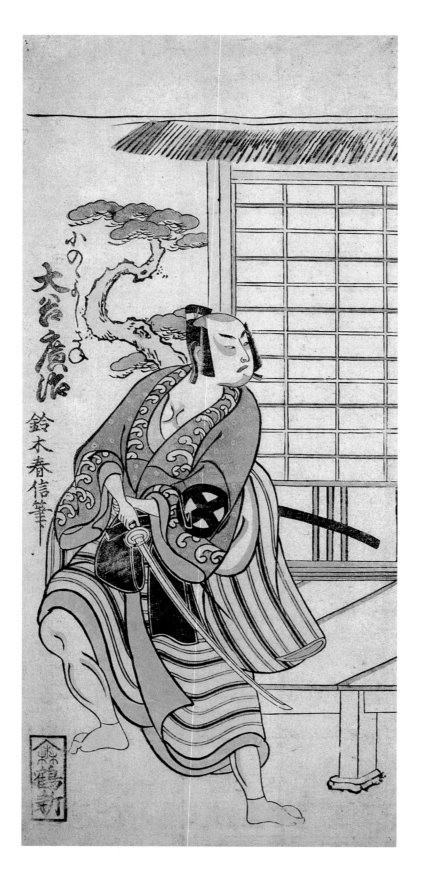

In his work "Hannichikanwa", the famous Edo writer Ota Nanpo (1749–1823) asserted that Harunobu had not portrayed any of the celebrated actors of his day. In fact however, of the 100 works dating from his apprenticeship up to the year Meiwa 2 (1765), when he began employing the *nishiki-e* polychrome technique, some 30 portray actors. The earliest example of which we have evidence is a picture of Bandō Kamezō and Bandō Sanpachi in a performance of "Soga bannen hashira", dating from the 3rd month of Hōreki 10 (1760). This was the start of the very decade when Harunobu was the most active. The Hōreki era was also the period in which Kiyomitsu was the leading portrayer of actors. Harunobu's works are strongly influenced by Kiyomitsu's compositions.

The work reproduced here is based on a performance of the play „Ono no Tōfū aoyaki suzuri" in the Morita theatre during the 8th month of Meiwa 1 (1764). Being one of the last works of this particular era, it exhibits features both of the traditional style of the Torii school – known as the "hyōtanashi" (pumpkin-leg) style on account of the portrayal of corpulent characters – and of the typical coloration techniques of *benizuri-e*. The character Ono no Yoshisane, played here by Hiroji, had allied himself with Tōfū and Yorikaze to bring down the ruthless Tachibana no Hayanari, and thus to avert the danger the latter posed to his lord. Devoted servants such as this were among Hiroji's favourite roles.

Suzuki Harunobu
Sagimusume
(p. 61)

"Sagimusume" is the title of a *kabuki* dance. A dancing-girl, clothed in a snow-white kimono, appears by the waterside as the incarnation of a white heron and, employing the gestures of the heron, performs the dance of a girl unhappy in love. After Kikunojō II had achieved popularity with this role in Edo's Ishimura theatre in Hōreki 12 (1782), the theme also became a motif for *ukiyo-e*. Harunobu, Koryūsai and Utamaro all used it. The tranquil scene with the white heron figure shrouded in a white kimono is a dream image far removed from reality. Neither clouds nor headscarf have a sharp outline; their contours are blurred. The contrast between the white kimono and the black *obi* is particularly striking. The *kimedashi* and *karazuri* techniques employed here, along with the polychrome technique, represent a further step forward in ink printing. They now became an element of the precisely carved woodblock print. To achieve such structuring effects, heavy pressure is needed; this required good paper, which from then on became a feature of *ukiyo-e*.

Suzuki Harunobu
Otani Hiroji as Ono no Yoshisane★
Hosoban 30.7 x 13.8
Benizuri-e
Published by Tsurushin
Meiwa 1 (1764)

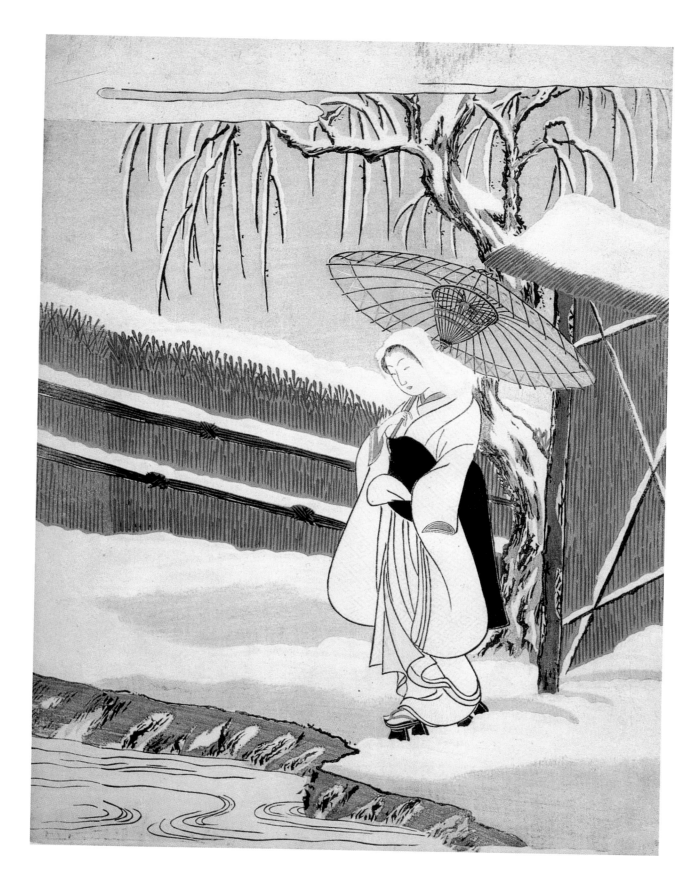

Suzuki Harunobu
Sagimusume★
Chūban 28.9 x 21.6
Nishiki-e
Publisher unknown
c. Meiwa 3 (1766)

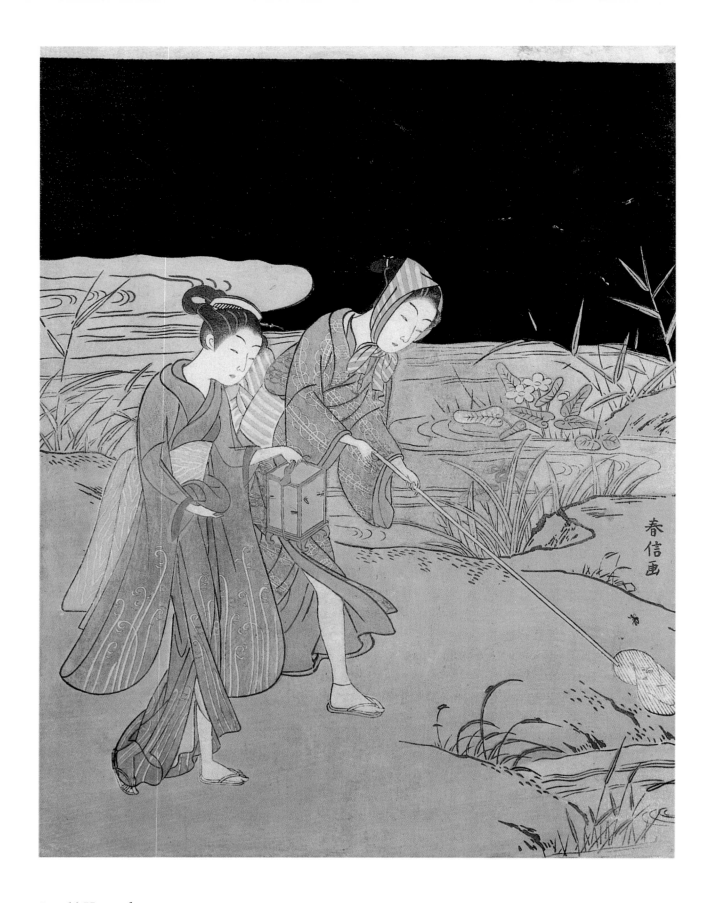

Suzuki Harunobu
Glow–worm Hunting★
Chūban 27.7 x 20.5
Nishiki-e
Publisher unknown
c. Meiwa 5 (1768)

Since time immemorial, the Japanese nobility had had a predilection for observing glow-worms, a passion which during the Edo period also spread to the mercantile and bourgeois classes. Glow-worm hunting became popular summer pastime. The scene depicted here was particularly popular: the girl counts how many glow-worms she has in her box, while the boy tries to trap the creatures in his net. Her *furisode-kimono*, with its fern pattern on a violet background, is so translucent that arms, feet and undergarment can be seen beneath it. The young man, who has tied a scarf around his head, is wearing a simple unlined kimono with the watsunagi pattern. Both, in other words, are wearing typical summer clothes. The surface of the water is rippling in the evening wind. The dense vegetation along the bank includes the yellow flowers of the marsh marigold, along with purple irises. In the darkness, the glow-worms can be faintly seem as shimmers against the night sky as they flitter noiselessly about. The whole scene is one of friendly silence. The dark background conveys an atmosphere of evening tranquillity, and along with the light blue of the water and the dense green of the vegetation, provides an effective contrast with the couple.

Suzuki Harunobu
Glow-worm Hunting
(p. 62)

"Mitate-e", or "travesty pictures", was the name given to pictures which took their inspiration from ideas and motifs drawn from ancient sources, such as legends, stories and *waka*, and which incorporated these into depictions of landscapes and other scenes. Here, the story of the classical Chinese poet Kinkō is enacted by a courtesan from Harunobu's own Meiwa era. Legend had it that Kinkō tried to capture a young dragon; in the process, he encountered a giant carp, and used its back as a stepping-stone to heaven.

The book which the courtesan is reading may perhaps have been given to her by her lover. The dreamy look on her face, typical of Haronobu's beauties, does not convey the impression that she would exclude the possibility of sitting on the back of a carp. The energetic movements of the fish as it rises out of the water, its flappings fins, the whirling current and the foaming spray, all form a dramatic contrast to the grace and poise of the girl herself. Her cloak is patterned with snow-laden pine-trees, while her kimono is bordered with ferns. The powerful colours of the figure stand out within the overall palette. In the top section of the picture, a cloud has been painted using a technique whereby no outlines are created. In many of Harunobu's works, such clouds contain a poem; this is not the case here, however.

Suzuki Harunobu
Mitate no Kinkō
(p. 64)

The letter in question – perhaps from a lover? – is just being handed to Oiren by a *kamuro*, to whom the courtesan is graciously turning her head. The *Nakonomachi*, which ran through the Yoshiwara pleasure quarter, was lined on both sides by tea-stalls with faded blue "noren", or awnings, which bore the name of the proprietor. The high-class courtesans would pass by these tea-stalls on their evening promenades when going to receive their regular clients, as was the custom in the quarter.

On the verandah in front of this tea-stall, rush-mats decorated with the ichimatsu (chequer-board) pattern have been laid out. The courtesan Oiren is just passing by in the company of her maids. The elder of the two is rolling a piece of paper to make a pipe-cleaner. Aged eight or nine and thirteen or fourteen respectively, the two girls are doing all they can to be of service to their mistress. When appearing in public with her, they wear kimonos of a new style, decorated with the yajirubei pattern, and, as was the fashion for younger girls at the time, they have their *obi* tied in a heijūrō bow. Oiren herself is prettily attired in her kimono with its shichidama pattern and a shawl decorated with irises. Her *obi* has a chrysanthemum pattern. Her coiffure, too, with its combs and hairpins, makes a very refined impression. Her figure, as she leans to one side in the centre of the picture, catches the eye immediately.

Suzuki Harunobu
A Letter for the Courtesan
(p. 65)

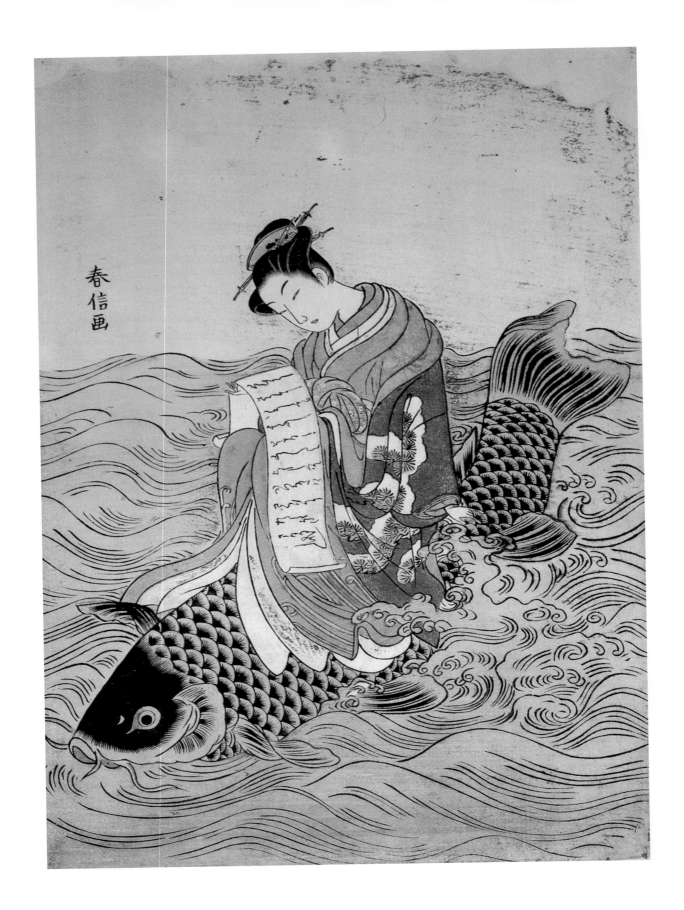

Suzuki Harunobu
Mitate no Kinkō
Chūban 28.5 x 20.5
Nishiki-e
Publisher unknown
Meiwa 2 (1765)

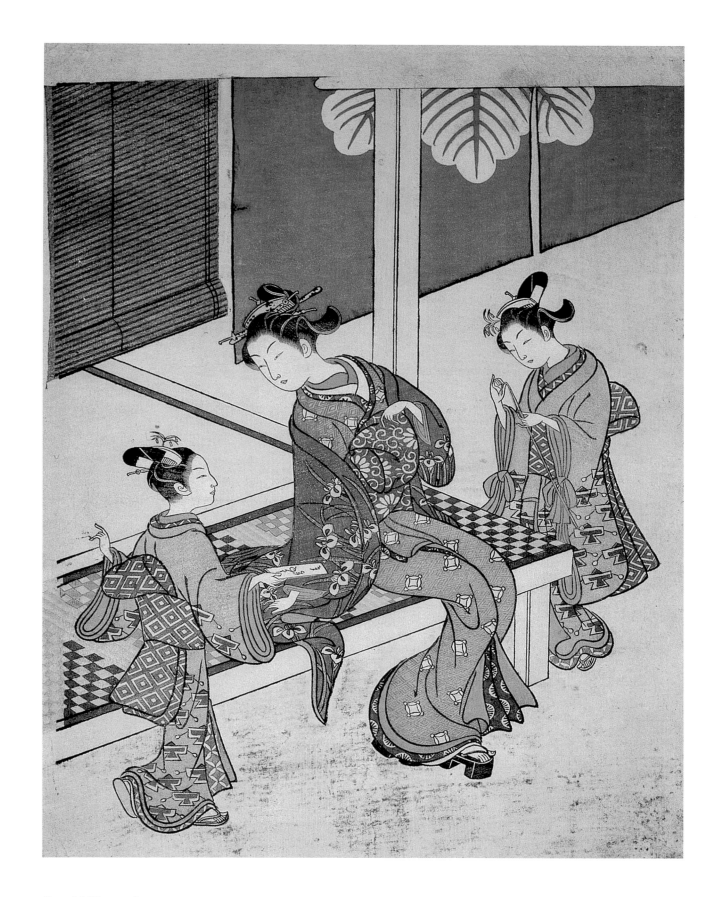

Suzuki Harunobu
A Letter for the Courtesan★
Chūban 28.4 x 21.7
Nishiki-e
Publisher unknown
c. Meiwa 3 (1766)

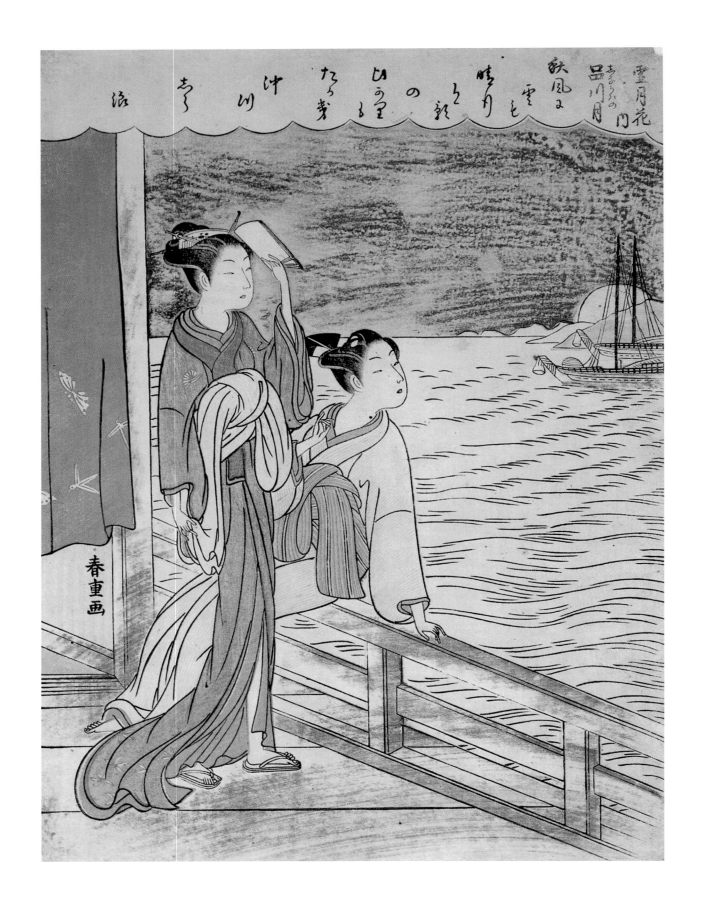

Suzuki Harushige
Snow, Moon and Flowers: The Moon over Shinagawa★
Chūban 27.6 x 21.2
Nishiki-e
Publisher unknown
c. Meiwa 8 (1771)

Shinagawa was the first stop on the *Tōkaidō*, the main route between Edo and Kyoto. Not only travellers between the two cities, but the inhabitants of Edo, too, were aware that Shinagawa had a flourishing pleasure quarter complete with brothels. This was not its only attraction: many people came out to see its famous blossoms and to watch the moon rising out of the sea from a vantage point above the sea. In honour of the full moon which rose, according to the old calendar, on the 26th day of the 7th month, a festival was held. Legend had it that the Buddha would appear in the moonlight. These festivals were always occasions for merrymaking. All this is a thing of the past: land reclamation has displaced the coastline, and the reclaimed land is covered with buildings.

This print depicts a prostitute and a young man watching the moon rise over the headland, and forms part of the triptych "Snow, Moon and Flowers". The inscription in the cloud is a *waka*, reading: "The autumn wind drives the clouds from the sky, the light of the moon strikes the waves of the open sea." The two persons depicted have left the room where they shared a bed in order to observe the moon. The composition of the woman, who is shading her eyes with a sheet of paper, is extremely effective, as is that of the man, sitting casually on the balustrade of the verandah outside the brothel.

The artist used the name Harushige during the early part of his career, when he was active as a producer of woodblock prints. In later years he turned to copperplate engravings and Western-style landscapes, and took the name of Shiba Kōkan. The portrayal of the figures is typical Harushige, but the perspective of the picture, apparent in the waves of the open sea, is more characteristic of Kōkan.

Suzuki Harushige
Snow, Moon and Flowers: Snow in
Yoshiwara *(p. 69)*

The Japanese enjoy the sight of nature and the landscape at every season. Especially popular are snow, moon and flowers. In pictures such as "Snow in Yoshiwara" (p. 69), "The Moon over Shinagawa" (p. 66) and "Cherry Blossom in Fukagawa", scenes with courtesans were combined with the natural attractions of these famous sites and preserved in woodblock print. The "Shin-goshūiwakashū" collection of verse includes in its chapter "Winter Poems" a piece which reads: "Unnoticed, snow has fallen, the way home will be hard to find." These lines, incorporated in this print in the cloud at the top of the picture, encapsulate the meaning of the scene depicted. The Japanese title of the picture has, preceding the word "yuki" (snow), the word "serō" – which signified the prostitute's room on the first floor of a Yoshiwara brothel – hence our title "Snow in Yoshiwara".

Through the bars of the open window can be seen a sedan chair, in which a Yoshiwara guest is being carried home along the Nihontei, the street which led to the gate which was the only way in and out of the pleasure quarter. There were no houses in the area around Yoshiwara, and the sight of snow was considered something special. If we turn our attention to what is going on inside, we might assume that the snow has fallen while the man in the sedan was indulging in the pleasures of love. On waking, he took no notice of the rice-wine or titbits which a young courtesan had brought him. The courtesan herself is using a "hibachi", or charcoal brazier, to warm up the left-overs of a meal in a small pot. She is using a hair-pin to poke the fire. Beside the hibachi is a red-lacquered table for the sake cups, while on the black tray, a white snow-rabbit is already beginning to melt.

Isoda Koryūsai
The Morning After
(p. 24)

In the years Tenmei 1 and 2 (1781, 1782) the highest title of honour which a print artist could receive was bestowed upon Koryūsai. In later life, he specialized in single-sheet pictures. The year Hōreki 1 (1751) had seen his first *hashira-e*, or post pictures (also known as "hashira-kake" or post scrolls, and "hashira-in" or post hangings). These were 69–75 cm long, and 12–13 cm broad, and as their name implies, they were hung on posts indoors. Koryūsai had an expert eye for the composition of such pictures.

"The Morning After" is a particularly fraught time for lovers, as it means separation is near. The scene depicted here will be taking place between 6 and 7 o'clock as dawn breaks, and the guest is taking leave of the girl with whom he has spent the night. Especially good guests, it should be said, were not left to depart from the brothel alone, but escorted to the gate which formed the entrance and exit to Yoshiwara. The expression on the faces of the couple shows how difficult is the parting now being heralded, inexorably, by the song of the early birds as the sun comes up. Could it be that the next assignation is being arranged?

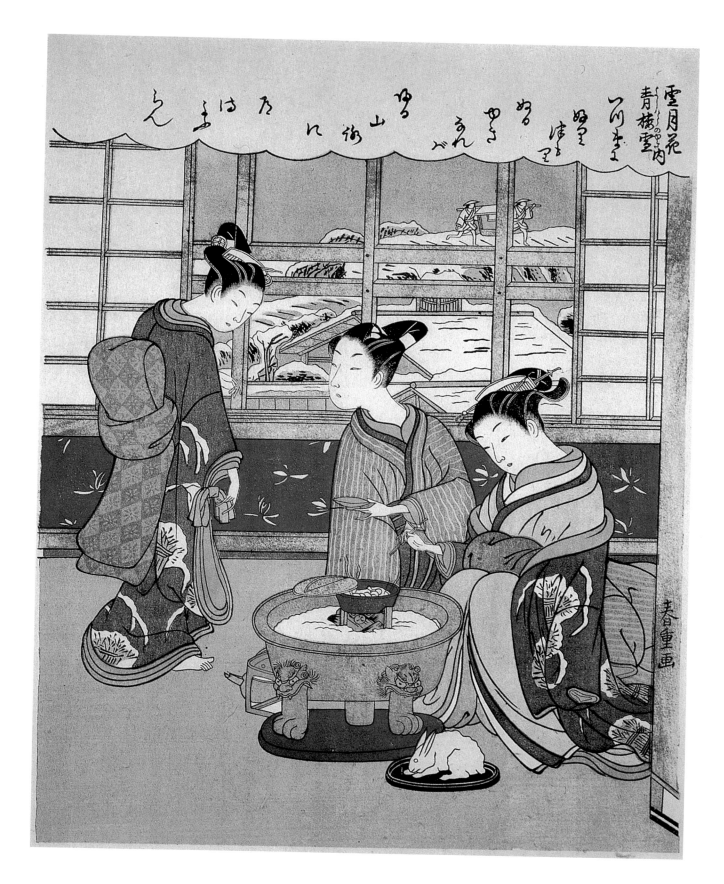

Suzuki Harushige
Snow, Moon and Flowers: Snow in Yoshiwara
Chūban 27.6 x 21.2
Nishiki-e
Publisher unknown
c. Meiwa 8 (1771)

Isoda Koryūsai
8 Pictures of Birds: Parakeet in the Early
Morning Mist
(p. 71)

Isoda Koryūsai
Tag
(p. 25)

Alongside pictures of beautiful women, Koryūsai also produced prints of animals and plants, and it is here that his great virtuosity is most apparent. The Edo period was notable as a time when the breeding of fashionable animals flourished, from dogs and cats to birds and fish and even insects. All these were among the motifs of the *ukiyo-e* artists. Books were published, giving instructions on methods of breeding birds, and competitions were held for the best birdsong.

The parakeet depicted here is not native to Japan: birds were imported in considerable numbers. The girl holding the parakeet is wearing her hair in what was, at the time, a very modern style. The *haori* is very long, another indication of the fashion prevalent among young women during the Tenmei era (from 1781), which was regarded as a particularly free and easy age.

The pictorial plane has been so skilfully organized that the beholder really does get the impression that the girl and the little boy are indeed playing tag around a screen. During the Edo period, boys had their heads shaved when they were three years old; a tuft was left to grow long. This urchin, then, is three or four years old, and has, besides the typical karashi hair-style, a cotton kimono with open sleeves. The girl's hair is done in the kamomezuto style, tied back into a looped bun, as was the fashion at the beginning of the An'ei era (from 1772). This composition by Koryūsai still bears clear signs of the influence of Harunobu.

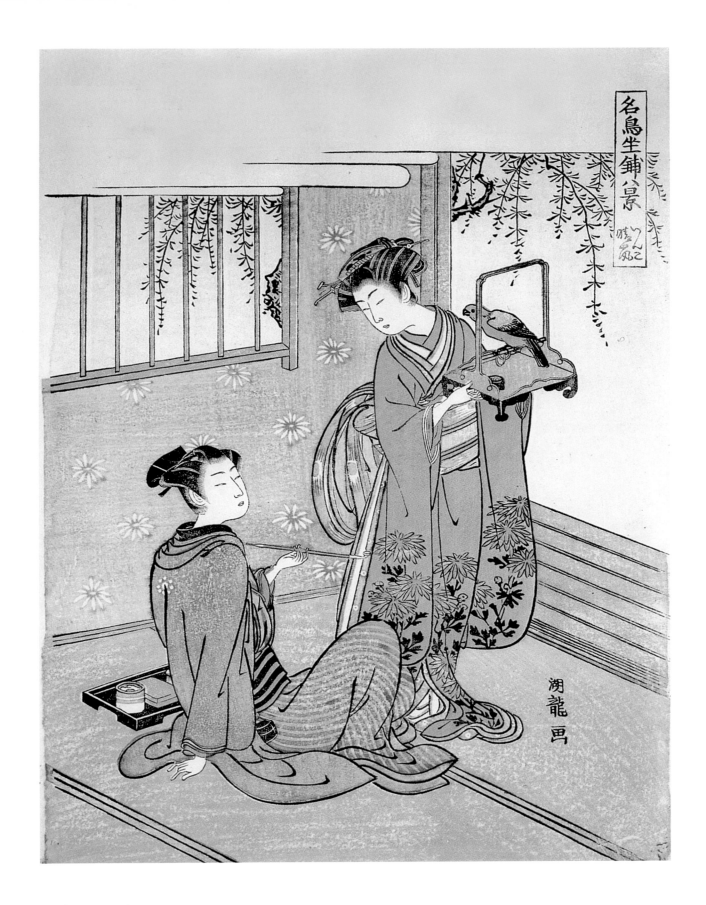

Isoda Koryūsai
8 Pictures of Birds: Parakeet in the Early Morning Mist★
Chūban 26.7 x 19.9
Nishiki-e
Publisher unknown
early An'ei era (1772–1781)

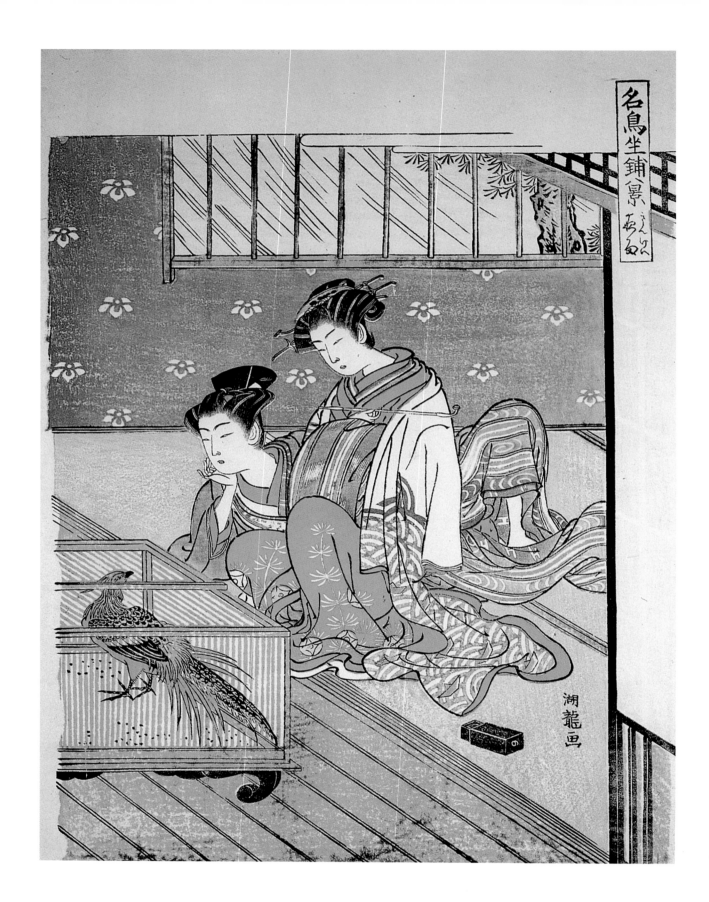

Isoda Koryūsai
8 Pictures of Birds: Pheasant in the Evening Rain
Chūban 26.2 x 19.7
Nishiki-e
Publisher unknown
early An'ei era (1772–1781)

The pheasant originally came from China, where it was famed for the splendid colours of its plumage. In this print, the colours on its back are not very clearly differentiated. In Koryūsai's *hashira-e*, however, where the pheasant is depicted sitting in a pine tree or on a giant peony, its colours are striking. Imported birds such as pheasants, parrots and parakeets were frequent motifs in Japanese painting of this period. The creatures themselves, however, fetched such high prices that it was difficult for the average citizen to acquire one. During the Kansei era (1789–1801) it was not infrequent for tea-houses to possess and exhibit rare birds.

On this print we see a courtesan and a servant girl on a rainy evening gazing at a pheasant in a cage. The hems of their kimonos are decorated with representations of water-plants, while the pattern on the kimonos themselves is known as "Blue Waves", and originated in China, where it was often used to decorate pottery. The striped pattern of the *obi* was also very popular. Indeed, the Edo period was all in all a very fashion-conscious epoch.

Isoda Koryūsai
8 Pictures of Birds: Pheasant in the Evening Rain *(p. 72)*

The title "Hinagata wakana no hatsumoyō" is a reference to the pattern on a garment which was worn for the New Year festivities. This print was doubtless subsidized by a tailor who wished to publicize a new fashion; that at least is what one would infer from the emphasis accorded to the magnificent kimonos. Presumably, too, the management of the brothel considered that by naming the wearer of this splendid garment, the reputation of the ladies of the house would also be enhanced. The fact that this work was commissioned from the Nishimuraya publishing house in the *oban* format led to more and more *bijin-ga* being brought out as large prints, rather than in medium size as hitherto. The whole series appeared between An'ei 4 (1775) and Tenmei 1 (1781), and comprises a total of 100 pictures. There also exist a few works of this format and subject by Kiyonaga and Shunzan.

This print depicts a courtesan and two *kamuro* who have taken a scroll picture out of its case to examine it. Their names are inscribed on the left. The courtesan's shawl is decorated with pine-trees, bamboo and a crane. The two *kamuro* are wearing identical kimonos. As personal maids of the courtesan, they would serve her with tea and refreshments and bring her tobacco. In return, they would be handed down their mistress' cast-off garments.

Isoda Koryūsai
Hinagata wakana no hatsumoyō *(p. 74)*

The extent of the popularity enjoyed by the beautiful subject of this print may be judged from the fact that her portrait was made the subject of more than 100 different woodblock prints. Koryūsai had by now liberated himself from Harunobu's technique, to become one of the first to produce sensuously realistic representations of beautiful women. The owl, modelled in the snow which covered the garden, has just been brought in from outside. The carefree manner in which the two *kamuro* are chatting to each other is indicative of the pleasant atmosphere in such houses of entertainment.

Isoda Koryūsai
Hinagata wakana no hatsumoyō: Shirayu *(p. 75)*

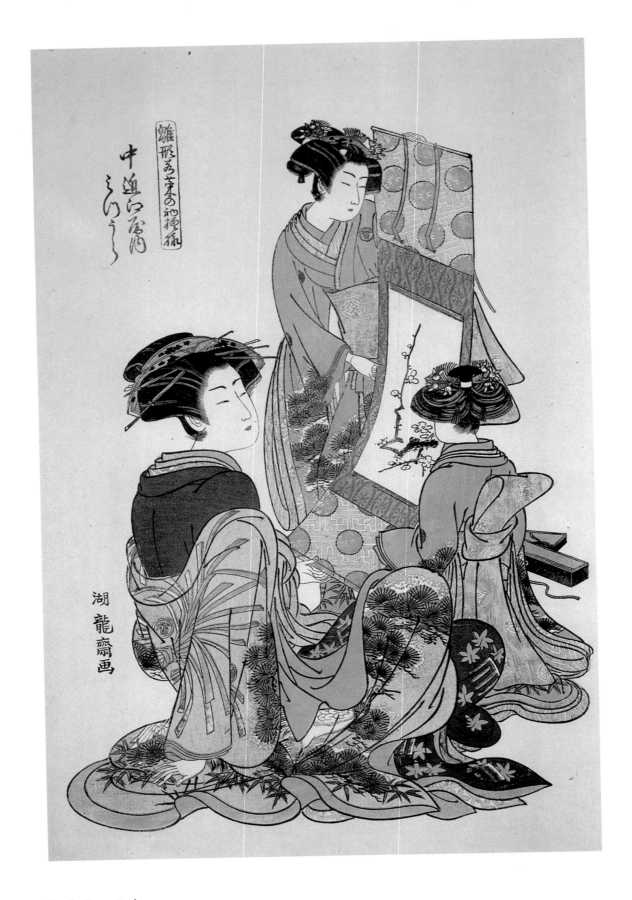

Isoda Koryūsai
Hinagata wakana no hatsumoyō★
Oban 38.4 x 25.3
Nishiki-e
Published by (Nishimuraya Yohachi)
An'ei 9–10 (1780–1781)

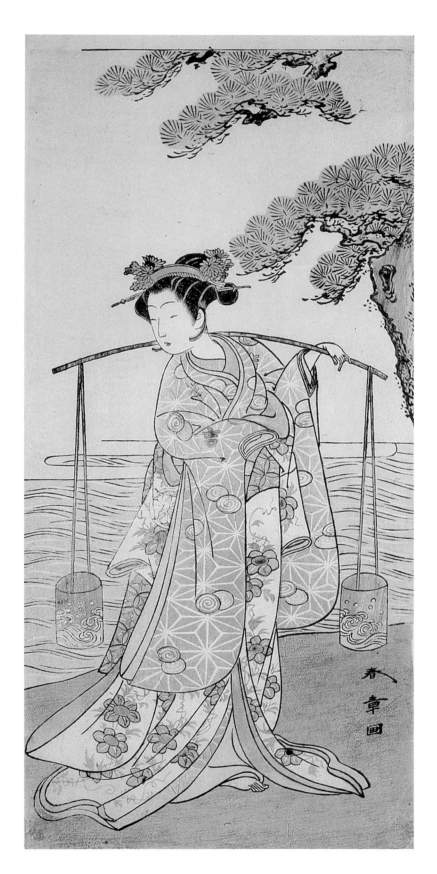

The character for Kichiji's name on the sleeve of the kimono is an indication that the actor portrayed in this print is Segawa Kichiji III. It is documented that he played the part of Murasame in the play "Gohiiki kanjinchō" at the Nakamura theatre in the 11th month of An'ei 2 (1773). This work is probably the right-hand side of a diptych, on whose left-hand side Matsukaze was portrayed.

The poet Ariwara no Yukihira was banished to Suma during the Heian period (794–1185). There, the sisters Matsukaze and Murasame became aware of their affection for him. Soon, however, his banishment was quashed, and he returned to the capital. This ancient story was absorbed into the repertoires of the nō, jōruri and kabuki theatres. The kabuki in particular made much of the "shiokumi" (salt-extraction) dance in its numerous variations. The play is still performed to this day on numerous occasions. It gives the kabuki actor an opportunity, as in this picture, to display a particular grace.

The shiokumi dance represents a stylization of the salt-extraction process. People would come from far and wide to draw water from the sea. The dance with the wooden buckets suspended from a yoke can be extraordinarily graceful. Kichiji III had previously specialized in elderly roles, but it was not until he took up onnagata parts that his youthful good looks made his name. In this print, Shunshō has succeeded in giving outstanding expression to Kichiji's extraordinary beauty. In the background can be seen the coast of Suwa, where the action takes place, and a pine grove.

Katsukawa Shunshō
Segawa Kichiji III as Murasame★
Hosoban 32.1 x 15.0
Nishiki-e
Publisher unknown
An'ei 2 (1773)

In the plays "Shokumoyō aoyanagi Soga" and "Shinobugusa koi no utsushie", which were performed at the Nakamura theatre in the 1st month of An'ei 4 (1775), Nakazō won considerable renown through his portrayal of the monk and the leek-seller of Seitenchō respectively, the first role being a *kabuki* dance, the second a theatre dance. Nakazō played the monk on subsequent occasions, too. If one considers the style and manner of this print, it is clear that this *kyōgen* will have served as the model. It is interesting to note that the archives of the Musée Guimet in Paris house a work by Shunshō depicting Nakazō as the leek-seller. Dainichibō is a mendicant monk, wandering from house to house begging for donations for a temple bell, which can be seen on the trolley he is pulling behind him. The characters on the box hanging round his neck state that he is asking for a donation for the temple bell. He is holding a small hand-bell, which he strikes as he goes along. The look on his face is pitiable, and suggest that he is being required to do lengthy penance for some wrong he has committed, for example the breach of a Buddhist precept. Nakazō, here depicted playing this part, was a popular performer of *aragoto* roles at this time. He also brought some innovative ideas to the production of dramatic works, some of which are still performed in his version to this day. For their part, Shunshō and Bunchō introduced a new style of actor portrait, in which the face and pose are reproduced with almost photographic realism. This print is an outstanding example of the new style.

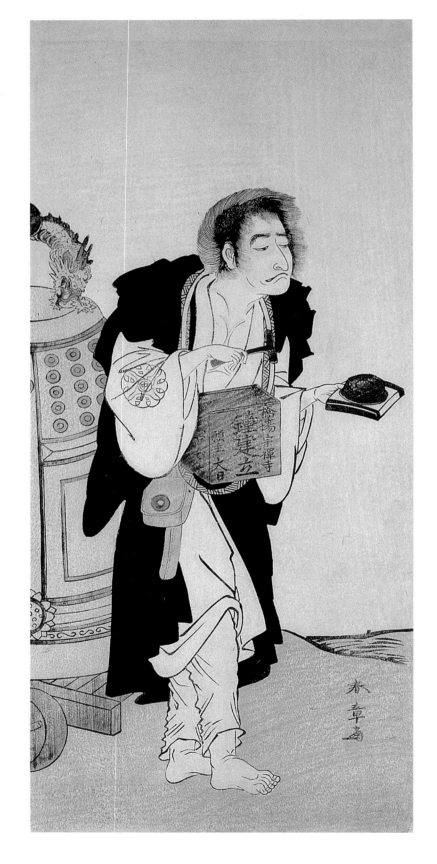

Katsukawa Shunshō
Nakamura Nakazō as Dainichibō★
Hosoban 32.3 x 14.9
Nishiki-e
Publisher unknown
An'ei 4 (1775)

The print artist Shunkō was stricken by paralysis in the late Tenmei and early Kansei eras, denying him the use of his right hand; he could therefore only hold the brush in his left. In the period between Tenmei 8 (1788) and the years Kansei 1 and 2 (1789–1790) in particular, he produced numerous actor portraits in the *oban* format. The work depicted here, showing the bust of an actor in this large format, may be described as one of the most progressive of its time. The two hanging paper strips bear the names "Hamamuraya" and "Rokō". The emblem on the sleeve of the kimono, along with the projecting lower lip, both suggest that the actor in question is Segawa Kikunojō III. He had added the epithet "the third" to his name in An'ei 3 (1774), and was one of the leading players of *onnagata* roles from the Tenmei through to the Bunka eras. His stage name was Rokō, and on account of his sensuous features he was known as "Senjo Rokō". In Edo he became so popular that people called him "the divine Hamamura". He played numerous courtesans. The sparrow-and-bamboo pattern of the kimono in this print indicates that the part being played here is that of the courtesan Takao, but it is uncertain which of the *kyōgen* about Takao, which were performed as from the 7th month of Tenmei 2 (1782), served as the basis for this portrait.

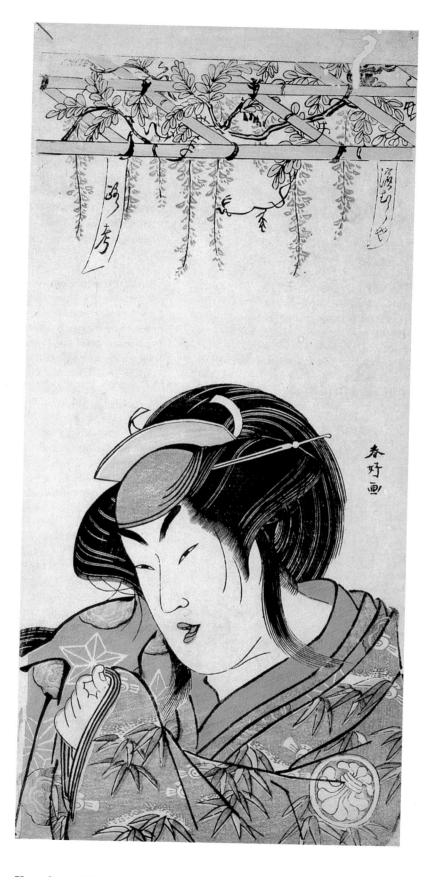

Katsukawa Shunkō
Segawa Kikunojō III★
Hosoban 33.0 x 15.2
Nishiki-e
Publisher unknown
early Tenmei era (1781–1789)

Kitao Masanobu
Ichikawa Monnosuke II as Chotto Tokubei
(p. 85)

During his period of creativity as a woodblock print artist, Masanobu illustrated numerous books, and until Tenmei 1 (1781) was also, along with Kitao and Kiyonaga, one of the best-known painters. Many of his albums illustrating stage plays have also been preserved, which is not the case, however, with most of the *yakusha-e* he produced from the late An'ei era (1772–1780) to the late Tenmei (1781–1788) era, few of which are extant. The work reproduced here shows Monnosuke II in the role of Tokubei the flowerseller in a *kyōgen* entitled "Soga matsuri Naniwa no Sugatami". This was performed at the Nakamura theatre in the 5th month of An'ei 9 (1779); so much can be deduced from the so-called "banzuke" for the play, in other words the bill or poster listing the performers. Masanobu's inaugural work was an illustration for "Kaicho Riyaku no Meguriai" dating from An'ei 7 (1778). At the time he was just twenty, and his technique had not yet matured. And yet, just two years later, he created this figure of the flower-seller, standing there with his elbows resting on the pole from which the flower trays are suspended, his chin resting on his hands – already the typical Masanobu atmosphere, which characterizes his portrayals of all the leading actors of the time. This work, with its fine colour composition, is very well preserved. Later, Masanobu took up a career as a writer of non-demanding literature, and changed his name to Santōkyōden.

Katsukawa Shūn'ei
Ichikawa Ebizō as Kamakura Gonogorō Kagemasa and Sakata Hangorō III as Hahazuno Yotahei
(p. 86)

In the 11th month of Kansei 6 (1794) the Kiri theatre staged "Otokoyama Oedo no Ishizue", in which Ebizō played Kagemasa and Hangorō played Yotahei. This double portrait was probably used as a poster to advertise the appearance of these two star actors, and it was also published in a large edition. In addition to this print, there exist a number of other double portraits: from the play "Uruou toshi meika no homare" at the Miyako theatre, we have Nisaemon VII as Kimeitora, Sōjūrō III as Kujaku Saburō, Noshio II as Tsurayuki no Musume and Chūzō II as Aramaki Mimishirō; from the play "Matsu wa Misao Onna Kusonoki" at the Kawabarasaki theatre, we have Hanshirō as Chihaya, Kaneyoshi's younger sister, and Matsusuke I as Yuasa Magoroku Nyūdō Sadatora.

Following the death of his master Shunshō, Shūn'ei reached the peak of his creative powers in the *yakusha-e* which he produced in the early-to-mid Kansei era (1789–1800). His works also had an influence on Toyokuni and Sharaku. Furthermore, there are pictures extant in which Shūn'ei portrayed three actors, representing a new style of portraiture. His faces are larger than those of Toyokuni and Sharaku. Almost tangible is the tension proceeding from the "shibaraku" (halt!) attitude of Ebizō and the look on Hangorō's face. We have, incidentally, another portrait of Hangorō, executed by Sharaku.

Katsukawa Shūn'ei
Segawa Kikunojō III as Osome and Iwai Hanshirō IV as Hisamatsu
(p. 87)

In the first two months of Tenmei 8 (1788), the Kiri theatre staged, as the second act of "Keiseiyū Soga", on alternate days the *kyōgen* "Osome Hisamatsu ukina no hatsugasumi" and "Oume Kumenosuke yonowasa yoku no yukidoke". In the first piece, Segawa Kikunojō III appeared as Osome and Iwai Hanshirō IV as Osome's lover Hisamatsu. In the second, they exchanged roles. The print reproduced here shows the two in the former casting. Hisamatsu is lost in thought, his elbows resting on an abacus, his chin on his hand. Osome stares at him melancholically, thus giving expression to their unhappy plight: their mutual love is crossed by the difference in social status between them. Osome is the daughter of an oil merchant, while Hisamatsu is merely an errand boy in his employ.

The play is based on a true event which happened in Osaka in Hōei 7 (1710), ending tragically in a double suicide. The *kyōgen* to which it gave rise was so popular that further plays on the subject of "Osome and Hisamatsu" appeared. During the middle of the Edo period, Kikunojō III played numerous *onnagata* roles – both young girls and courtesans – in the *jōruri* and *kabuki* theatres – roles for which his feminine good looks and coquettish manner made him particularly suitable. Hanshirō IV for his part had a round enough face, but his mellifluous voice made him equally suitable both for *onnagata* and for male roles, whether as *aragoto*, male lead, or youth. Together on stage, the two complemented each other wonderfully.

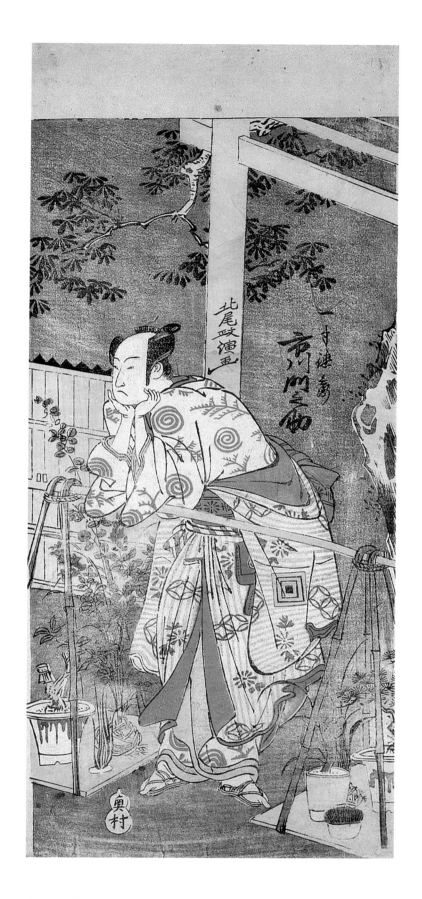

Kitao Masanobu
Ichikawa Monnosuke II as Chotto Tokubei★
Hosoban 31.4 x 13.8
Nishiki-e
Published by Okumura Genroku
An'ei 9 (1780)

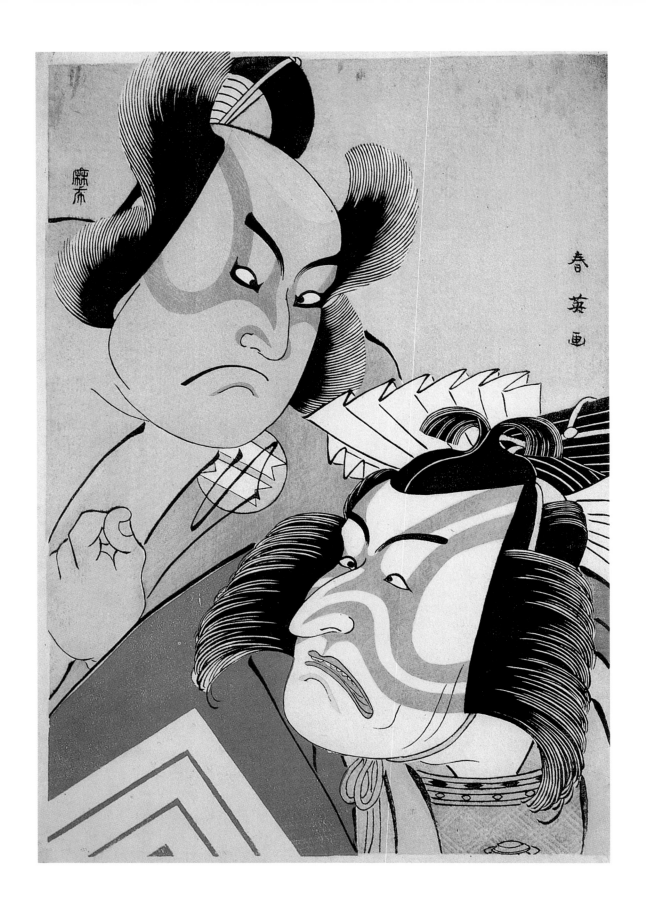

Katsukawa Shūn'ei
Ichikawa Ebizō as Kamakura Gonogorō Kagemasa and
Sakata Hangorō III as Hahazuno Yotahei★
Hazama-ban 32.8 x 22.8
Nishiki-e
Published by Azabu
11th month of Kansei 3 (1791)

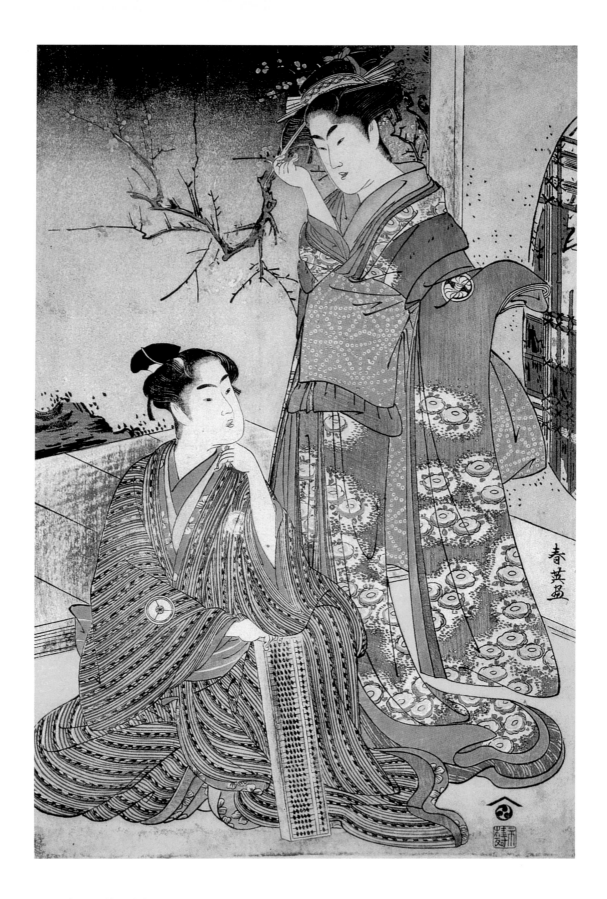

Katsukawa Shūn'ei
Segawa Kikunojō III as Osome and
Iwai Hanshirō IV as Hisamatsu★
Oban 37.9 x 24.1
Nishiki-e
Published by Nishimuraya Yohachi
Tenmei 8 (1788)

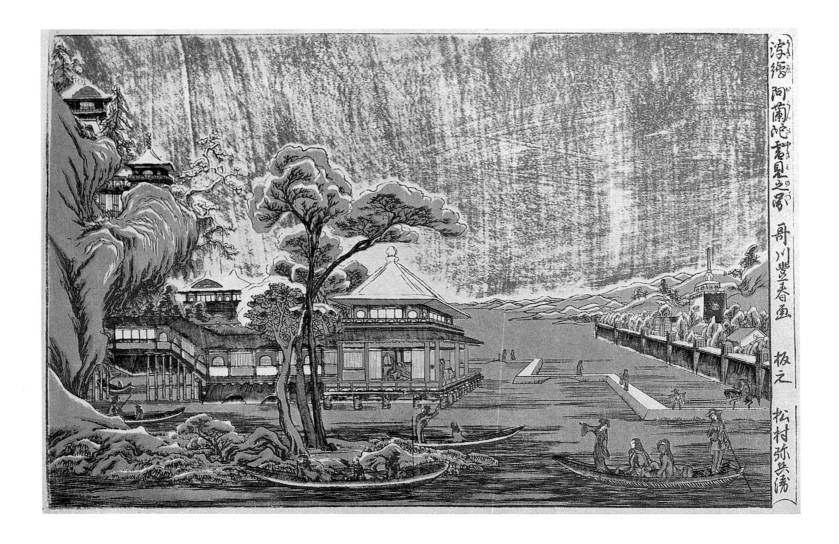

Utagawa Toyoharu
Uki-e of a Foreign Scene
Yoko-ōban 26.0 x 38.8
Nishiki-e
Published by Matsumara Yohei
An'ei era (1772–1781)

During the period of Japanese isolation (1639–1858), all contact with foreign countries was forbidden. The sole exception to this was the trade permitted with representatives of China and Holland, conducted on a small island off Nagasaki. It was during this period, and via this route, that knowledge of the new "Dutch" (i.e. Western) scientific discoveries came to Japan. It has been known for some years now that Toyoharu copied Chinese prints and Western paintings, producing woodblock prints of his own in large numbers. The picture reproduced here depicts a palace and a dyke in the Chinese style, and, on the right, a pagoda in the Western style. The details of the picture are also Western and Chinese in origin. For the off-white of the clouds, Toyoharu used calcium carbonate. The perspective technique had hitherto only been used for interior views.

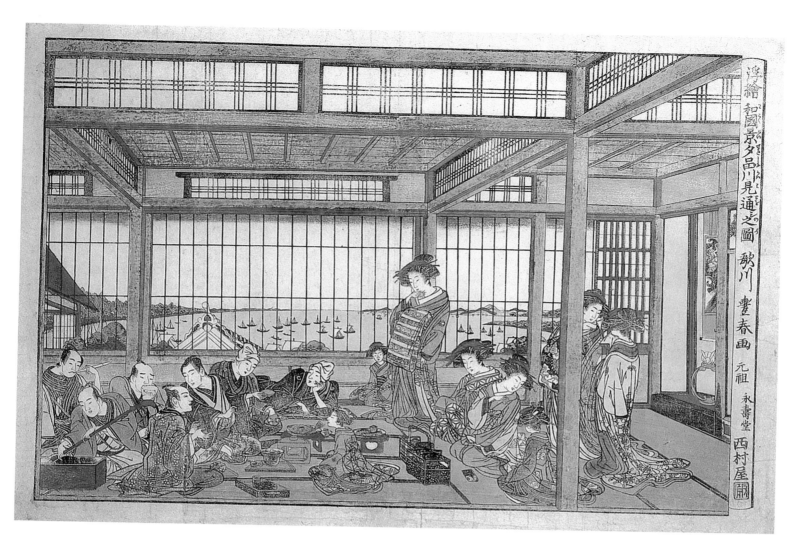

The *uki-e* in the title of this picture refers to a current within *ukiyo-e* painting in which Western techniques of perspective were used. It was introduced into Japanese art by Okumura Masanobu. Unlike other artists, however, Toyoharu produced direct imitations of Chinese and Western techniques, thus promoting further evolution. In the print reproduced here, the total effect of depth is enhanced by the view through the window at the rear to the scene beyond. The room itself is occupied by seven men, five prostitutes and their maids; it is located on the first floor of a brothel in Shinagawa, whose pleasure quarter rivalled Yoshiwara in every respect and attracted a large clientele. In front of the girls can be seen two black containers holding smoking materials; the men are using ash-trays. The provision of tobacco was a standard part of the service in the pleasure districts.

Utagawa Toyoharu
Uki-e Yamato no kuni: Evening View of Shinagawa★
Yoko-ōban 29.8 x 43.6
Nishiki-e
Published by Nishimuraya Yohachi
2nd half of the Meiwa era (1764–1772)

Torii Kiyonaga
Tea-Stall Girl with Guest
(p. 91)

"Mizuchaya" were stalls set up outside shrines and temples, in front of which simple stools and benches were placed for the benefit of pilgrims who wished to take some rest. Refreshment was provided in the form of tea, served by attractive young women in splendid kimonos and broad aprons who would compete for custom. The girl in this picture, wearing a long apron, has her hair done up in the fashion of the time. Boys and men, dressed in fashionably long kimonos, would also come to the tea-stalls for no other reason than to visit the waitresses, two particularly popular ones being Osen and Okita, who were used as favourite motifs for woodblock prints by, for example, Bunchō, Harunobu and Utamaro (see p. 78).

It cannot be determined for certain where this particular tea-stall was located, but the characters spelling out "bosatsu" on the lantern on the left indicate that it was by a temple; these lanterns served as street-lighting. On the lantern on the right would be written the name of the proprietor, but unfortunately part of it is hidden from view. The guest has a pipe in his hand, and beside him is an ash-tray. The girl is pictured as she turns to face him; in front of her is a cabinet which would have contained different varieties of tea.

Torii Kiyonaga
Figure of a Woman beneath Wistaria
(p. 26)

Kiyonaga produced some 120 *hashira-e*, in other words pictures of long and narrow vertical format which were affixed to a post (hashira). These "post pictures" were at the peak of their popularity during Kiyonaga's time; he was succeeded as an exponent of the genre by Koryūsai.

This work is also known under the title "Shy Beauty beneath Wistaria". The fluttering hem and the wistaria blossoms waving in the spring wind are pictures of what really happens. This wind blows in April and May, and people in the streets suffer a degree of embarrassment when their skirts are raised by a sudden gust; it plays havoc, too, with the blossoms which have only just appeared. There are numerous prints of this theme of women caught out by the wind, for example Kiyonaga's "Kites in the Wind." and "Figure of an Embarrassed Woman beneath Willows".

The woman depicted here is walking along by the side of a ditch, using her right hand to try to keep in place the garment which is being ruffled up by the wind. With her left hand she is holding her protective hood close to her face. In so doing, she is unconsciously radiating a natural coquettishness. At the same time, however, her embarrassment is evidenced by the whiteness of her face, especially in contrast to the black hood. The generally subdued coloration is accentuated by the red of her under-kimono, which can be seen under her sleeves and around her ankles. The red sash around her hips served the purpose of hitching up to a convenient length the loose cape which was worn over the kimono at this period.

Torii Kiyonaga
Geisha Leaving Heiroku's Shop
(p. 27)

The poem in the top left corner of the picture reads: "Why not ask Heiroku? Someone has been sent from the boat". It comes from an eleven-volume collection of songs known as "Yanagi-daru", which appeared in An'ei 5 (1776). Heiroku was an apothecary in the third block of Tachibanachō, where many *furisode* dancing-girls lived at the time. As the *geishas* often visited Heiroku's shop, the young ones were occasionally invited to take a boat ride. The nearby Sumida river was a favourite destination for day-trippers from Edo. In the vicinity of the river were a number of centres of entertainment, including not only the pleasure houses of Yoshiwara and Fukagawa, but also some renowned restaurants. Inviting *geishas* to join one on a pleasure trip up the river was a favourite pastime. The shop awning, or "noren", bearing the inscriptions "medicines" and "Heiroku", is fluttering in the wind. The girl is turning gracefully towards the interior of the shop; presumably somebody has called to her from there. She is a young *geisha*, as indicated by the fact that her hair is not completely pinned up. She is wearing curlers in her hair, in order to give it a wave. This hair style, along with the pattern of the kimono, are in accordance with contemporary fashion. Beneath the light-coloured *furisode* can be glimpsed the speckled red under-kimono; the difference in the quality of the fabric between these garments and the plain *obi* is very apparent.

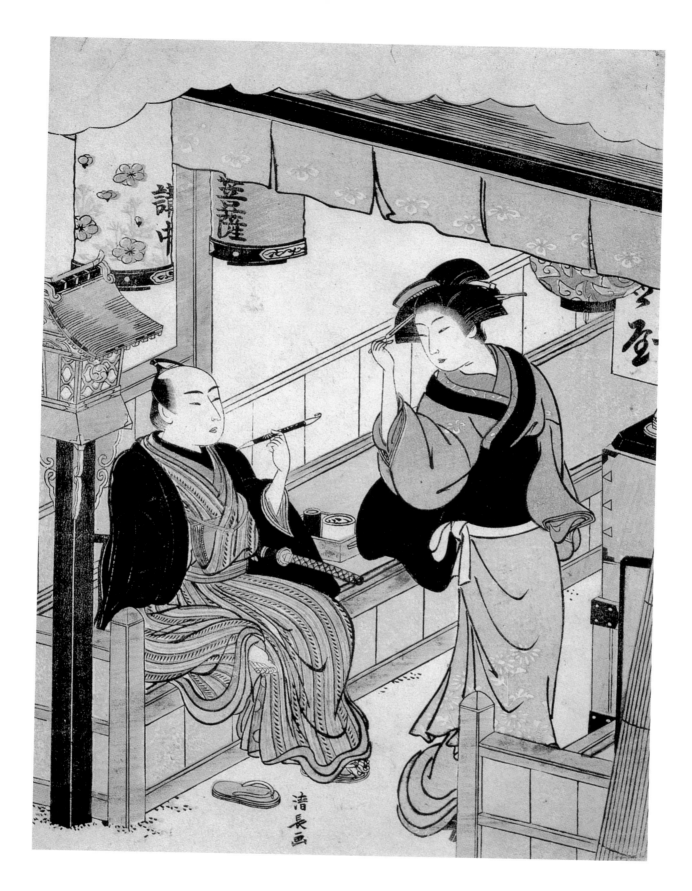

Torii Kiyonaga
Tea-Stall Girl with Guest
Chūban 26.0 x 19.0
Nishiki-e
Publisher unknown
c. An'ei 7 (1778)

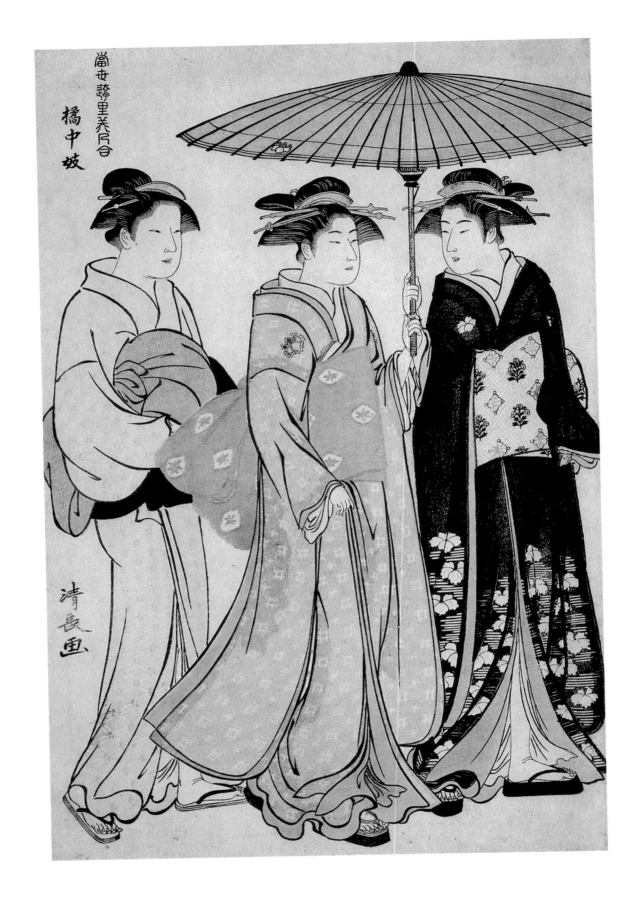

Torii Kiyonaga
Contest of Beauties from the Pleasure Quarters:
Courtesans of Tachibanachō*
Oban 38.2 x 25.4
Nishiki-e
Publisher unknown
c. Tenmei 2 (1782)

The three great works of Kiyonaga are considered to be the large-format series "Everyday Scenes in the City of Edo", "12 Pictures of Beauties from the South", and that illustrated here, "Contest of Beauties from the Pleasure Quarters". Of the 21 pictures in this series, five are diptychs. These works represent Kiyonaga's successful debut in the field of large-format (ōban) woodblock prints. He went on to create three-sheet, five-sheet and other large-scale works. In the years Tenmei 2–4 (1782–84) he took as models not only courtesans from Yoshiwara, but also those from the unlicensed pleasure districts of Shinagawa, Fukagawa and Tachibanachō, as well as geishas from the towns. Thus during the Tenmei era society discovered Okabasho as a place which excelled even the officially-approved pleasure district of Yoshiwara, insofar as its brothels had even better things to offer. Nearby was Tachibanachō, with its numerous geisha houses. For the exercise of their profession, the geishas studied singing, dancing, music and literature; and as was customary for young unmarried women, they wore the furisode.

The two young geishas depicted here strolling along in their furisode beneath a raised parasol are presumably on their way to a festival in Tachibanachō to which they have been summoned; blue parasols like this were made using thick, light-blue Japanese paper from Kōchi, known as "aodosa". Blue parasols had the advantage that in strong sunlight they made the pale faces of the ladies beneath appear even more delicate. The geishas are being followed by a maid, who is carrying a change of clothing wrapped in a cloth or "furoshiki" under her arm. Beneath the kimonos of the geishas can be glimpsed the thin under-kimono, typical summer wear. This work brings across very well the special quality of Kiyonaga's beauties as they wander carefree along the street.

Yoshiwara was Edo's only pleasure district with an official licence. In addition, however, large brothels also grew up at Shinagawa, Shinjuku, Itabashi and Senjū, in other words at the entrances and exits to the city, the country's political centre, to which all roads led. Every traveller wishing to spend a night in one of these establishments would know that girls would also be on hand to entertain him – indeed, they were officially engaged by the management for this purpose. Shinagawa was on the southern edge of Edo. To distinguish it from Yoshiwara, the latter – situated to the north of Edo Castle – was known as the "nothern pleasure quarter", while Shinagawa was known as the "southern pleasure quarter", or simply "the South".

The series from which the present print is taken illustrates the numerous pleasure houses of Shinagawa during the twelve months of the year. This picture, representing the fifth month, depicts a woman stepping out of a litter, on top of which is a bunch of twigs decorated with coloured sweets – a speciality of the district. They are the symbol of the famous temple of Meguro Fudōson, which was about three kilometres away from Shinagawa. On the 28th day of the fifth month, the local "Green Day" festival was celebrated there, and pilgrims would gather on the evening before. It may be that the proprietress of the house of entertainment is returning from a visit to the temple, either on the eve of the festival, or in the early morning of the day itself. The girl behind her is wearing a comfortable "yukata", or cotton kimono, which suggests a morning occasion.

During the Edo period, visiting shrines and temples was a popular activity. Outside their precincts, as well as at well-known beauty spots, tea-stalls would be set up. Ten such tea-stalls were employed by Kiyonaga as motifs for a series of woodblock prints. That reproduced here depicts a tea-stall on the road to the Tomigaoka Hachimangū shrine, which was dedicated to the war-god Hachiman. Stools and benches have been placed outside, on which, beneath a cherry-tree in blossom, the waitresses are sitting. With the broad aprons which were the mark of their trade, and with their hair piled up into an elaborate bow, they present a typical picture of the everyday life of the time. The stone lantern on the right is, as the inscription on the board next to it reveals, a gift from the collection of the Nakamachi tea-house, a famous pleasure house in Fukuyama. The road to the shrine would have been lined with such lanterns. Behind it can be seen a kettle with a novel handle designed in the shape of a spiral to prevent its getting too hot to hold. Sitting in front of the tea-stall is a woman in a short-sleeved kimono bearing a family emblem. She is looking in the direction of the two younger women. It may be that these two, in the cheerful costume of the geisha world, have come from Fukuyama with other geishas to pay their respects to Hachiman. It may also be that they have been summoned to the two famous tea-houses in the neighbourhood of the shrine. Whatever the case, they represent for the artist the central motif of the picture.

Torii Kiyonaga
Contest of Beauties from the Pleasure Quarters: Courtesans of Tachibanachō
(p. 92)

Torii Kiyonaga
12 Pictures of Beauties from the South: 5th Month (p. 94)

Torii Kiyonaga
10 Views of Tea-Stalls: Tomigaoka (p. 95)

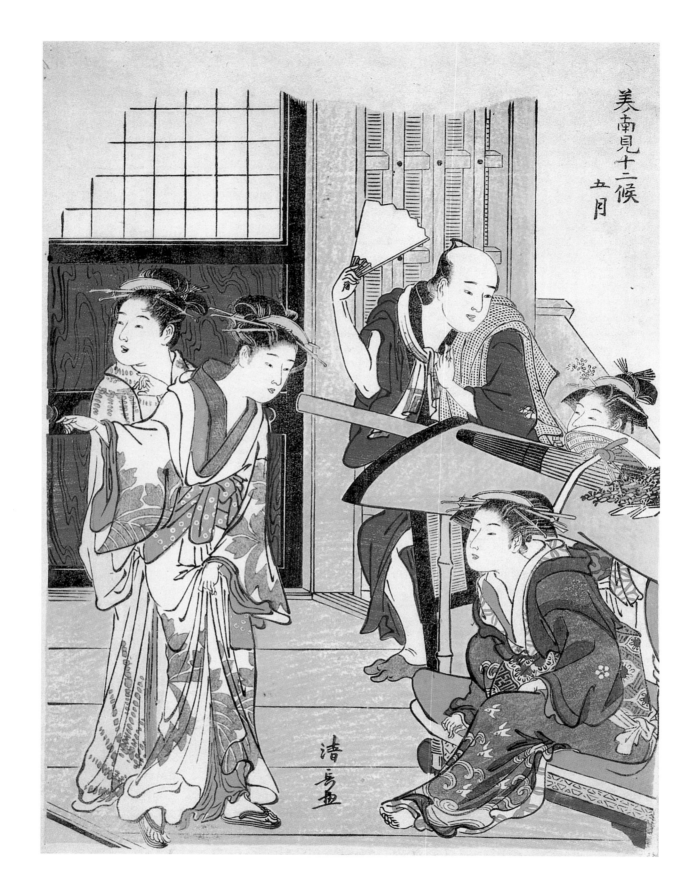

Torii Kiyonaga
12 Pictures of Beauties from the South: 5th Month
Chūban 26.6 x 19.7
Nishiki-e
Published by (Izumiya Ichibei)
c. Tenmei 3 (1783)

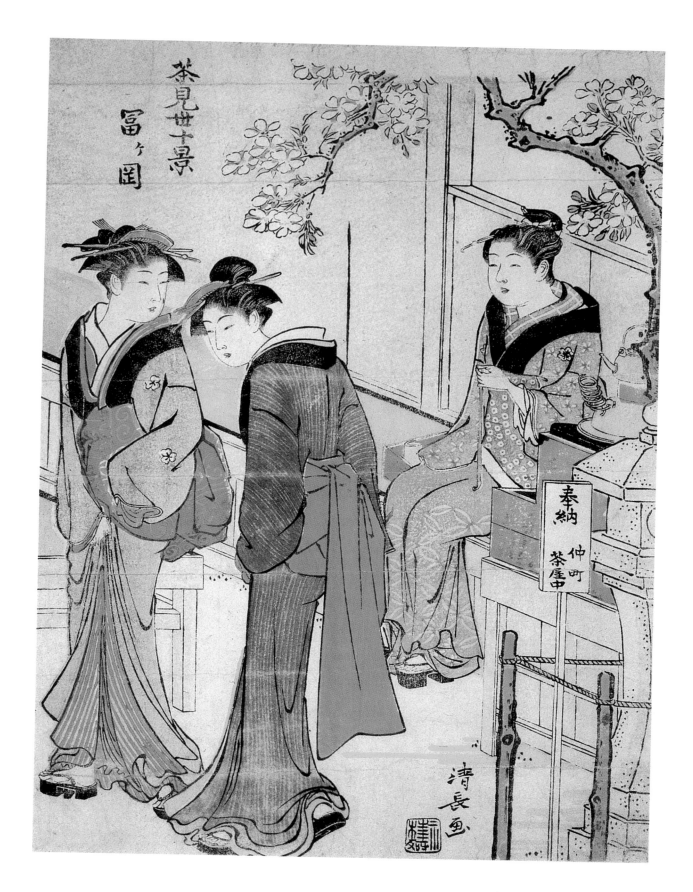

Torii Kiyonaga
10 Views of Tea-Stalls: Tomigaoka
Chūban 25.2 x 18.7
Nishiki-e
Published by Nishimuraya Yohachi
c. Tenmei 3 (1783)

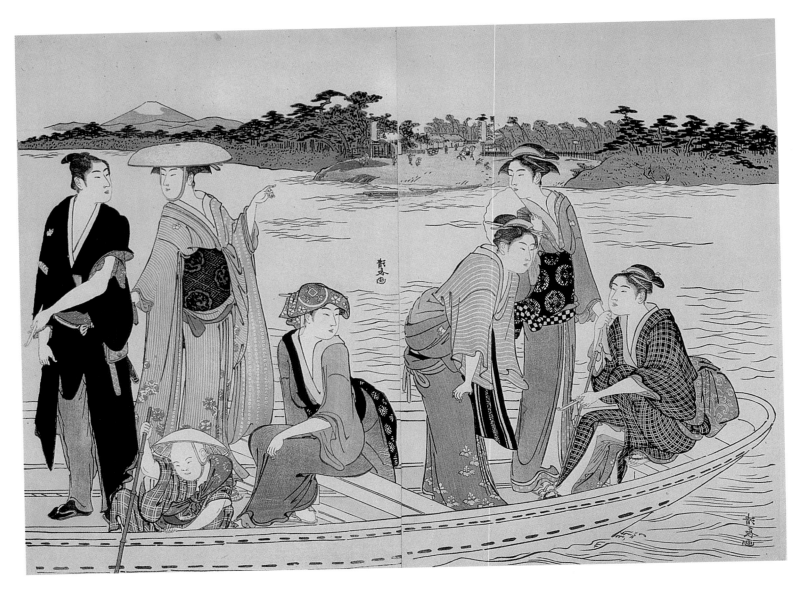

Torii Kiyonaga
Ferry across the Rokugo River★
Oban, central and right-hand sheets
of a triptych, each 39.1 x 26.3
Nishiki-e
Published by (Takatsuya Isuke)
c. Tenmei 4 (1784)

It was Kiyonaga who was responsible for introducing large formats to *ukiyo-e* painting, many such works being preserved from the mid-Tenmei era (1781–1789). He is regarded as unsurpassed in this area, and his strength of composition as incomparable. The work reproduced here depicts human figures by means of freely drawn lines and rhythmic arrangements. Clear colours create a peaceful atmosphere. The compositional structure, along with the two stamped inscriptions, suggest that a third sheet once existed which would have continued the scene to the left, but unfortunately only these two are known.

The distant view of Mount Fuji, along with the inscriptions on the lanterns on the further shore, indicate that the scene cannot be far from the Kawasaki-taishi temple. The *Tōkaidō* was the most important route in Japan, linking Edo the capital with the whole country and in particular with Kyoto. Between Shinagawa and Kawasaki stations, the road crossed the Tama river, then known as the Rokugo. Today, this point is a 24-minute train ride from Tokyo.

Kubo Shunman
View of 6 Rivers: Kōya
(p. 97)

"Mutamagawa", the Japanese title of the series, refers to the six rivers Yamashiro, Nogi, Kōya, Ide, Chōfu and Kinuta. Their clear waters have been praised since time immemorial in *waka*, and in combination with *bijin-ga*, they were favourite motifs for *ukiyo-e* artists. The picture reproduced here is the extreme left-hand sheet of a work conprising six sheets in all, and depicts the Tama river in Kōya. In the upper part of the picture the pagoda and roof of the Kōya temple can be discerned through the haze. The women are depicted against the background of a tranquil landscape. The woman on the right is tightening her shoe.

Few colours are used. The pale green ground lends a fresh feeling to the lighter and darker inks. This technique is known as *benigirai*, in which *beni* red is avoided, and the ink hues mixed with violet and green instead.

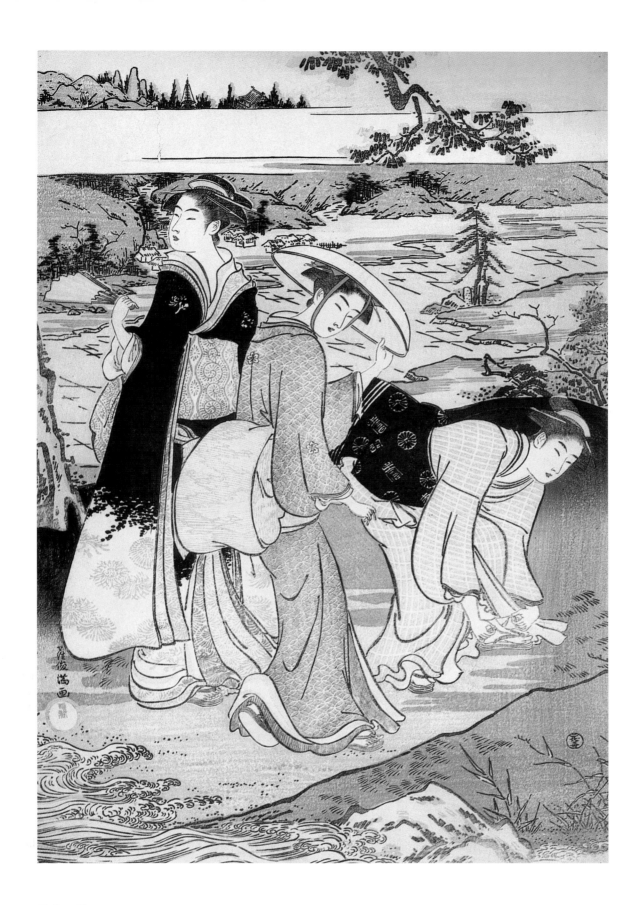

Kubo Shunman
View of 6 Rivers: Kōya★
Oban 37.9 x 25.5
Nishiki-e
Published by Fushimiya Zenroku
mid Tenmei era (1781–1789)

Kitagawa Utamaro
Three Famous Beauties
(p. 99)

From the outset, scenes from the pleasure districts were among the favourite themes of the *ukiyo-e* painters. The depiction of the courtesans and their magnificent garments was extremely popular. However, the girls known in Utamaro's day as "The Three Beauties of the Kansei Era" were not prostitutes at all, but quite ordinary young women. Gradually, waitresses and *geishas* also came to be the subjects of *ukiyo-e* painting. The picture reproduced here portrays Nanbaya Okita, Takashimaya Ohisa and Tomimoto Toyohina. Okita was a dancing-girl in a tea-house in front of the Zuishinmon gate in Asakusa. Ohisa was the daughter of a tea-house proprietor in the Ryōgoku Yagenbori district of Edo. Fujimoto Toyohina was a *geisha* in Yoshiwara. At first sight, Utamaro's figures appear somewhat idealized, but they neverthelesss reflect the three different types of sitter: the tea-house enployee, the "normal" woman, and the *geisha*.

Kitagawa Utamaro
In the Pleasure Quarter: 2nd Block of Kyōmachi. Kiyomi, Sekiya and Takoto from the Kadokanaya Establishment
(p. 100)

"Niwaku" was the name given to the festival that took place in Yoshiwara every August. The pleasure-houses and tea-houses would then be filled with noise and dancing. One of the dances performed on these occasions is known as the "katoma" dance, which, while based on a religious dance proper to the Katomajingū shrine, had spread throughout the country. Later, the dancers would hold *gohei* in their hands to ward off misfortune.

This work dates from Utamaro's early period, and does not reflect his mature style. The two seated persons are wearing priestly hats and splendid garments. In front of them a third is squatting, holding a lantern and a *gohei*. The scene creates the impression that the three are resting after a dance. As the Niwaku festival was one of the outstanding events of the Yoshiwara year, the lively goings-on and the participants were depicted by numerous artists. Following the completion of this series depicting scenes from the pleasure-quarter, Utamaro went on to create numerous other masterpieces.

Kitagawa Utamaro
Wakaume from the Tamaya Establishment
(p. 101)

In the first block on Yoshiwara's Edo-machi street there were a number of houses of entertainment, in one of which Wakaume worked as a courtesan. According to "Yoshiwara Saiken", a guide to the pleasure quarter which appeared each spring and autumn, Wakaume was employed there from Kansei 2 (1790) until Kansei 10 (1798). Her personal maids were originally called Onami and Menami, but during the course of Kansei 4 (1792), they changed their names to Umeno and Irokan. On the basis of these data together with the style of painting, we can date this picture accurately to Kansei 5 (1793).

Kitagawa Utamaro
Takashimaya Ohisa
(p. 28)

The girl standing beneath the door-sign, which reads „Takashima", and holding a fan bearing the oak-leaf family emblem in her right hand, is Takashimaya Ohisa, one of the "Three Beauties of the Kansei Era". Her father was the proprietor of a "senbei" (rice-cake) shop. He was the richest man in the neighbourhood, and apart from the tea-house, owned a number of other venues for functions in the vicinity of the Ryōgoku bridge. His daughter Ohisa inherited the tea-house. She was often compared to the famous beauty, Nanbaya Okita – although Okita was reputed to have the more pleasant personality. According to the book "Mizuchaya hyakunin issho", which appeared in Kansei 5 (1793) and compared 100 tea-house girls, Okita was at that time 16 and Ohisa 17. The patterns on their kimonos and *obis* were similar, likewise their dark-green aprons. Originally these latter garments were worn to keep the kimono from getting dirty, but in the course of time they became the uniform, so to speak, of girls who worked in tea-houses. They were made of silk or crêpe.

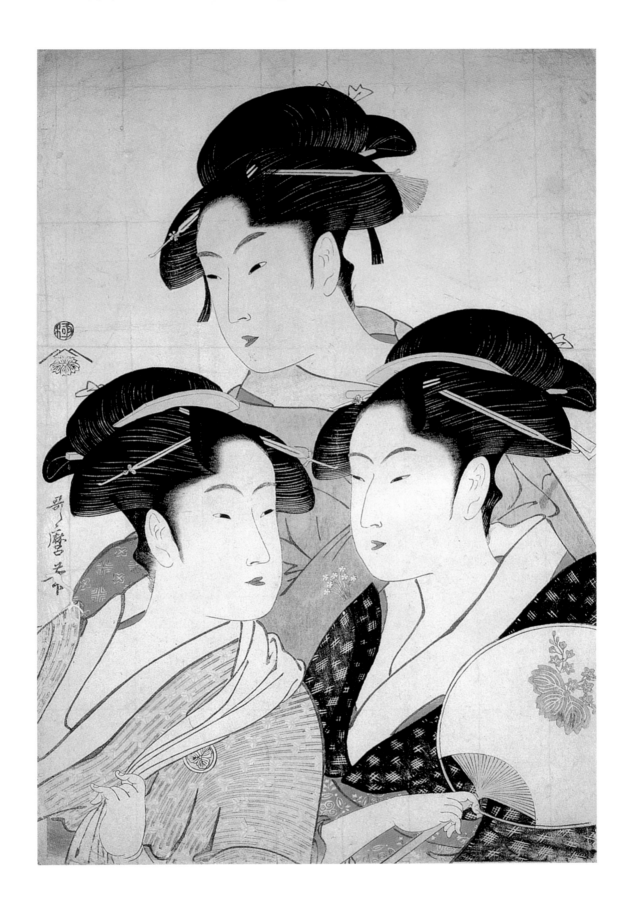

Kitagawa Utamaro
Three Famous Beauties★
Oban 39.0 x 25.8
Nishiki-e
Published by Tsutaya Jūzaburō
c. Kansei 4–5 (1792–1793)

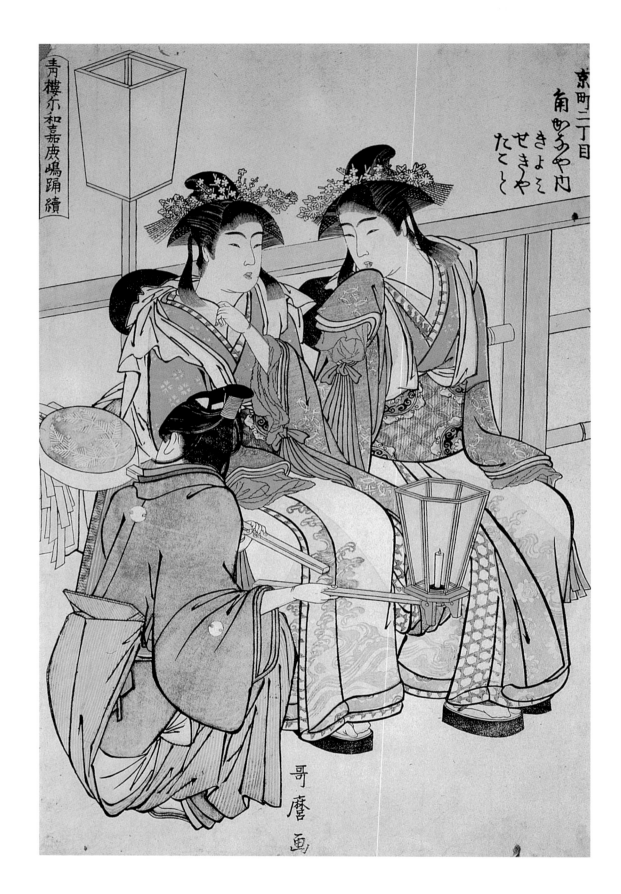

Kitagawa Utamaro
In the Pleasure Quarter: 2nd Block of Kyōmachi.
Kiyomi, Sekiya and Takoto from the Kadokanaya Establishment★
Oban 38.2 x 25.3
Nishiki-e
Published by (Tsutaya Jūzaburō)
c. Tenmei 3 (1783)

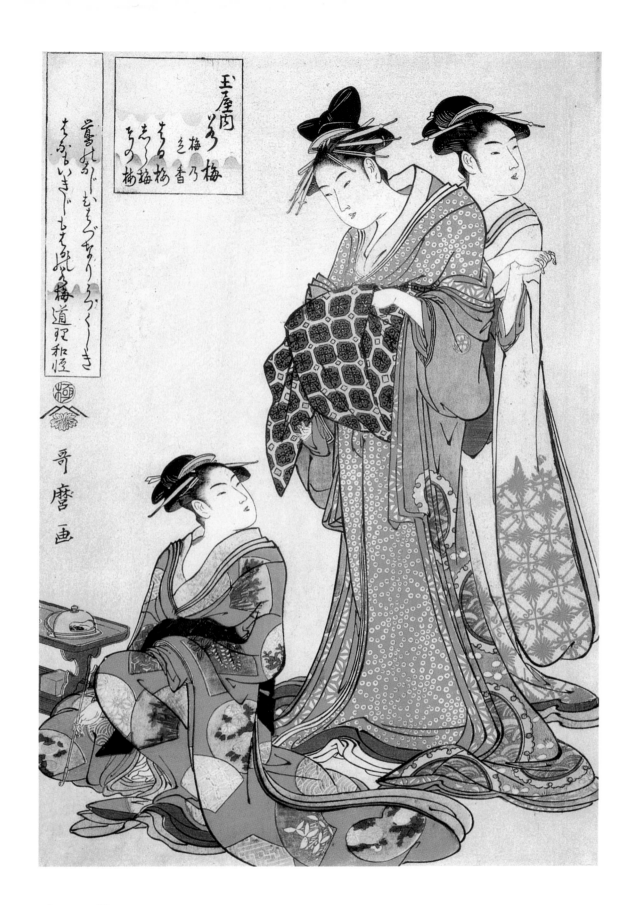

Kitagawa Utamaro
Wakaume from the Tamaya Establishment
Oban 37.0 x 24.6
Nishiki-e
Published by Tsutaya Jūzaburō
c. Kansei 5 (1793)

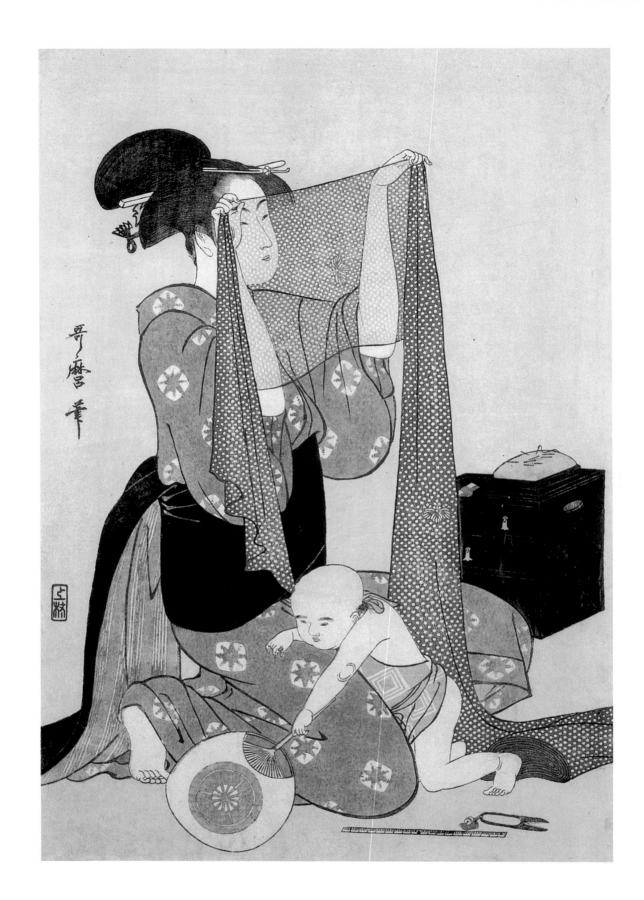

Kitagawa Utamaro
Sewing
Oban, left-hand sheet of a triptych, 38.1 x 26.3
Nishiki-e
Published by Uemura Yohei
c. Kansei 7 (1795)

This print is part of triptych depicting the everyday lives of carefree citizens. The Edo period (1603–1868) was marked by a certain affluence. There was a flowering of bourgeois culture, and more and more girls came to enjoy the advantages of a good education. Sewing in particular became one of their obligatory activities, as it was regarded as a necessary skill for a married woman. From their earliest childhood they would learn the craft from their mothers and other older women, as well as from sewing mistresses, and in the temple schools.

On the print reproduced here, a piece of fabric is being inspected for tears. As through a veil, the white face and arms of the mother shimmer with a characteristic beauty as she holds up the thin silk *haori*. Utamaro enjoyed the expressiveness which the woodblock print afforded. The littel boy in his apron is getting restless. His mother is trying to calm him by rocking him on her thigh, a typical motherly gesture which did not escape Utamaro, evidence of his superbly keen eye for detail.

Kitagawa Utamaro
Sewing
(p. 102)

The evergreen theme of love has occupied artists since time immemorial, and the Edo period was no exception. This particular work is one of a five-part series, whose other titles are "Secret Love", "Rare Love", "Blossoming Love" and "Everyday Love". The series is one of Utamaro's masterpieces. The large faces, composed of fine lines and delicate colours, betray the innermost feelings of the women thus portrayed. Before Utamaro, artists had emphasized figure and dress, but with him, there was a shift towards the depiction of hidden feelings. In this picture we see a mature woman resting her head on her hands, so that her lower arm is exposed to view. In so doing, she casts her gaze dreamily into the distance. Her eyebrows are shaven, her black hair tied up into an exquisite bun. Her simple check kimono also suits her well.

Kitagawa Utamaro
Selection of Love Poems:
Love which one cannot put out of one's
mind *(p. 104)*

Ten years after the appearance of his two major series in the early Kansei era (1789–1801), "10 Different Female Figures" and "Sketches of 10 Women", Utamaro took up the same theme during the Kyōwa era (1801–1804) with his series "Sketches of Women". As its conception is similar to that of his earlier works, it provides a useful yardstick against which to measure how far Utamaro's beauties have changed over time. The print reproduced here is typical of his later period; one can see how his own taste changed and adapted to popular demand.

Older (married) women used to tie their hair into a bun, rarely wore brightly coloured garments, and blackened their teeth with an amalgam of iron-filings, rice-starch, tea and vinegar, to which, after it had oxidized, was added pulverized gall-nut. The resulting black liquid was then used to paint the teeth. At first, this form of beautification was restricted to the nobility, but during the Edo period it became customary for all married women. In his pictures Utamaro succeeds in masterly fashion in capturing the expressions on the faces of women entirely absorbed in their outward appearance: full of feeling, intensely concentrated on what they are doing and yet reticent.

Kitagawa Utamaro
Sketches of Women: Women Gathering for a
Tooth-Blackening Ceremony *(p. 105)*

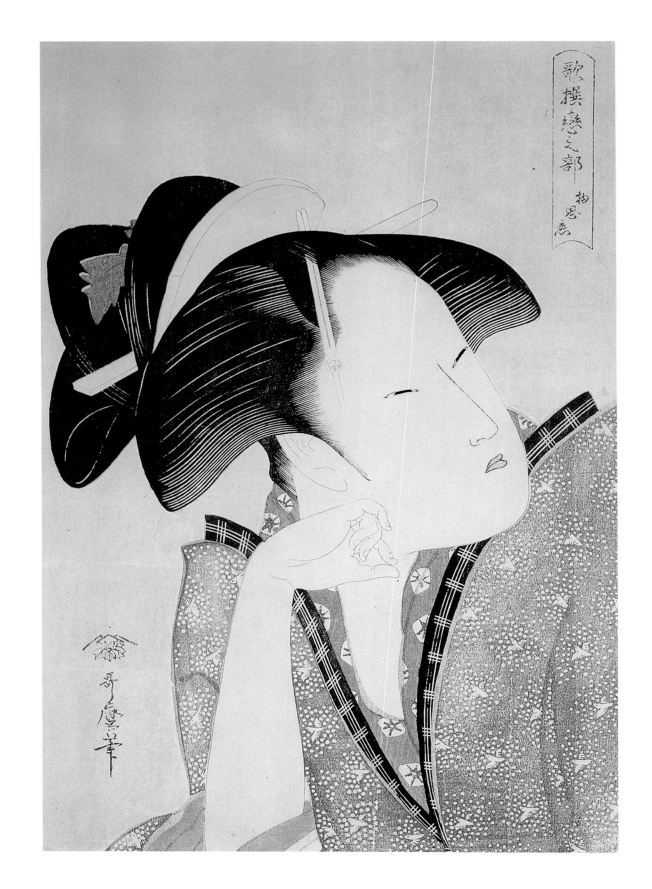

Kitagawa Utamaro
Selection of Love-Poems: Love which one
cannot put out of one's mind★
Oban 38.5 x 26.2
Nishiki-e
Published by Tsutaya Jūzaburō
c. Kansei 5 (1793)

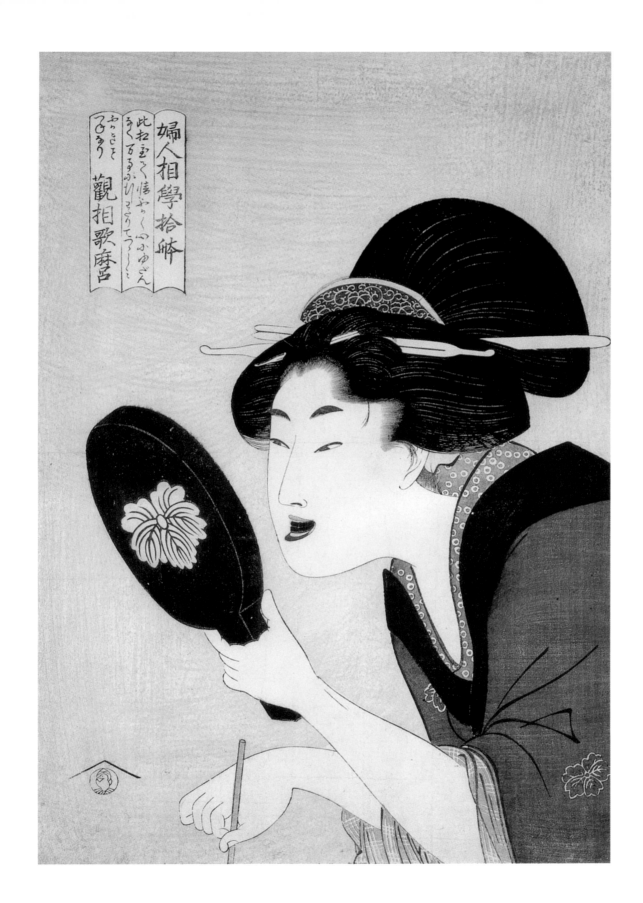

Kitagawa Utamaro
Sketches of Women: Women Gathering for
a Tooth-Blackening Ceremony★
Oban 37.1 x 25.4
Nishiki-e
Published by Tsuruya Kiemon
c. Kyōwa 3 (1803)

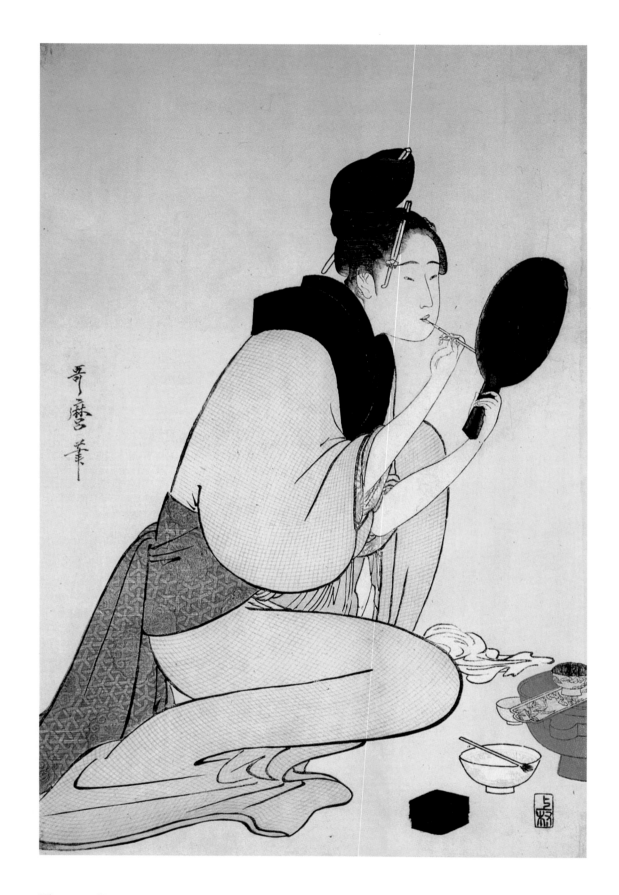

Kitagawa Utamaro
Applying Lipstick★
Oban 38.2 x 24.8
Nishiki-e
Published by Uemura Yohei
c. Kansei 6–7 (1794–1795)

The woman in this picture is depicted in a half-kneeling position; her figure is soft with flowing contours. Hand-mirror, protective collar and powder box are glossy black. For the powder box in particular, bone-glue has been mixed with the ink to heighten the gloss. The hair has been done up into a bun with a long pin. Wearing indoor clothes with a check pattern, she is looking into the mirror and concentrating entirely on the matter in hand, namely the application of her lipstick. The contrast between the red of the lipstick and the white of her skin has been handled by Utamaro most successfully. He demonstrates his mastery not only with elegant ladies, but also with women dressed in ordinary everyday clothes.

By the woman's knee can be seen the implements used for blackening the teeth, as was customary among married women. Lipstick, incidentally, was extremely expensive at this time.

Kitagawa Utamaro
Applying Lipstick
(p. 106)

This single sheet has an inset in its top right-hand corner showing Edo Bay in the vicinity of Shinagawa, as is apparent from the "kyōka" (short humorous poem) which accompanies it: "The yukata (cotton kimono) is like the kimono worn by Princess Otohime, and Kamekichi looks highly refreshing". This is a play on words, to be explained as follows. The coastline near Shinagawa has the shape of a sleeve; the sleeve thus has associations with the word "ura" (bay), and "ura" in turn conjures up associations with the story of Urajima Tarō, and this in its turn brings us to Princess Otohime. Utamaro produced another single-sheet print where he combined a kyōka with the portrait of a beauty, this time a *geisha* named Takawa.

Shinagawa was just to the south of Edo, and at this period was in the process of losing its position as the first stop on the *Tōkaidō*. As ships and travellers from all parts of Japan put in at its harbour, however, a pleasure quarter grew up there. It attracted numerous visitors, as the entertainments offered were cheaper than in Yoshiwara, and less importance was attached to etiquette. As Utamaro used many of its celebrated courtesans as models, it is likely that the *geisha* Kamekichi was a courtesan here. With her hands clasped together and her gaze directed over her left shoulder, she conveys an impression of lofty grace, an impression enhanced by the economy and harmony of colour.

Kitagawa Utamaro
The Geisha Kamekichi
(p. 108)

Kintarō the wonder-boy was a popular motif for woodblock print artists. Many pictures portray him as a warrior, while others depict him as a wild, intrepid child. He is the subject of many surviving prints by Kiyonaga, for example. Unlike many other artists, Utamaro's Kintarō pictures – of which some fifty are known, in various settings and formats – almost always include the mountain woman who, the story goes, was Kintarō's mother. Some of his works have as their theme the pure motherly love which was said to have existed between her and Kintarō, while others portray her as an enchanting female figure. Others yet again make reference to a *kyōgen* about her which was being performed at the time.

In the print reproduced here, one can feel the true motherly love emanating from the woman as she seeks to calm the boy with chestnuts while caressing him as he clings to her, giving him a loving smile. Her slim body is wrapped in a cloak patterned with leaves, while her hair falls loosely over her exposed breasts. The quiet, gently melancholic effect of the overall colour composition is interrupted by the strong colours used for the boy, who positively radiates health and strength. It is this contrast which gives the picture its peculiar charm.

Kitagawa Utamaro
Yamamba the Mountain Woman with Kintarō *(p. 109)*

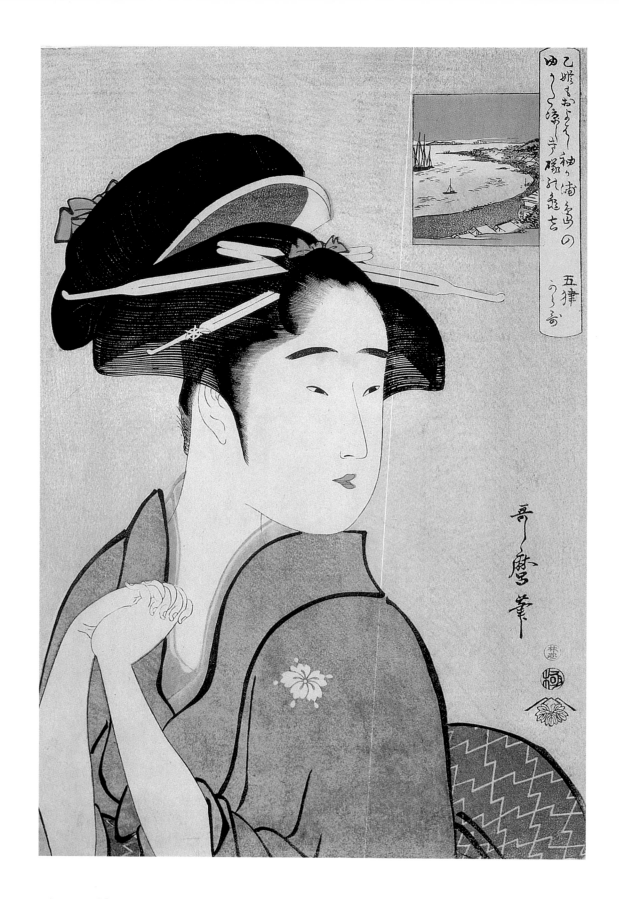

Kitagawa Utamaro
The Geisha Kamekichi★
Oban 38.2 x 24.8
Nishiki-e
Published by Tsutaya Jūzaburō
c. Kansei 6 (1794)

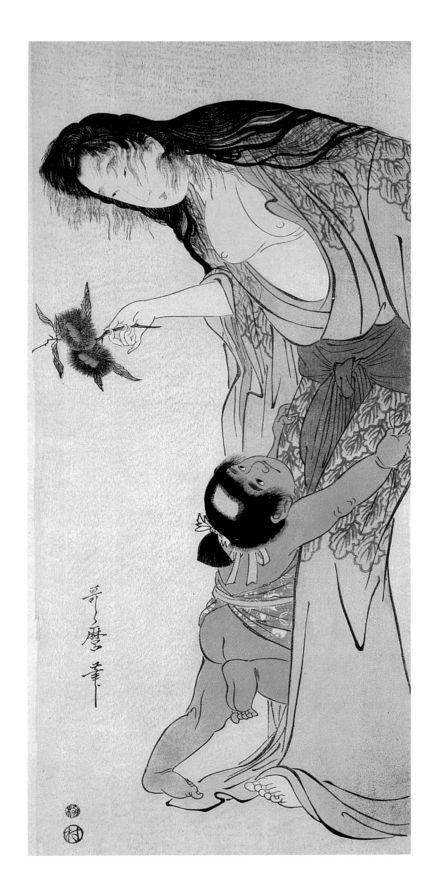

Kitagawa Utamaro
Yamamba the Mountain Woman with Kintarō★
Naga-ōban 52.8 x 23.8
Nishiki-e
Published by Murataya Jirōbei
Kyōwa era (1801–1804)

Chōbunsai Eishi
Hanaogi, Yoshino and Tatsuta from the
Ogiya Establishment
(p. 111)

Chōbunsai Eishi
6 Immortal Poets: Kisen Hōshi
(p. 112)

Chōbunsai Eishi
6 Beauties from the Pleasure Quarter:
Echizenya Morokoshi *(p. 113)*

There were officially licensed pleasure quarters in Kyoto (Shimabara), Osaka (Shinmachi) and Edo (Yoshiwara). Yoshiwara was a self-contained district which developed a culture of its own. It was subdivided into a number of neighbourhoods. The main street, which ran southwards from the gate, was the *Nakanomachi*. The highest-ranking courtesans would dress at four in the afternoon, when the lanterns were lit, and, wearing their sumptuous garments, would parade as far as the *Nakanomachi* and back to the establishments where they were based. They would be accompanied by their young maids who would be wearing *furisode* kimonos; some of the maids were in fact apprentice courtesans, while others were simply servant-girls. The parade of the high-ranking courtesans was one of the daily sights of Yoshiwara.

This print depicts the courtesan Hanaogi from the Ogiya establishment parading with her two servants Yoshino and Tatsuta. She is captured in the middle of a conversation with a trainee courtesan (shinzō). The names Yoshino and Tatsuta are derived from two towns in the province of Nara famous for the splendour of their cherry blossoms and autumn colours. Since time immemorial, they have been an inspiration to artists. The fact that girls were even named after them is evidence that a sense of poetry was present in Yoshiwara.

Of the six celebrated *haiku* poets, we know only three by name: Ono Komachi, Saihara Gyōhei and Kisen Hōshi. This series comprises portrayals of women seeking to emulate these poets. Each picture contains in the top right-hand corner the title of the series, and to the left of this the name of the individual poet concerned, and a *waka* composed by him. The poem in the picture reproduced here reads: "My little house stands in the south of Kyoto, and there deer live. But the people of the capital who do not like this place say that where I live is the back of beyond." From the title and the poem, the name of the poet can be inferred.

Even a beholder ignorant of the meaning and content of the poem can comprehend the content of the picture: the lady at her writing table, on which is laid out the draft paper for her poem, is toying with her writing brush as she thinks hard to choose precisely the right words. The objects on the table – an edition of the "Tale of Genji", a lamp, writing materials and a small box – together with the woman's hairstyle, her costume and her blackened teeth – all point to her being the wife of a *bushi*.

The courtesan Morokoshi from the Echizen establishment, which was in the first block of Edomachi in Yoshiwara, was well-known as a partner versed in Japanese short poems or *waka*. In Yoshiwara there were numerous high-ranking courtesans skilled in such arts as dancing, kangen (Japanese wind and string instruments), the tea ceremony, ikebana (flower arranging), *waka, haiku,* and shodō (calligraphy). In addition they would make their own costumes and even some items of furniture. In the course of time, many of these skills were lost, but in this picture, lying on the red-lacquered writing table at which Morokoshi is sitting reading, we see many books, complete with bookmarks, waiting to make their contribution to a many-sided education. In order to prevent her hair falling into her face, Morokoshi has done it up into a bun. Odd strands of hair are highlighted, and together with her thin kimono, which is only loosely held in place by a relatively narrow sash, these convey an impression of grace. The colour-combination of the diaphanous, pale black kimono, white sash and red under-kimono is also highly successful. The way the lines are drawn is typical of Eishi's depiction of seated women. He also painted the other courtesans who sought to emulate the six famous poets: they too were known to be outstanding *waka* partners, and had written verses on six different flowers. In this series, these flowers form a thread linking the pictures together. To the right of the flower is the name of the establishment, while to the left is the name of the courtesan.

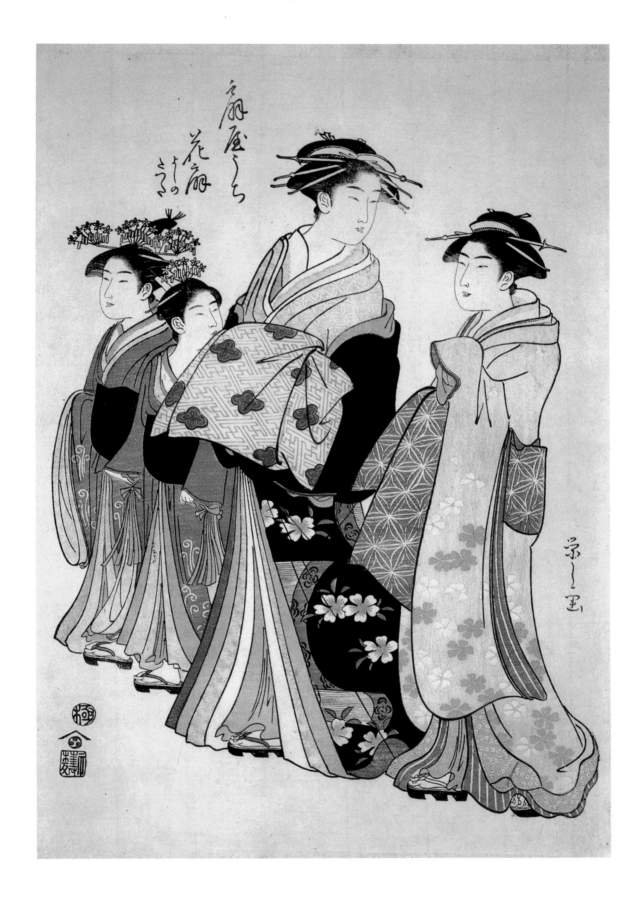

Chōbunsai Eishi
Hanaogi, Yoshino and Tatsuta from the Ogiya Establishment★
Hazama-ban 33.1 x 22.6
Nishiki-e
Published by Nishimuraya Yohachi
mid Kansei era (1789–1801)

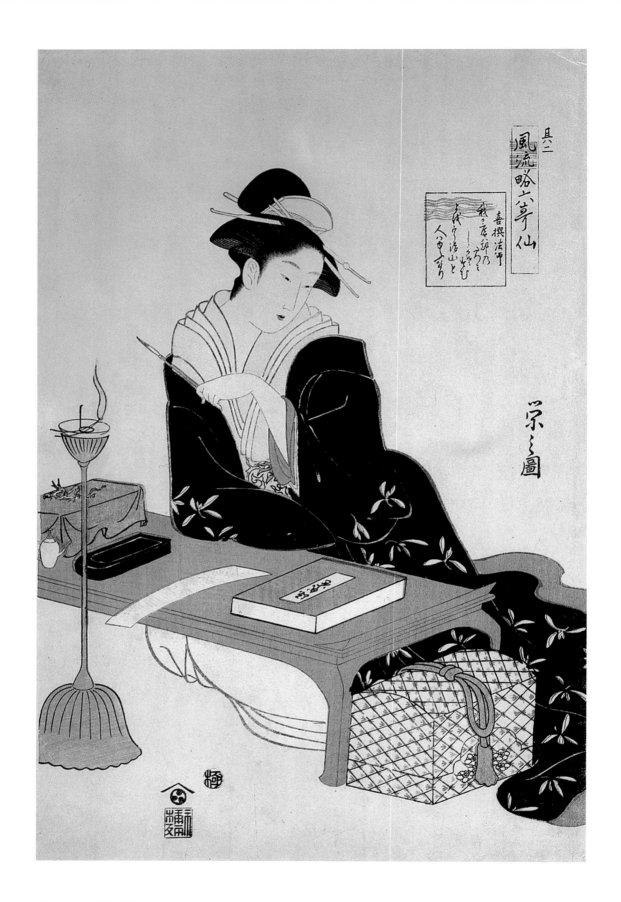

Chōbunsai Eishi
6 Immortal Poets: Kisen Hōshi★
Oban 38.1 x 24.7
Nishiki-e
Published by Nishimuraya Yohachi
c. Kansei 5–6 (1793–1794)

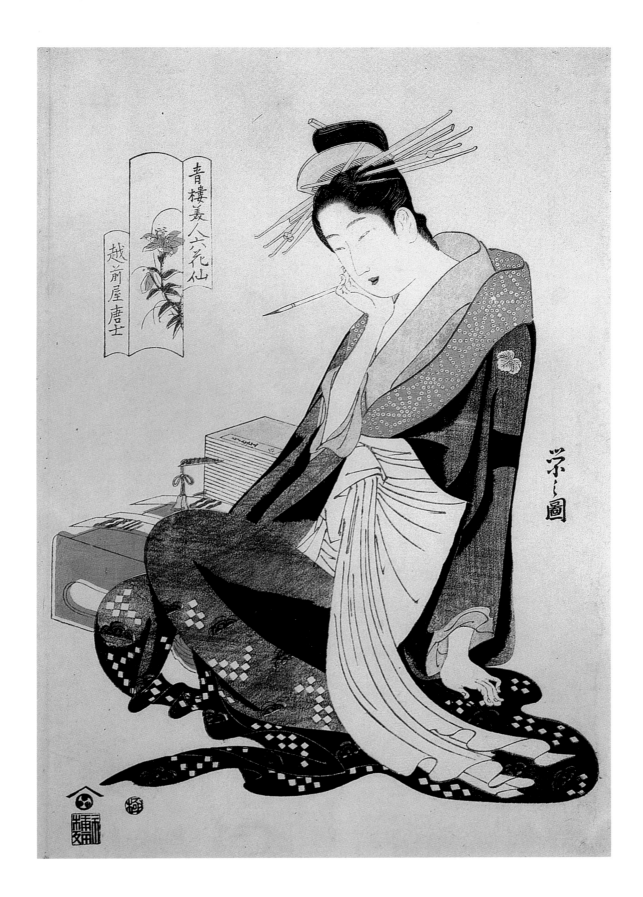

青楼美人六花仙
越前屋唐土

Chōbunsai Eishi
6 Beauties from the Pleasure Quarter:
Echizenya Morokoshi★
Oban 37.0 x 25.3
Nishiki-e
Published by Nishimuraya Yohachi
c. Kansei 6–7 (1794–1795)

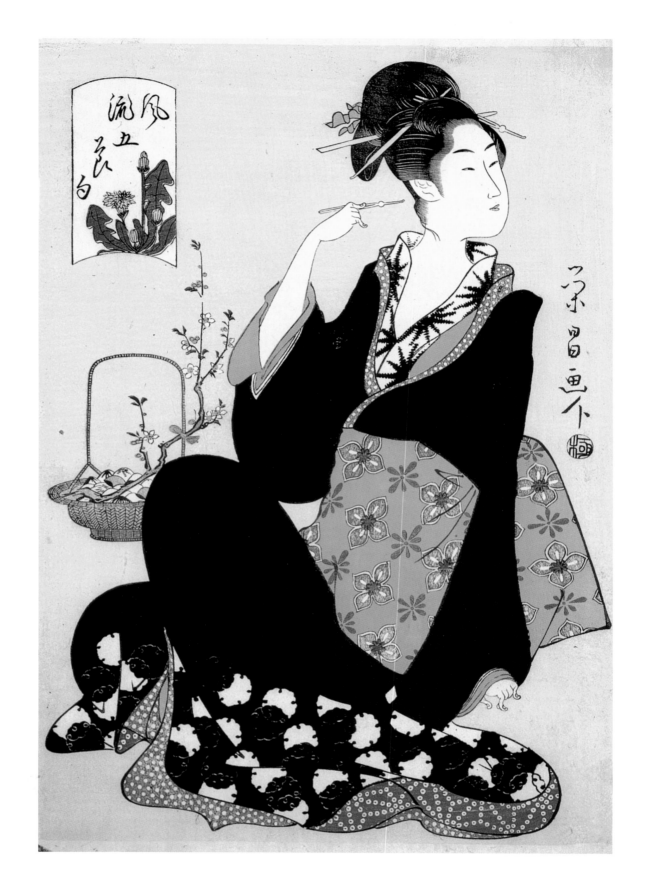

Chōkōsai Eishō
The 5 Festivals of the Year: The Doll Festival★
Oban 33.9 x 22.7
Nishiki-e
Published by Yamaguchiya Chūsuke
mid Kansei era (1789–1801)

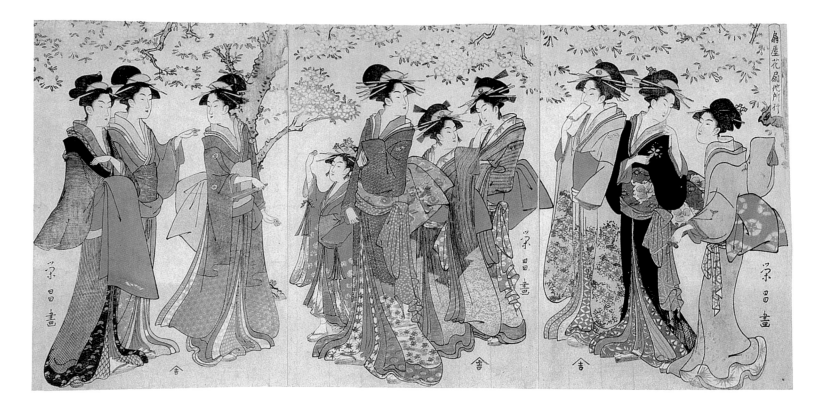

In Japan the spring cherry blossom is celebrated with "hanami", or flower-viewing excursions in which people sit around under the cherry trees and drink and sing while enjoying the splendour of the blossoms. During the Edo period, it became very popular to go in groups to some site renowned for its blossom. Favourite "hanami" sites, then as now, were Ueno, Koganei and Karasuyama.

   This print depicts a group of courtesans from Yoshiwara. Normally they would not have been allowed to leave the pleasure district, but the cherry-blossom period was an exception, when they were given days off to relax and celebrate. In the centre of the group, wearing an *obi* with a cloud and dragon pattern, is the famous Hanaogi, who was frequently painted by Utamaro, Eishi and other *ukiyo-e* artists. Behind her, two "shinzō" (trainee courtesans) in identical attire are conversing. Eishō painted numerous busts, but more typical of his style are group pictures such as this triptych.

Five of the traditional festivals in the Japanese year were adopted unchanged from China. Under the old calendar, New Year was celebrated on the 1st day of the 1st month. On this occasion, the traditional meal was a rice soup with seven herbs (nanakusa-kayu), which was supposed to ensure good health in the year to come. On the 3rd day of the 3rd month came the Doll Festival, when little girls prayed for long life. On the 5th day of the 5th month, irises were attached to the roofs of verandahs, in order to ward off evil. (Later, this festival became Boys' Day, which it still is.) The 7th day of the 7th month was the Star Festival, when people prayed for greater skill in crafts and calligraphy, while the 9th day of the 9th month was the day when people went out to view chrysanthemums. The popularity of all these festivals among woodblock-print artists may be measured by the number and variety of works devoted to them.

   The series from which this picture is taken concentrates on the flowers and smaller objects which were of particular importance in the context of the festival. Symbolic of the Doll Festival (hinamatsuri) in this picture are the dandelion, the clams and the branch of peach blossom. The elegant kimono with its pattern on a black background, which is held in place by a broad floral-patterned *obi*, and whose collars are overlapped in broad succession, is typical of the Chōkōsai school, as is the elegant posture of the lady, sitting upright with the left knee raised.

Chōkōsai Eishō
Hanaogi from the Ogiya Establishment and Others★
Oban, triptych, each sheet 36.9 x 25.9
Nishiki-e
Published by Enomotoya Kichibei
mid Kansei era (1789–1801)

Chōkōsai Eishō
The 5 Festivals of the Year:
The Doll Festival
(p. 114)

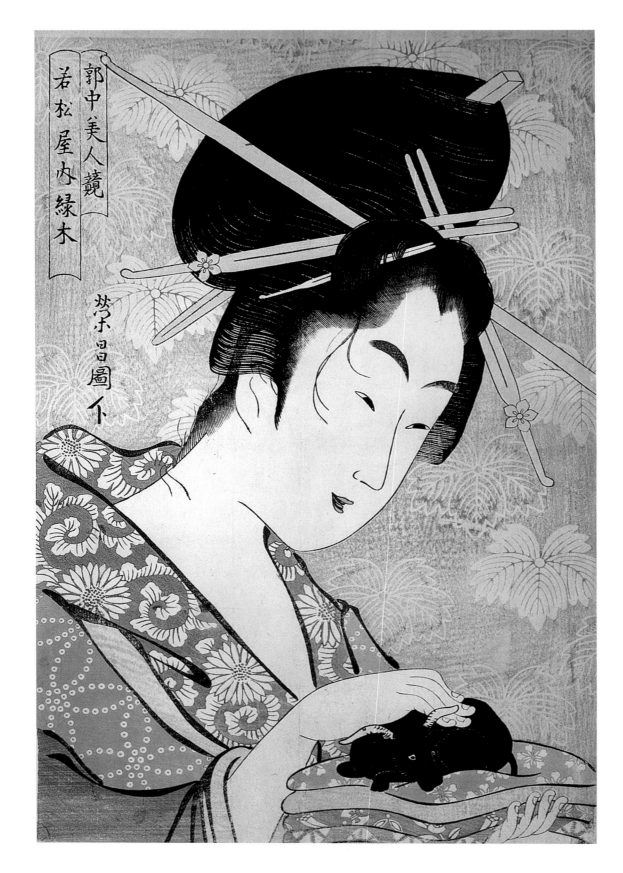

Chōkōsai Eishō
Contest of Beauties in the Pleasure District:
Midoriki from the Wakamatsuya Establishment★
Oban 39.7 x 26.0
Nishiki-e
Published by Yamaguchiya Chūsuke
c. Kansei 7–8 (1795–1796)

The series "Contest of Beauties in the Pleasure District", which comprises a total of 19 portraits, depicts the most popular courtesans in Yoshiwara at the time. Eishō depicted his subjects more tenderly than did his master, Eishi. Chōkōsai Eiri also produced three woodblock prints on this theme. Their style is similar, since both were products of the same school: areas of the picture use the *kira-e* technique, or else, as here, are covered in an ivy motif; objects such as pipes or sake beakers are also included. The object of all of these devices is to avoid any sense of monotony when the main subject is a large-format bust. The girl in this picture is holding a cushion on which is a toy cow. In the Edo period, it was believed that this would bestow the ability to foretell the future on the Day of the Cow (1st or 3rd day of the month of the Ushi festival). Midoriki has pinned her ample hair into a large bun in the form of a shell. At this period she was known throughout Edo as the leading courtesan in the Wakamatsuya establishment, and was very popular.

This picture is part of the same series as that reproduced on p. 119. It shows a *geisha* who has been invited to a party in a *tatami* room. With the plectrum in the fold of her garment at her breast, she is about to get a *shamisen* out of its box. The poem on the scroll in the top left-hand corner of the picture reads: "Parting is difficult, but I turn my head once more. Since we shall meet again soon, life goes on." At parties, poems such as this were declaimed to the accompaniment of a *shamisen*. Perhaps the gentle smile on the face of the *geisha* indicates some other, more secret, feeling. Her ivy-bordered kimono with its broad black *obi*, set against a pale yellow background, draws attention towards her and away somewhat from the splendour of the party itself. Almost every famous work of *oban* size was printed by Tsuruya Kiemon, and this was no exception. It was published by Tsutaya Jūzaburō, who also recognized the talents of Utamaro and Sharaku.

Although Chōki was working contemporaneously with Utamaro and Einosuke during the Kansei era, his *bijin-ga* are stylistically different from theirs. In common with many print artists, the details of his life are unknown. His speciality was the depiction of elegant women with pretty faces and gently sloping shoulders. His courtesans and *geishas* from Osaka, with their hint of luxury, along with his actor portraits *(yakusha-e)*, are not dissimilar to those by Sharaku. Chōki's typical *bijin-ga* include both "seasonal" works using the *kira-e* technique, and seated portraits of female figures from ballads and folk songs.

The lines of poetry in the top right-hand corner explain the sitter's pose: "Actually, you are my client, but that is not how I feel. When with you I should like to be dressed as a wife with two collars. But you do not like the idea, since your letter is so short." The woman, lost in thought, with both sleeves rolled down, tending a fire beneath a pot in order to boil clams, evokes various emotions. She arouses our sympathy, with her elegant garment, her turned-down collar, and her skilfully-bound bun, which is just beginning to come loose.

Chōkōsai Eishō
Contest of Beauties in the Pleasure District: Midoriki from the Wakamatsuya Establishment *(p. 116)*

Eishōsai Chōki
Geisha
(p. 118)

Eishōsai Chōki
Geisha Behaving like a Married Woman
(p. 119)

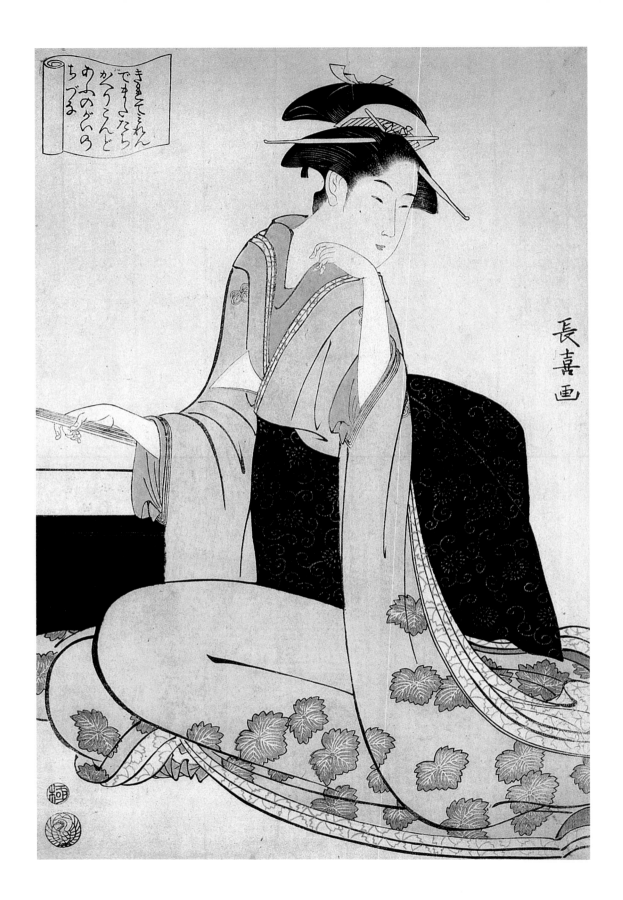

Eishōsai Chōki
Geisha★
Oban 36.6 x 24.1
Nishiki-e
Published by Tsutaya Jūzaburō
c. Kansei 6 (1794)

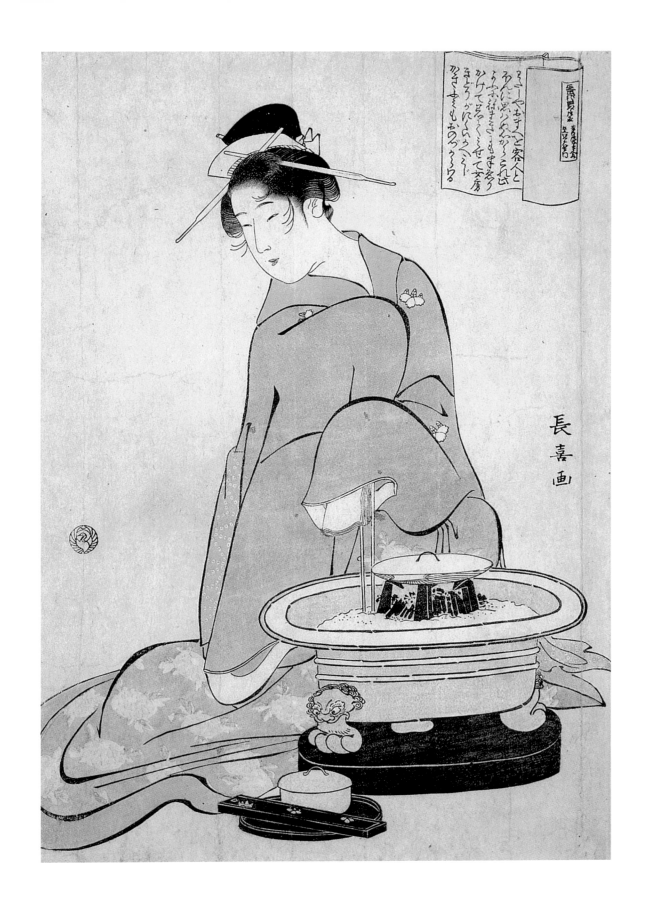

Eishōsai Chōki
Geisha Behaving like a Married Woman★
Oban 37.2 x 25.5
Nishiki-e
Published by Tsutaya Jūzaburō
c. Kansei 6 (1794)

Tōshūsai Sharaku

Segawa Tomisaburō II as Yadogiri, the Wife
of Ogishi Kurando, and Nakamura Mansei
as Wakakusa the Lady's Maid
(p. 121)

During his first period of artistic activity, in the 5th month of Kansei 6 (1794), Sharaku produced 28 works based on theatrical performances, five of them depicting two actors facing each other in profile. These works give excellent expression to the different characters of the actors concerned and of the roles they are playing.

The print reproduced here is based on the play "Hanaayame Buroku Soga", performed at the Miyako theatre. In it, Ogishi Kurando assists the hero of the story in his revenge. His wife Yadogiri, played by Segawa Tomisaburō II, is of course also a good woman. Another of Sharaku's major works depicts a woman who typifies even more strongly the serene dignity of a warrior's wife. Tomisaburō II has a noble face with narrow lips and high cheekbones. His pose – with his right hand touching his collar – is expressive of dignity. By contrast, Mansei in the role of Wakakusa has a round face and a robust figure. His back bent, both hands hanging down, this figure lacks any hint of elegance, albeit expressing loyalty. The colour composition is well thought out. Tomisaburō II is drawn largely in pastel shades: the shawl, in pale red with a spring pattern, hangs over a long beige garment; Mansei by contrast is depicted in strong colours, dressed in a bright green kimono with a violet stripe and a bright red under-kimono.

Tōshūsai Sharaku

Segawa Kikunojō III as Oshizu, the Wife of
Tanabe Bunzō
(p. 122)

The story of the play "Kashōjū bunroku Soga", in which the part of Oshizu is played here by Kikunojō, goes as follows: In a battle to avenge a wrong perpetrated on his lord, Tanabe Bunzō, the husband of the subject of this picture, had been crippled by his enemy; thereafter he was forced to spend his days in abject poverty, and later had his wife avenge the wrong. In this *kyōgen*, which has marital loyalty as its theme, Kikunojō III appears emaciated, his hair dishevelled and kept in place by a "hachimaki" (headband); this symbolizes sickness.

Kikunojō and Gishii Hanjirō IV were rivals for the status of leading *onnagata*. In a review of actors compiled in the year Kansei 1 (1789), the *onnagata* are ranked in order; the following year, the Nakamura and Ichimura theatres are newly listed among those with takings of 1,800 ryō or more, a substantial sum. Kikunojō III was 43 years old at the time, good-looking and well-known for his chubby cheeks and projecting lower lip. Beneath the garment in the Narumi batik style, the green under-kimono allows a glimpse of a chrysanthemum, Kikunojō's hallmark ("kiku" = chrysanthemum).

Tōshūsai Sharaku

Sanokawa Ichimatsu III as the Geisha Onayo
of Gion
(p. 123)

During the Kansei era (1789–1801), the extravagantly sumptuous fashion of the day reached the *kabuki* stage, thus forcing up the salaries of the actors and the expenses for costumes. As a result, the venerable Nakamura, Ichimura and Morita theatres were unable to keep going.

It was in the 5th month of Kansei 6 (1794), in the midst of this depression in the *kabuki* theatre, that the figure of Tōshūsai Sharaku and his actor portraits suddenly appeared. The actors portrayed did not play on any of the three stages mentioned above, but at the Miyako, Kiri and Kaharazaki theatres. The only subject of conversation in the *kabuki* and *ukiyo-e* communities in the weeks to come must have been Sharaku and his 28 amazing woodblock prints using the *kira-e* technique. It was said of him that he could catch the dramatic powers of an actor precisely.

Here we see Ichimatsu III playing a courtesan from Gion in the play "Kashōjū bunroku Soga" produced at the Kiri theatre. Through the strong, robust masculine face there shines the beauty which was typical of the *onnagata* of the *kabuki*, conveying all the sensuousness of a man dressed as a woman. Ichimatsu III changed his name twice in the subsequent period; however, because it was the favourite of the first-generation Ichimatsu, the check pattern on the collar and cuffs of the kimono became known in popular parlance as the "Ichimatsu pattern".

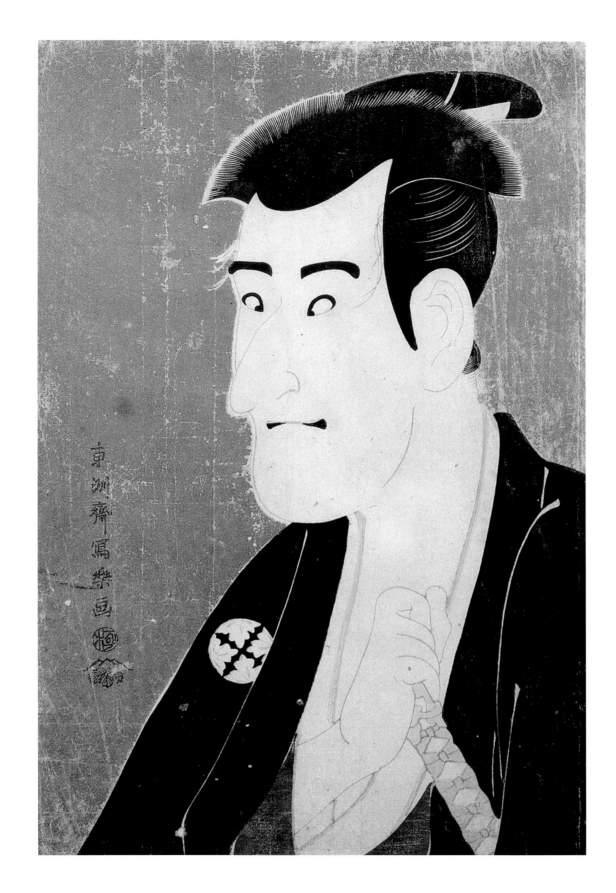

Tōshūsai Sharaku
Ichikawa Komazō III as Shigano Daishichi★
Oban 37.1 x 24.0
Nishiki-e
Published by Tsutaya Jūzaburō
5th month of Kansei 6 (1794)

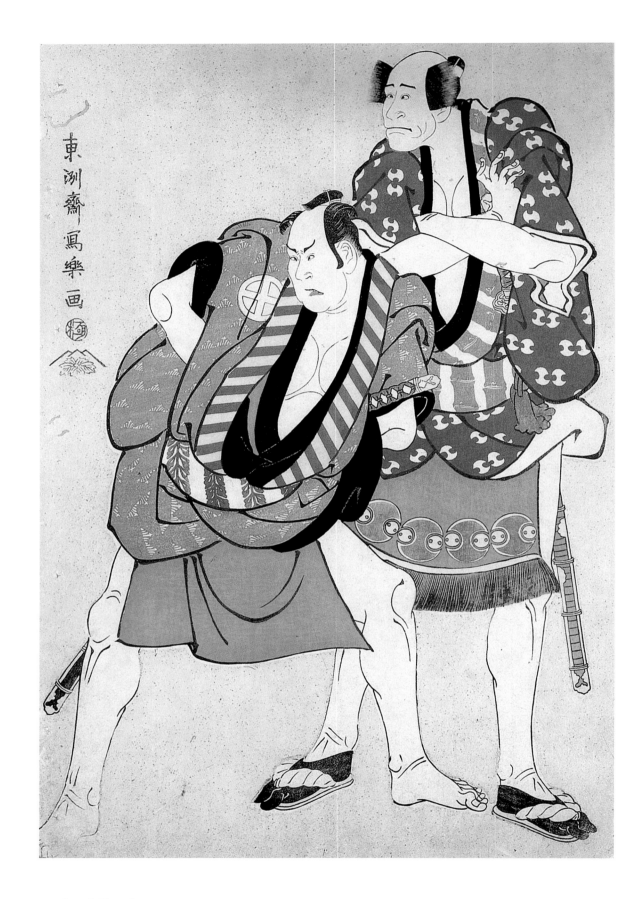

Tōshūsai Sharaku
Arashi Ryūzō II as the Servant Ukiyo no Matahei
and Otani Hiroji III as the Servant Tosa no Matahei
Oban 37.0 x 25.4
Nishiki-e
Published by Tsutaya Jūzaburō
7th month of Kansei 6 (1794)

This work dates from Sharaku's third period of activity in the 11th month of Kansei 6 (1794); it depicts Kinsaku II as Iwate, the wife of Abe Sadatō, in the play "Otokoyamago Edo Banseki", which was performed at the Kiri theatre. Kinsaku originally came from Kyoto, and spent a short time in Edo as an actor, achieving considerable popularity before returning to Kyoto in the year An'ei 9 (1780). It was 15 years before he came back to Edo, now aged 66. The charm of his youth, captured on paper by Shunshō, may have vanished, but his acting was nonetheless received with great popular acclaim in the capital (as too was Sharaku's print of the young Sumō wrestler Daidōsan). Having waited so long for his comeback, the theatregoers of Edo greeted Kinsaku with rapturous applause.

As an actor, he was extremely versatile, but his robust figure made him more suitable for the parts of warrior's wives, versed in the martial arts, and for villains' roles. In this picture, we see him holding an umbrella as a shield against the snow, and gazing down at his raised wooden sandals, or "geta". It is assumed that Iwate, whom he is portraying here, practised the martial arts, and in so far, this picture gives outstanding expression to Kinsaku's versatility on stage.

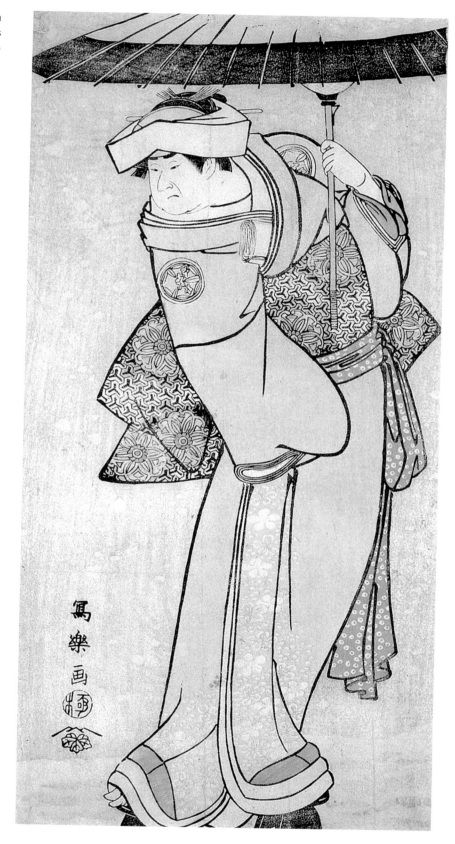

Tōshūsai Sharaku
Arashi Ryūzō II as the Servant Ukiyo no Matahei
and Otani Hiroji III as the Servant Tosa no Matahei
(p. 128)

From Sharaku's second period of activity in the 7th and 8th months of Kansei 6 (1794), eight *oban*-size full-length portraits are known, and 30 *hosoban*-size busts. These works are different in character from those he produced during his first period two months earlier. The print reproduced here shows the antagonists Ukiyo no Matahei and Tosa no Matahei in the play "Keisei Sanbongasa", which was staged at the Miyako theatre in the 7th month of Kansei 6 (1794). Ukiyo was an evil servant and Tosa a good servant in the employ of one Nagoya, who is said to have had an affair with the courtesan Kazuragi, although no text is extant to confirm this. The use of line and colour by Sharaku has produced an outstanding portrayal both of the actors and of the roles they are playing.

Tōshūsai Sharaku
Yamashita Kinsaku II as Iwate, Wife of Sadatō
Hosoban 30.7 x 15.2
Nishiki-e
Published by Tsutaya Jūzaburō
11th month of Kansei 6 (1794)

The second *kyōgen* staged by the Kawarazaki theatre in the 7th month of Kansei 6 (1794) saw Iwai Kiyotarō IV in the role of Osode, the daughter of Futamiya. The story is based on a performance on the 12th day of the 4th month of Hōreki 11 (1761), in which a love affair between the 14-year-old Osode and 38-year-old Obiya Chōeimon ends tragically on account of the difference in their ages. The romance had begun when Chōeimon, returning from a pilgrimage, stopped at Futamiya's inn and met the daughter of the house.

Kiyotarō was a pupil of Iwai Hanshirō V, and assumed the name Ichiwaka Yaozō IV in the year Bunka 1 (1804). He died in Kōka 1 (1844) at the age of 73. At the time of this performance, then, he was just 23. Osode is captured in flowing lines as she turns round; the colour combination – tea-green and yellow for the kimono, and bright green for the *obi* – reflects her beauty and gentle character. This is one of Sharaku's masterpieces, and one of his few single-sheet prints in the *hosoban* format.

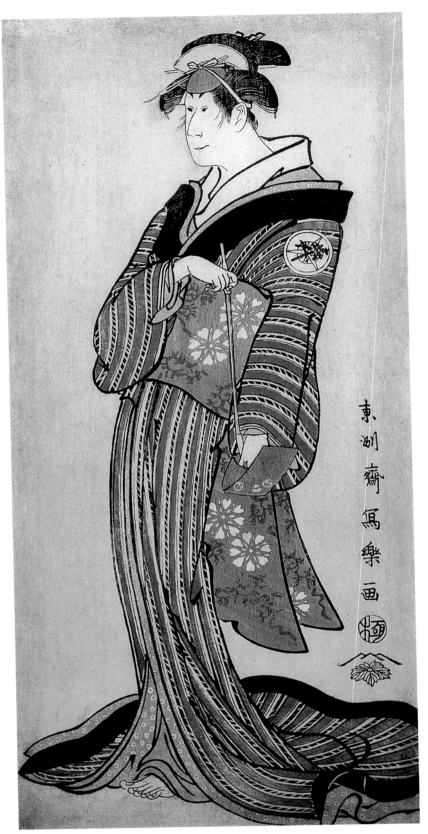

Chōensai Eishin
Falconer
(p. 131)

Eishin left very few works; some ten of them can be described as major pieces. He was influenced by, among others, Utamaro. The most frequent theme of his major works is the life of the young people of his day, for example this young falconer, breeding and training his birds for the sport of hawking. At the beginning of the Edo period, hawking was a popular pastime among the aristocratic warrior class. Gradually, as the shogunate drew to a close, more and more *bushi* took up the profession of falconer. As the portrayal of falconers was attracting increasing interest among the bourgeoisie, they came to be a frequent theme of woodblock prints and ink drawings. This friendly-looking falconer is holding his falcon on a perch in his left hand. On the sleeve of his *haori*, among the finely printed aubergines of the pattern, there is an unexpected representation of Mount Fuji. But Fuji, falcon and aubergine were all symbols of good luck, promising peace and prosperity in the year to come.

Tōshūsai Sharaku
Iwai Kiyotarō IV as Osode, Daughter of Futamiya★
Hosoban 31.5 x 15.0
Nishiki-e
Published by Tsutaya Jūzaburō
7th month of Kansei 6 (1794)

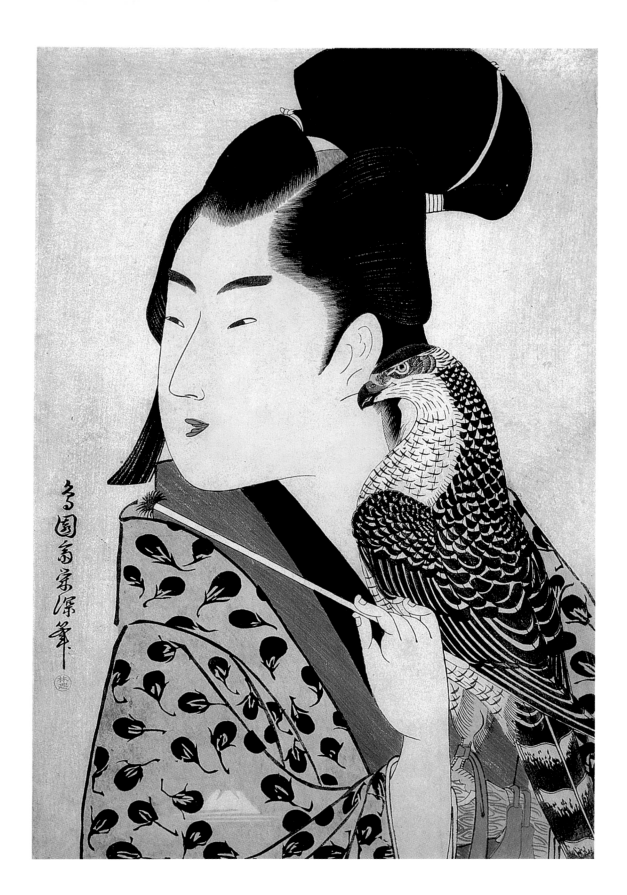

Chōensai Eishin
Falconer★
Oban 38.9 x 25.8
Nishiki-e
Publisher unknown
2nd half of the Kansei era (1789–1801)

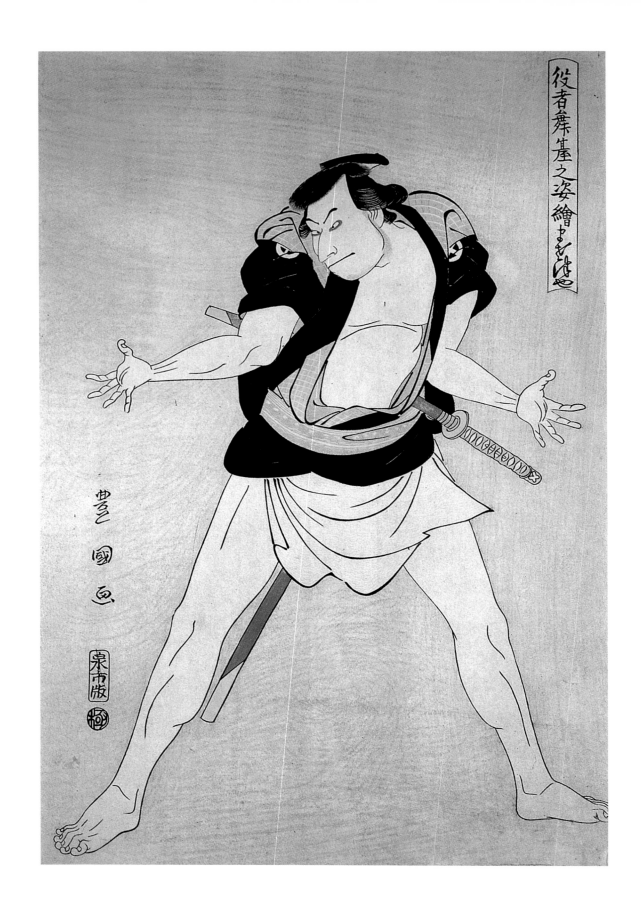

Utagawa Toyokuni
Actors on Stage: Masatsuya★
Oban 37.5 x 25.3
Nishiki-e
Published by Izumiya Ichibei
Kansei 6 (1794)

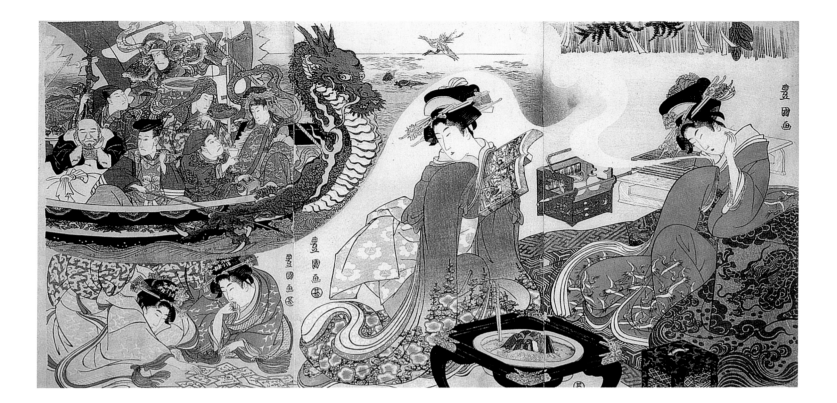

This scene is set in a room in a pleasure quarter which has been sumptuously decked out for the New Year festivities. The newly-employed girl is reciting poems by the imperial lady-in-waiting Sei Shōnagon, while two others are playing the card game "100 Famous Poems by 100 Famous Poets". Meanwhile a courtesan has reclined against the table to sleep. From the fans in her hair, she can be identified as the courtesan Ogiya from the 1st block in the Yoshiwara pleasure district in Edo. From her breast there emerges the dream of the title. The depiction of dream images in clouds or bubbles was a favourite convention.

This courtesan is dreaming of a treasure ship sailing on the open sea, above which a crane is dancing, the symbol of Kisshō, the God of Good Fortune, while turtles are swimming in the waves. On board the ship, with its many treasures, are the seven gods of Good Fortune. By lying down to sleep at the New Year on a cushion beneath which this picture had been placed, it was believed that one could experience this dream. Here, however, the seven gods are not portrayed in their usual form, but with the faces of celebrated actors. From the right, these are Iwai Kumezaburō as Benzaiten, Ichikawa Omezō as Daikokuten, Onoe Eizaburō as Fukurokuju, Matsumoto Kōshirō V as Bishamonten, Ichikawa Yaozō III as Ebisu, Sawamura Gennosuke III as Jūrōrin and Arashi Sanpachi as Hotei.

The actor portrayed here under the name of Masatsuya is Otani Oniji II. Tradition has it that in the 9th month of Kansei 6 (1794), he played the part of Teikurō in the play "Kanadehon Chūshingura" at the Kawabarasaki theatre. This corresponds to the part of Edohei the servant in the play "Koinyōbo somewake no tazuna" which is performed at this same theatre every May.

Sharaku's portrayals of Oniji II in roles he played at that time were extremely popular. One of these masterpieces is this *oban*-format figure of Oniji, with his characteristic piercing look and his mouth drawn to a thin line. Here Toyokuni has given us a full-length portrait of Oniji II as, in a tense moment, he tries to steal money and is being challenged by his opponent. The powerful gesture with the open arms was probably also characteristic of Oniji: certainly both Sharaku and Toyokuni depicted him in this pose. In his series "Portraits of *Kabuki* Actors", Toyokuni showed his subjects in the same pose, perhaps under the influence of or in reaction to Sharaku. In any case, it is interesting to compare the two. The extent of the popularity of Toyokuni's realistic actor portraits can be gauged from the fact that these series were continued even after Sharaku's disappearance from the scene.

Utagawa Toyokuni
The First Dream
Oban, triptych, each sheet 39.0 x 26.0
Nishiki-e
Published by Maruya Jinpachi
early Kyōwa era (1801—1804)

Utagawa Toyokuni
Actors on Stage: Masatsuya
(p. 132)

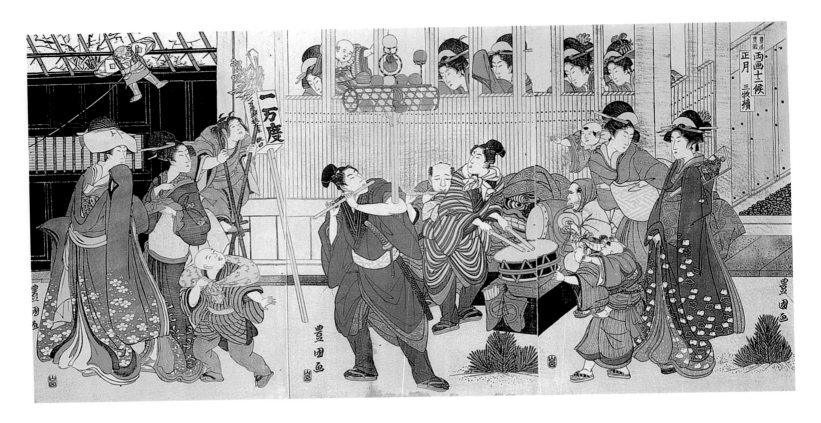

Utagawa Toyokuni

12 Views by Toyohiro and Toyokuni:
New Year★

Oban, triptych, each sheet 38.8 x 26.1
Nishiki-e
Published by Yamadaya Sanshirō
Kyōwa I (1801)

Utagawa Toyokuni

Actors on Stage: Kōraiya
(p. 135)

The series of "12 Double-page Views" of popular customs over the twelve months arose as the result of a painting contest between Toyohiro and Toyokuni. Both were pupils of Utagawa Toyoharu. Towards the end of the *Tokugawa* shogunate, they decided to put their woodblock-print styles to the test in mutual competition; in so doing, they brought about a flowering of the Utagawa school. Toyohiro was responsible for the 2nd, 3rd, 6th and 7th months in the series, while Toyokuni depicted the 1st, 4th and 5th. From the written characters on the picture of the 4th month, it can be deduced that the series must have been produced in the 1st year of the Kyōwa era (1801).

The print "New Year" shows the start of a procession of *daikagura* dancers to celebrate the feast, along with people lining the street to watch the procession. The *daikagura* was originally only performed at the Ise shrine, but it was spread thoughout the country by Ise pilgrims. To the accompaniment of flutes and drums, lion dances and *kyōgen* were performed.

The "Pictures of Actors on Stage" – which also included the print reproduced on p. 132 – were published in the years Kansei 6–7 (1794–1795). The series comprises a total of 40 sheets, and established Toyokuni's position as a painter of actor portraits. In many of these stage portraits there is no background scenery, except perhaps a lone tree, focussing our attention fully upon the actor. Compared with Toyokuni's later work, the style is unselfconscious, and the planes of colour remain large.

The actor depicted here was well-known on account of his mask with its large nose and hawk-like eyes. He is staring at his partner on stage with animosity, while his pose, with sword raised, heightens the tension. This actor also popularized the grid-iron pattern for the kimono, which soon became very widespread.

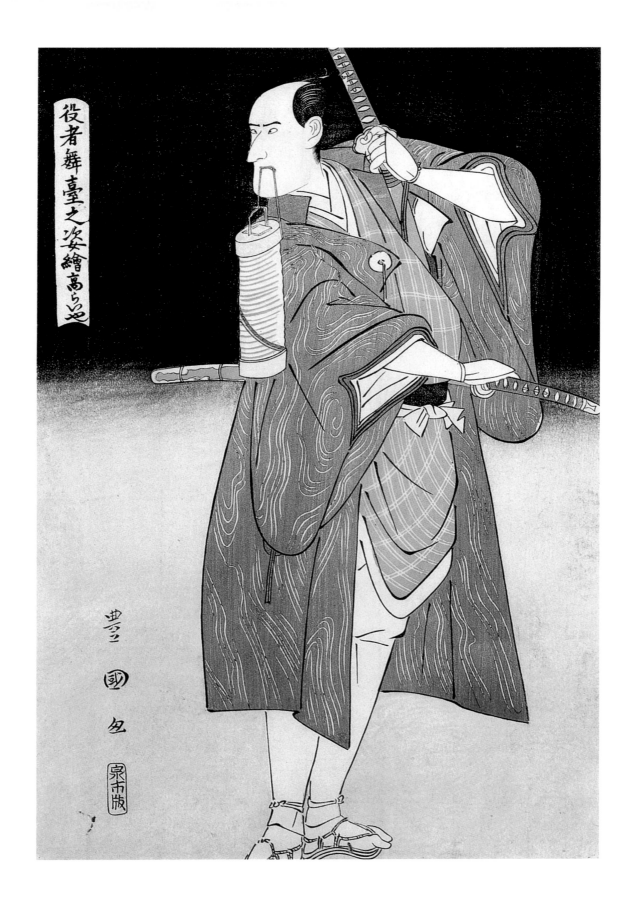

Utagawa Toyokuni
Actors on Stage: Kōraiya★
Oban 36.0 x 24.1
Nishiki-e
Published by Izumiya Ichibei
Kansei 7 (1795)

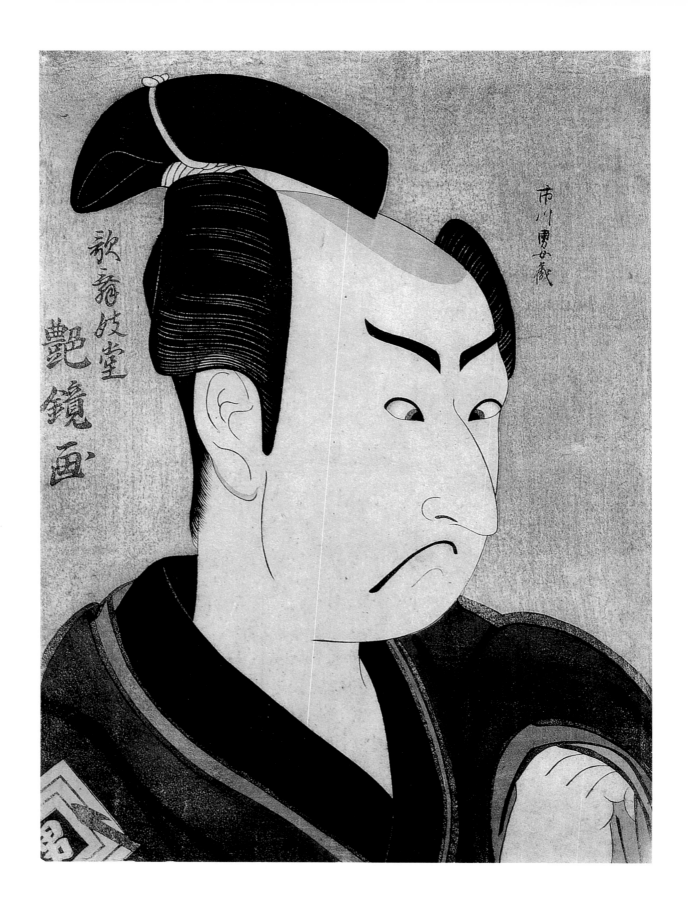

Kabukidō Enkyō
Ichikawa Omezō★
Oban 35.5 x 25.6
Nishiki-e
Published by Tsutaya Jūzaburō
c. Kansei 8 (1796)

The emblem on the kimono in the bottom left-hand corner of the picture bears the character for "otoko" (man). As the facial features are very similar to the known features of Ichikawa Omezō, he is probably the actor portrayed here. According to one version, Omezō is identical with the *kyōgen* author Nakamura Jūsuke II, but there is no documentary evidence of this, and his dates are unknown. This particular work, dating from around Kansei 8 (1796), bears neither a seal of the artist's name nor that of the publisher, and was thus unlikely to have been produced for sale.

The colour tones against the grey background have been carefully chosen. Omezō is dressed in a dark brown kimono, beneath which we have a glimpse of a green undergarment. The facial features are typical of him. The lines are simple and strong, and bear witness to outstanding draughtsmanship. A number of theories exist as to the role being played here, but none has been proved. The same pose has been chosen here as in the works of Kunimasa. The composition resembles those of Sharaku, but the use of a dark and a light shade of black, along with the red ear lobes, are more reminiscent of the work of Toyokuni and Kunimasa.

According to Roger S. Keyes, the 11th month of Kansei 7 (1795) witnessed the performance at the Miyako theatre of the play "Kaeribana yuki no Yoshitsune", in which Tokuji took the part of "Mibu no kozaru" (The Monkey of Mibu). There exist three other works by Kunimasa based on the same play and published by Uemura Yohei, portraying the actors Nakamura Noshio II, Ichikawa Yaozō III and Ichikawa Danjūrō IV. The print reproduced here, however, bears no publisher's mark, suggesting that it was added later to the group just mentioned. It is also thought that this work is part of a triptych, whose remaining two sheets have been lost. Kunimasa produced a great number of actor portraits in profile or full face. It is often difficult to determine the identity of the subject. Tokuji's portrait in the role of the "Monkey of Mibu" also appeared in an album entitled "Nigao ehon yakusha gakuyatsu", to which Kunimasa and Toyokuni each contributed 18 bust portraits of actors, and which was published in Kansei 11 (1799). That portrait bears a substantial resemblance to the one reproduced here.

In this print – unlike many other, for him more typical pictures – Kunimasa has not used thick and thin incisions or sweeping strokes of the brush, but has rather sought to convey a gentler, almost soft impression, doubtless in order to give adequate expression to the subject's character.

Ichikawa Ebizō was the son of the actor Danjūrō IV and himself used the name Danjūrō V for a time. When he retired from the theatre in the 11th month of Kansei 8 (1796), this picture was published, showing him in the role of Usui Sadamitsu in the play "Seiwa nidai ooyose genji", performed at the Miyako theatre. The play reaches its climax when the villain seeks to kill a weak, defenceless man. At this moment the *aragoto* hero appears on the "flower-walk" (in the *kabuki* theatre, a catwalk through the auditorium providing access to the stage), and, on reaching the stage, shouts "Halt!". Ever since the time of Danjūrō I, the role of the *aragoto* had been the most important part of the repertoire of this acting dynasty. They did not have a monopoly, however, and to play the *aragoto* was regarded as the high point of an actor's career.

Kunimasa has here filled almost the whole picture with the face and shoulders of Ebizō, who has put his whole soul into the part. In the top left-hand corner, he has just left room for the title, his signature, and the publisher's seal. The left sleeve of his coat is cut off by the edge of the picture, and the profile has no ink contour – both features are distinctive aspects of Kunimasa's style. This work combines beauty of composition with beauty of coloration, enhancing its attractiveness.

Kabukidō Enkyō
Ichikawa Omezō
(p. 136)

Utagawa Kunimasa
Otani Tokuji as the Monkey of Mibu
(p. 138)

Utagawa Kunimasa
Ichikawa Ebizō
(p. 139)

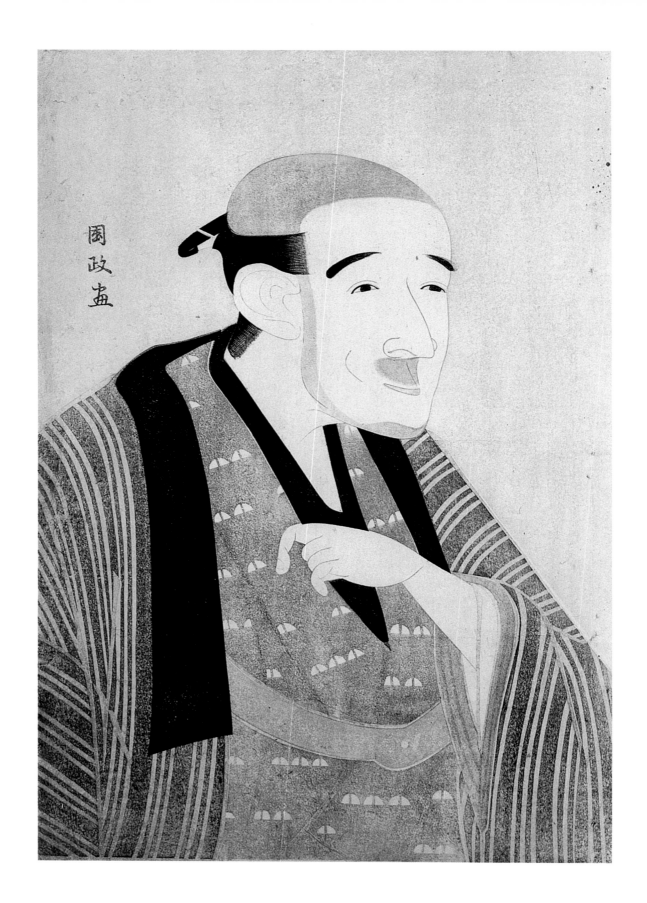

Utagawa Kunimasa
Otani Tokuji as the Monkey of Mibu★
Oban 36.9 x 25.4
Nishiki-e
Publisher unknown
2nd half of the Kansei era (1789–1801)

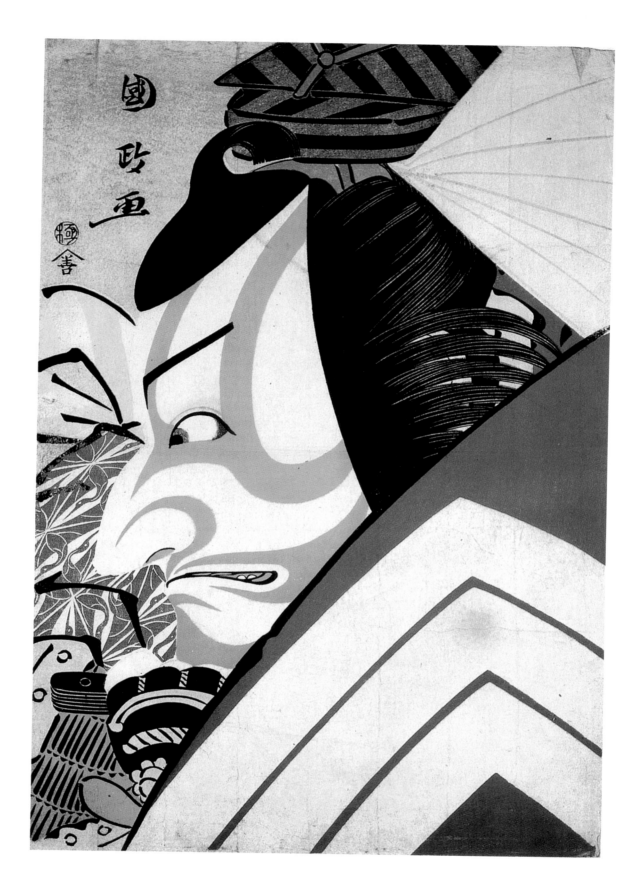

Utagawa Kunimasa
Ichikawa Ebizō★
Oban 38.1 x 26.1
Nishiki-e
Published by Yamazen
Kansei 8 (1796)

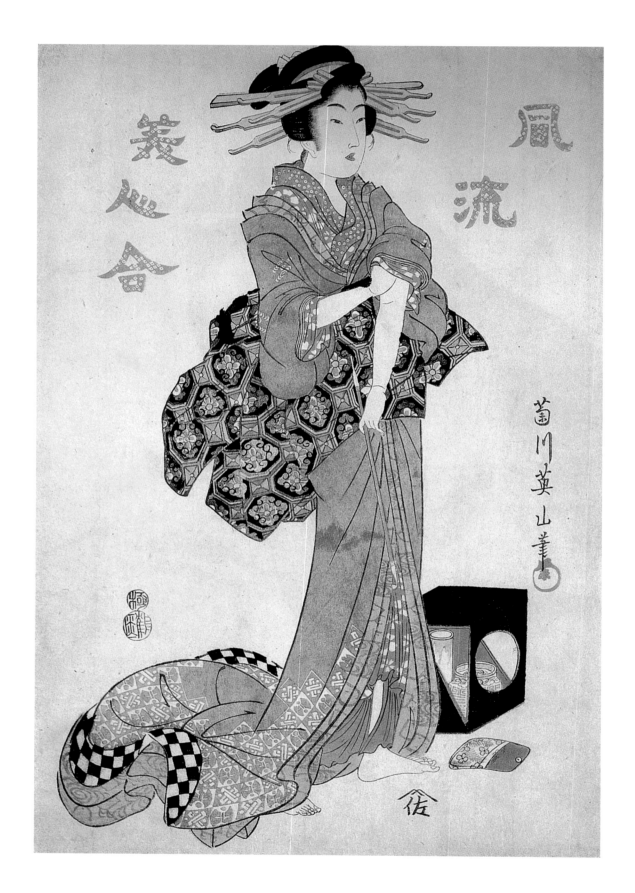

Kikukawa Eizan
Encounters with Elegance: Long Pipe
Oban 38.8 x 26.2
Nishiki-e
Published by Izumisa
c. Bunka 9 (1812)

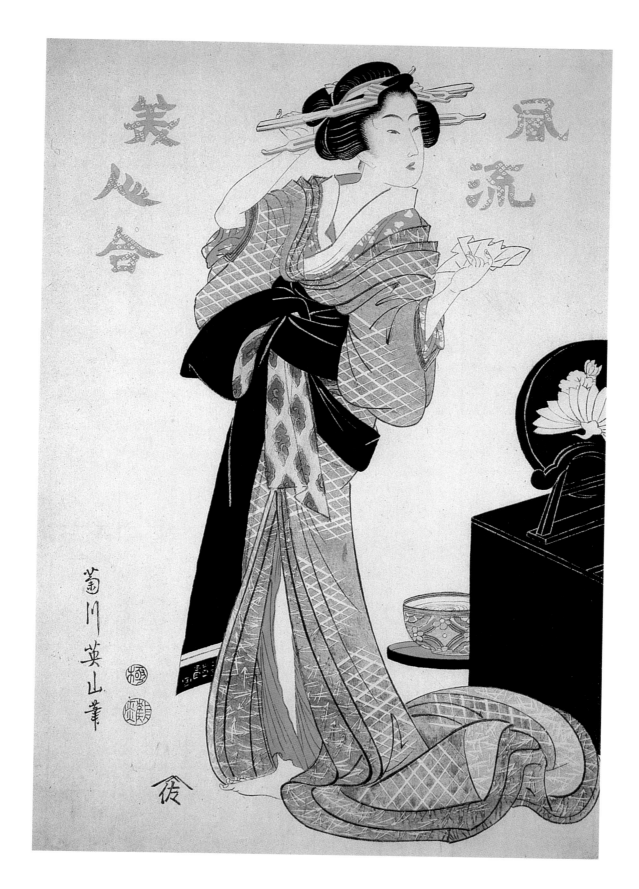

Kikukawa Eizan
Encounters with Elegance: At the Dressing Table
Oban 39.0 x 26.3
Nishiki-e
Published by Izumisa
c. Bunka 9 (1812)

Utagawa Toyohiro
Summer Evening
(p. 145)

Woodblock prints often portrayed courtesans from the pleasure quarters who had made themselves ready for the evening. This picture, however, shows a young girl holding a round fan turning towards a young mother sitting beside her. The main structure of the composition is a long arc linking the faces of the girl, the young mother, the child, and a rotating lantern. The light from the lantern both illuminates the room and reveals, on its shade, the shadow figures of two foxes and the gate to a shrine, the *Inari*-Torii.

This arc mechanism links two pictorial levels, and the apparent rotation thereby produced gives an interesting impression of an animated cartoon, lending the picture a cheerful harmony.

The picture constitutes a poem on a summer evening: a child, reaching out for the lantern, and the mother gently laying her hand on his *obi* to stop him from straying, are evidence of the attention given by the artist to the details of this very natural mother-child relationship. The composition of bright red kasumi pattern, white stripes, black hair and dark *obi* conveys a feeling of freshness while relaxing the eyes. The shimmering face of the girl is likewise marked by a natural freshness.

Toyohiro worked in the school of Utagawa Toyoharu, and sometimes used the name Toyokuni. Compared with Toyoharu, he is regarded as a conservative painter, who has left a huge number of illustrations to text books and books dealing with stories of revenge.

Keisai Eisen
Mirror of the Age: The Courtesan
(p. 146)

This woodblock print is painted in the *aizuri* style. Shading is applied in indigo blue and combined to considerable effect with *beni*-red lines. Towards the end of the Bunsei era (1818–1830), Eisen introduced this style for single-sheet woodblock prints. Here, the lips and eyebrows have also been drawn in *beni*. By that time the woodblock-print technique as such was highly developed, and in consequence, the inhabitants of Edo, already accustomed to polychrome prints, quickly developed a taste for the new indigo style with its fresh colours. This was also the technique employed by Hokusai in his celebrated "36 Views of Mount Fuji".

The popularity of the print reproduced here can be gauged from the fact that similar pictures with different landscapes and different kimono patterns are also extant. Eisen wrote in a letter that he was particularly fond of portraying courtesans in *uchikake*. This courtesan is wearing an *uchikake* with a moon and bamboo pattern; the *obi* is decorated with bamboo and tiger motifs.

Keisai Eisen
Contest of Beauties:
A Geisha from the Eastern Capital
Oban 37.2 x 25.6
Nishiki-e
Published by Sanoya Kihei
mid Bunsei era (1818–1830)
(p. 2)

There exist a whole series of half-length figures by Eisen, representing women of various occupations and social class. The other titles in this series are "Tsujigimi", "Shinsō no musume", "Mizuchaya", "Courtesan" and "Oyashikisugata". Usually they are known by their collective name of "Imayō mime kurabe", which means something like "Contest of Beautiful Women of the Present Day". Each of Eisen's works bears, as subtitle so to speak, a circle with the character for "izumi", or "source"; the alternative reading of this character is "sen", a component of the artist's name. In addition to this series, Eisen was also responsible for half-length portrait series entitled "Ukiyo fūzoku mime kurabe", "48 Views of Ukiyo" and "Collection of 8 Favourites".

The *geisha* depicted here has a mirror in her hand and is painting her eyebrows. Typical of Eisen's style are the sideways look and the fact that the eyes are not looking in the same direction. He not only put across the play of facial features, but also attached great importance to the depiction of gestures. It is precisely this aspect, along with his predilection for variety in kimono patterns, that distinguishes his work from that of other artists.

Katsushika Hokusai
Ariwara no Narihira
(p. 147)

The books "Sanjū rokkasen" (36 Immortal Poets) by Fujiwara no Kintō and "Rokkasen" (6 Immortal Poets) by Ki no Tsurayuki contain the verses of celebrated poets known for their mastery of the *waka* form. The portrayal of these poets each with one of their poems was a standard motif of the woodblock print. *Ukiyo-e* include many depictions of beautiful women seeking to emulate the poets, but here we have one of the six immortals himself, Ariwara no Narihira. He is portrayed in a type of picture known as "moji-e", in which the figure is composed of written characters. This tradition goes back to the Heian period (roughly the 8th and 9th centuries A.D.); among woodblock-print artists, its main exponents were Kiyomasu and Masanobu. In the year Kyōwa 3 (1803), these "moji-e" were published by Santō Kyōden as an album of caricatures. Hokusai too, though, was an accomplished "moji-e" artist, and in his books gave a detailed description of the method.

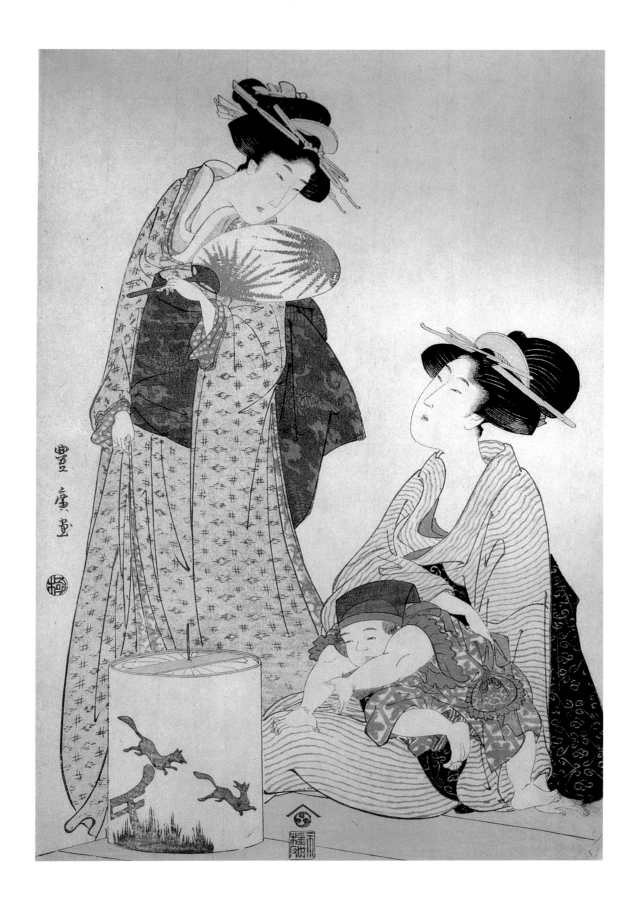

Utagawa Toyohiro
Summer Evening★
Oban 38.6 x 25.6
Nishiki-e
Published by Nishimuraya Yohachi
Kyōwa era (1801–1804)

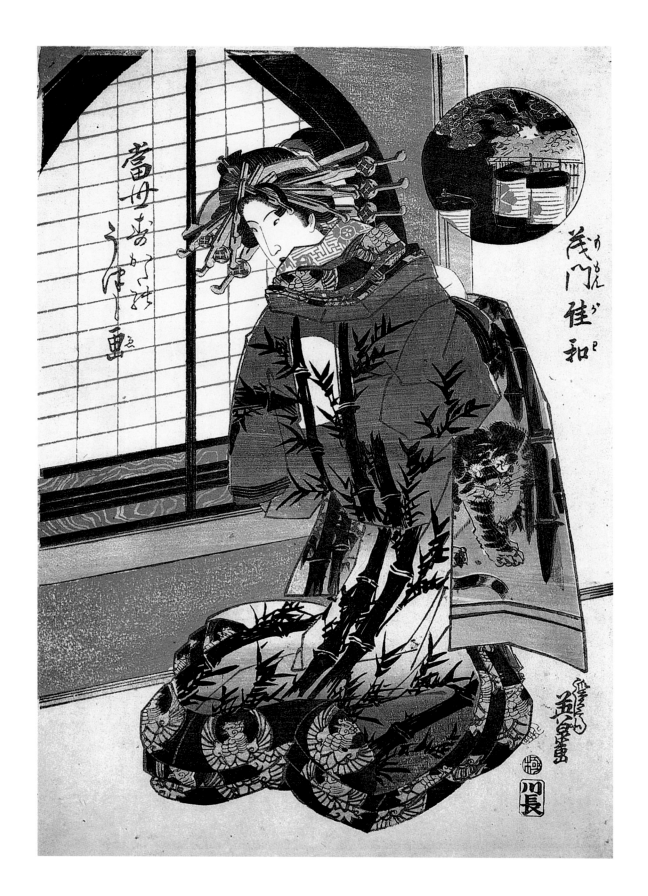

Keisai Eisen
Mirror of the Age: The Courtesan
Oban 39.4 x 26.8
Nishiki-e
Published by Kawaguchiya Chōzō
late Bunsei era (1818–1830)

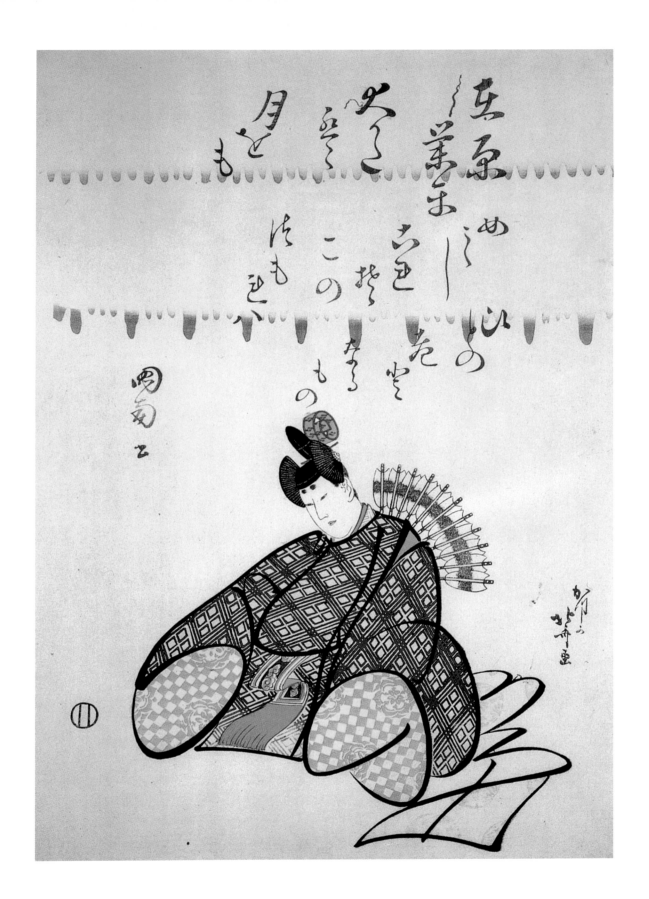

Katsushika Hokusai
Ariwara no Narihira
Oban 38.8 x 25.7
Nishiki-e
Published by Ezakiya Kichibei
mid Bunka era (1804–1818)

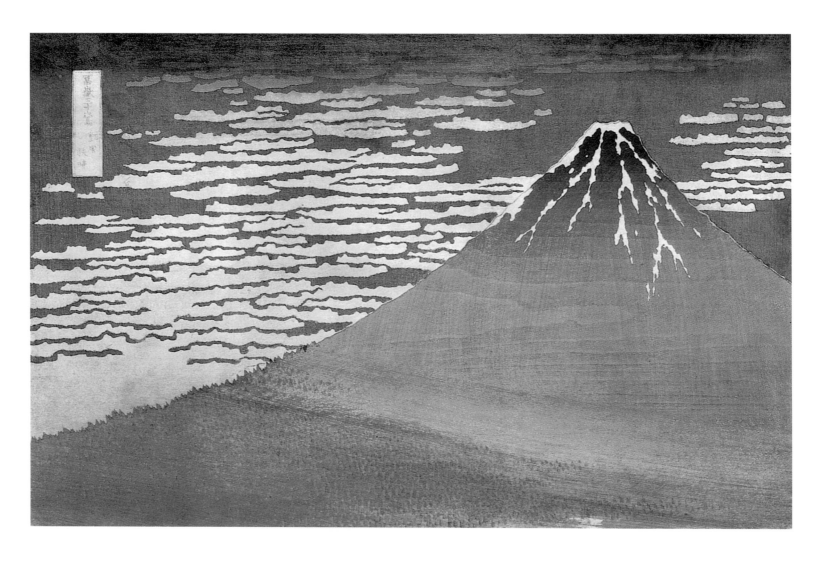

Katsushika Hokusai
36 Views of Mount Fuji:
The South Wind Dispels the Clouds
Yoko-ōban 26.1 x 38.1
Nishiki-e
Published by Nishimuraya Yohachi
Tenpō 2–5 (1831–1834)

Ryōtei Tanehiko, a contemporary of Hokusai's and a well-known writer, introduced this series in Tenpō 2 (1831) as follows: "'36 Views of Mount Fuji' by Hokusai Tanehiko [his original name]: a series of woodblock prints showing the mountain from a broad array of different viewpoints. These pictures show views of Mount Fuji...seen from different places, whereby no one is the same as another, and are for all those who devote themselves to the study of mountains, rivers and lakes. Were one to assemble all Hokusai's views, there would be more than 100 and not just 36." Indeed, if one adds to these 36 views the 10 he produced of the mountain seen from its other side, one comes to a total of 46. In addition, he produced a series of paintings entitled "100 Views of Mount Fuji". In other words, he pursued his quest to portray Japan's highest mountain in all its aspects with a certain obsessiveness.

Against a background of soft clouds blown along by the south wind at the beginning of summer, the bare summit of Mount Fuji is here portrayed in russet tones, for which reason it is also known as the "Red Fuji". Perhaps, for Hokusai, this was *the* view, the true aspect of the mountain. The feeling of tension produced by the steep slopes rearing up into the sky has caused this picture to be regarded not merely as Hokusai's masterpiece, but as *the* masterpiece among Japanese woodblock prints.

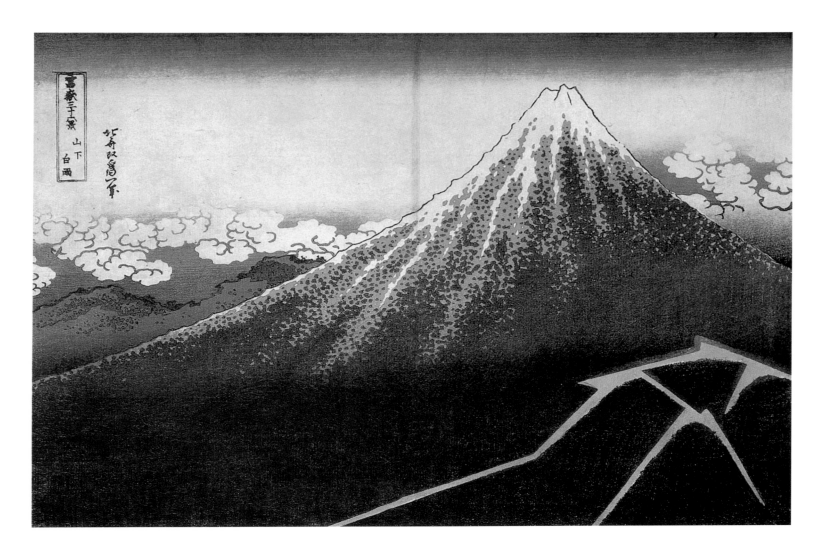

"Shower at the Foot of the Mountain" forms the evening counterpart to the morning view of the "Red Fuji" reproduced on the previous page. A violent thunderstorm is in progress among thick banks of cloud, accompanied by a sudden downpour. Hokusai has given outstanding expression to the evening atmosphere of Mount Fuji. In contrast to the tranquil landscape seen stretching away to the left of the mountain, the black clouds hugging the base of the mountain and the bizarre flashes of lighting appear sinister and threatening. The loftiness of the mountain is emphasized by the fact that the summit looms up into a clear blue sky, where it is crowned by wispy white clouds. The slopes, by contrast, are black and red, increasing the tension within the picture to outstanding effect. Comparing the silhouette of the peak in this view to that of the previous one, it will readily be seen that the mountain is depicted here from the opposite side. In view of the contrasting times of the day – evening and morning – and the contrasting weather conditions – stormy and fair – it is fair to assume that Hokusai was aiming for a conscious contrapuntal effect, and that these two prints belong together.

Katsushika Hokusai
36 Views of Mount Fuji:
Shower at the Foot of the Mountain
Yoko-ōban 26.1 x 37.0
Nishiki-e
Published by Nishimuraya Yohachi
Tenpō 2–5 (1831–1834)

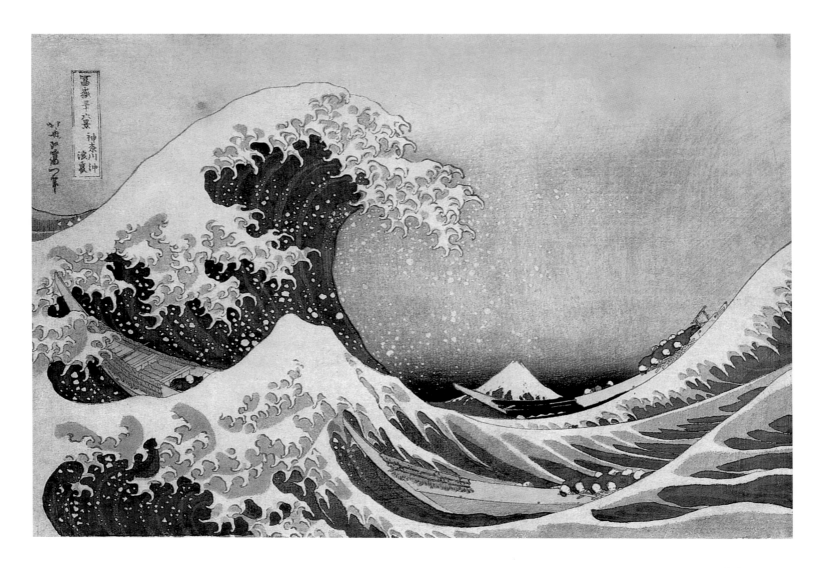

Katsushika Hokusai
36 Views of Mount Fuji: Back of a Wave on
the Open Sea off Kanagawa
Yoko-ōban 26.5 x 38.1
Nishiki-e
Published by Nishimuraya Yohachi
Tenpō 2–5 (1831–1834)

Ryōtei Tanehiko continued his introduction to the "36 Views of Mount Fuji" (cf. the text on p. 148) as follows: "The pictures portray Mount Fuji differently in respect both of form and place. Whether seen from Shichirigahama, Tsukudajima or elsewhere, no two views are the same." Fuji is not only depicted from different viewpoints, but also at different times of the day and year. This picture, showing the mountain as seen from the open sea off mainland Kanagawa, is the third of the three masterpieces in the series, the other two being those reproduced and described on the two previous pages. As with his pictures "Small Punts" and "Woodcutters on the Open Sea off Kanagawa", where small boats are similarly seen being tossed about by giant waves, this picture too was produced in *yoko-ōban* format. The curvature of the waves as they break over the sailors conveys a vivid impression of the power of nature against which the power of man has little defence. In the midst of the waves Mount Fuji can be seen, small and distant, but yet majestically asserting its presence. Whether Hokusai ever actually saw Fuji from the sea, however, is very much open to question.

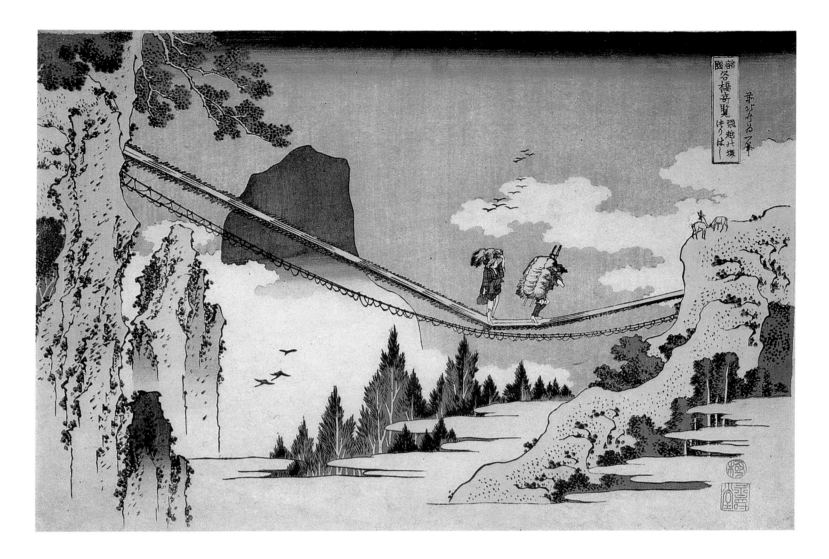

Following his "36 Views of Mount Fuji", Hokusai painted numerous other landscapes, among them "Views of Famous Bridges". Eleven pictures are known from this series, all published by Nishimuraya Yohachi. It is safe to assume, therefore, that a full dozen were actually produced.

The valley forms the boundary between Hida and Etchū. In this picture, the bottom is not visible. On one side, deer can be seen. The valley is spanned by a suspension bridge, which is being crossed by two local people apparently unconcerned by their precarious passage. The flock of birds high in the distance lends a sense of depth and expanse to the scene, as do the hazy mountains on the horizon. The depth of the gorge, with its precipices rising out of the clouds, is left to the beholder's imagination. Hokusai himself, incidentally, never visited this area.

Katsushika Hokusai
Famous Bridges of Various Provinces:
The Suspension Bridge between the
Provinces of Hida and Etchū
Yoko-ōban 26.2 x 38.0
Nishiki-e
Published by Nishimuraya Yohachi
Tenpō 5–6 (1834–1835)

Katsushika Hokusai
Horseman in the Snow
(p. 153 left)

This work is part of a series on "immortal poets", or rather on their poems; nine other titles are known. They all illustrate ancient Chinese and Japanese stories and the characters that appear in them. This is the only work for which no title has been preserved. A man is journeying on horseback through a snowy landscape, accompanied by his servant. Hence the print is usually simply referred to as "Horseman in the Snow". The rider may be Sobu, who wrote under the pen-name of Tōba. He had rebelled against his lord Oanseki and retired to the country. Later he returned to the capital, where he was deceived by followers of Oanseki and sent into distant exile. Alternatively, the subject may be Kanyu; he too was banished after differences of opinion with his lord.

Katsushika Hokusai
Poem of Youth
(p. 153 right)

In the top left-hand corner, the short poem tells the story illustrated in the picture. The young horsemen want to get back home after a visit to the pleasure quarter, but their horses are reluctant. The lads have not bought their riding crops, but as it would involve too much effort to go home and get them, they have broken off sticks from a tree to whip the horses with. On the bank of a river sits an angler. In contrast to his tranquillity, the young horsemen appear animated, almost hectic. The picture convincingly reflects the contrasting moods expressed in the poem.

In addition to this print, Hokusai produced numerous other works portraying historical personnages and events from classical poems. Basing his art on Chinese models, he developed a characteristic style of his own.

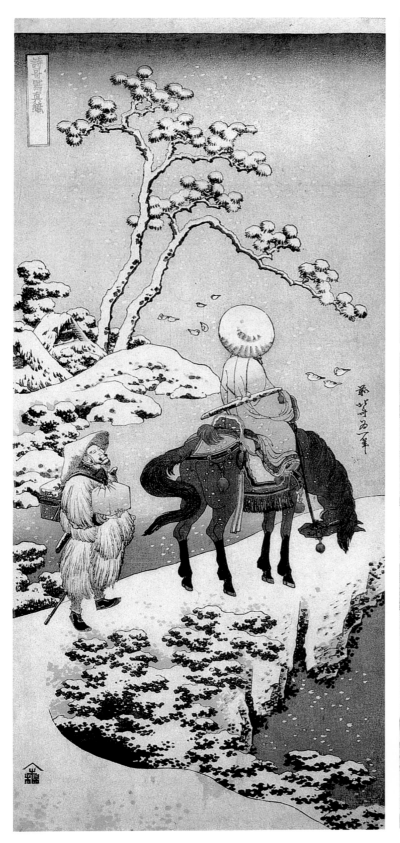

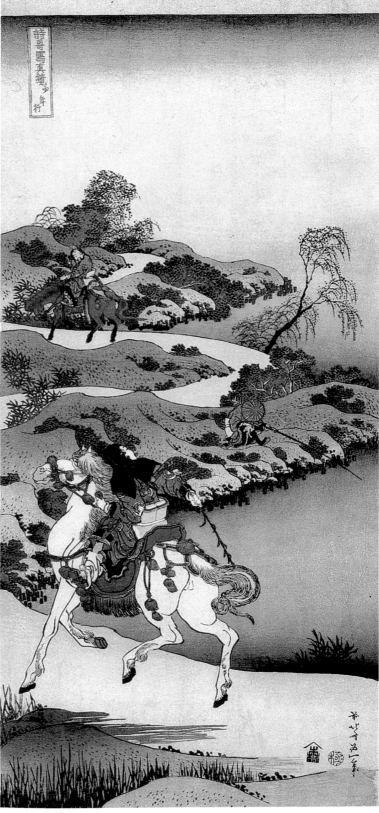

Katsushika Hokusai
Horseman in the Snow★
Naga-ōban 51.9 x 22.6
Nishiki-e
Published by Moriya Jihei
Tenpō 4–5 (1833–1834)

Katsushika Hokusai
Poem of Youth★
Naga-ōban 52.0 x 26.3
Nishiki-e
Published by Moriya Jihei
Tenpō 4–5 (1833–1834)

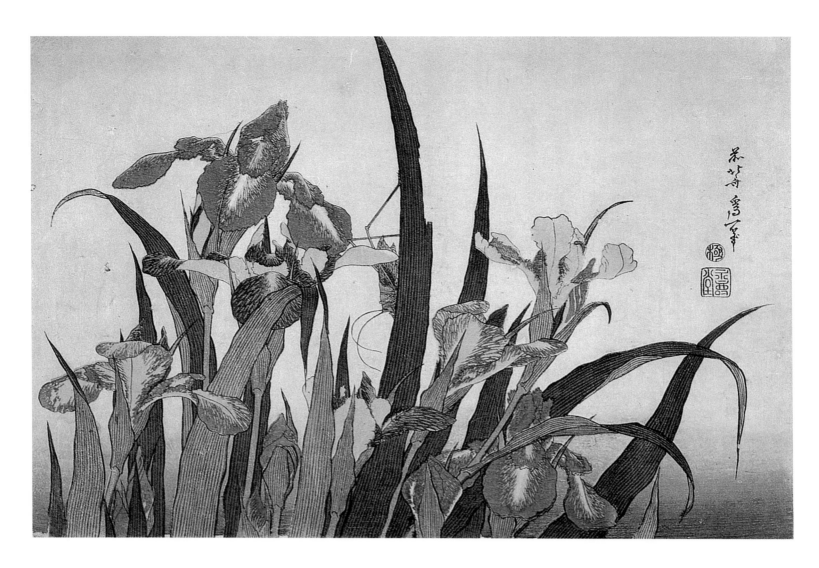

Katsushika Hokusai
Irises and Meadow Cicada★
Yoko-ōban 26.5 x 38.2
Nishiki-e
Published by Nishimuraya Yohachi
c. Tenpō 3 (1832)

From the earliest days of the woodblock print, artists took birds and flowers as motifs, albeit on a modest scale. The standard techniques were developed further by Harunobu and Koryūsai. The chief exponents of the genre, though, were Hokusai and Hiroshige. Hokusai acquired his reputation through the realistic expressivity of his pictures, which were mostly published in *oban*-format series by Nishimuraya Yohachi. The work reproduced here is part of one series, which also includes prints entitled "Morning Dew and Frog", "Fritillary and Dragonfly", "Peony and Butterfly", "Hibiscus and Sparrow" (ill. p. 155), "Poppies", "Lilies", "Japanese Cypress", "Chrysanthemum and Bee" and "Hydrangea and Swallow".

In this work we can see the veins of the leaves of the irises, the pattern on their petals, and a cicada which has settled on the underside of a leaf. The artist has even noted small tears in the leaves. It is Hokusai's ability to go beyond the mere reproduction of precise detail, however, that raises this picture to the level of a work of art.

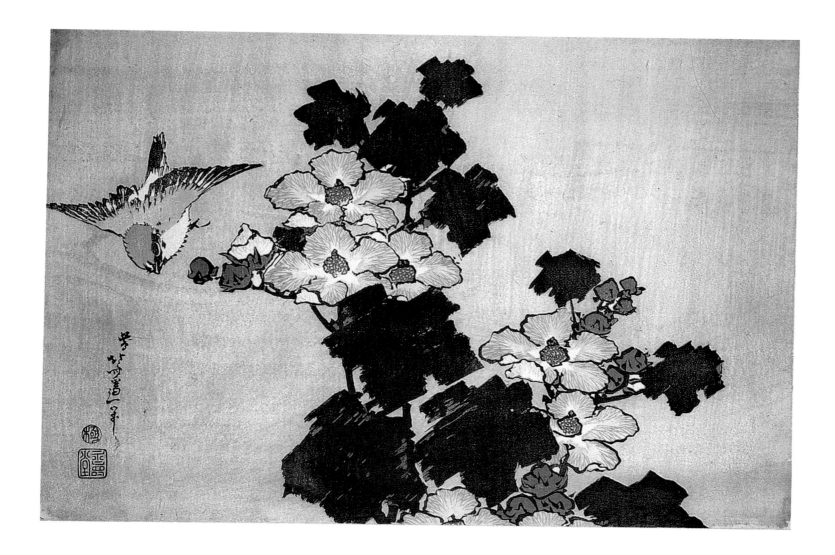

This is one of the works from Hokusai's series of pictures of flowers and birds in the *yoko-ōban* size, published by Nishimuraya Yohachi. In other works in this series, for example in the leaves of the irises in the print reproduced opposite, fine lines are used. Here, by contrast, the lines are predominantly coarse; the hibiscus leaves have no contours at all, appearing simply as planes of colour. The pale colour of the water in the background conveys an idea of freshness. Hokusai – whose wish it had been to paint every creature during his lifetime – wrote in Tenpō 5 (1834), in an epilogue to his "100 Views of Mount Fuji", that he did not feel fulfilled with the works published before his 70th birthday, and that he had therefore decided, at the age of 73, to paint a series of flowers and birds, with the inclusion of fish, insects, plants and animals. This series, and another comprising colourful Chinese landscapes in *chūban* format, were a source of particular pride to him.

Alongside these single sheets, Hokusai illustrated various books. Worthy of mention here are the "Hokusai manga" sketches, which astonished a number of Western painters on account of their versatile expressivity and lively composition.

Katsushika Hokusai
Hibiscus and Sparrow★
Yoko-ōban 26.1 x 38.7
Nishiki-e
Published by Nishimuraya Yohachi
c. Tenpō 3 (1832)

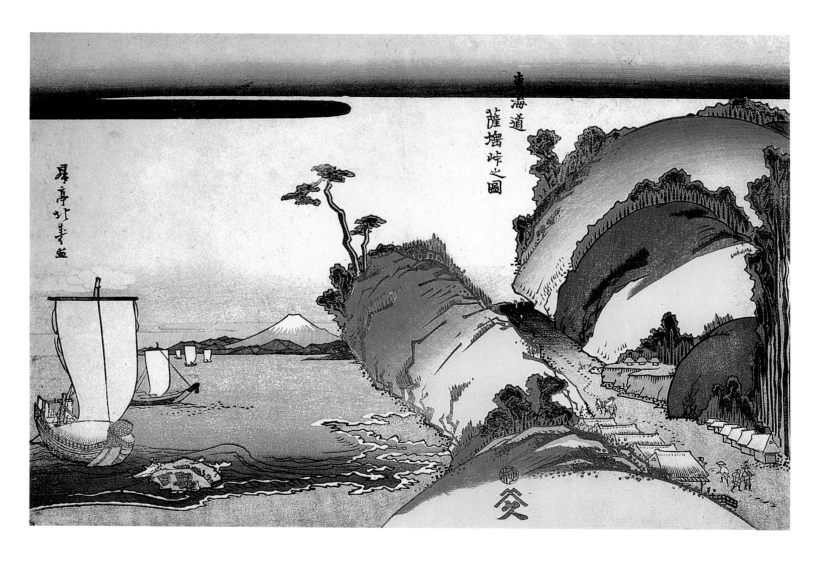

Shōtei Hokuju
12 Views of Famous Places near the Eastern
Capital: The Satta Pass on the Tōkaidō
Yoko-ōban 20.6 x 38.1
Nishiki-e
Published by Yamamotoya Heikichi
c. Bunka era (1804–1818) – Bunsei era
(1818–1830)

Hokuju was a pupil of Hokusai. During the Kyōwa era (1801–1804), he enjoyed the reputation of being an excellent *ukiyo-e* painter. But since Hokusai was such an outstanding genius, his pupils made every effort to imitate his style and techniques. Thus Hokkei took up elements of the Chinese landscape style, while Hokuju concentrated on the methods of Western painting and developed them for himself.

Among his scenes in the Western landscape style, the "12 Views of Famous Places near the Eastern Capital" (i.e. Edo) are doubtless the best known. Alongside the works reproduced here and on the page opposite, those entitled "View of the Kawasaki Inn", "Ferries on the Rokugō at the Kawasaki Station on the Tōkaidō" and "View of the Oi River on the Tōkaido" are still extant.

Hokuji's distinctive stylistic features include his simple coloration technique for light and shade, the distribution of the various colours, and a pictorial composition based on triangles and circles. These characteristics are not in fact so obvious in the work under discussion here, but the valleys and peaks and the shadows of the pine groves certainly provide a hint of them.

The Satta Pass lies between Okitsu, the town of Shimizu and Yuimachi; it was one of the most difficult stretches along the entire length of the *Tōkaidō*. Before the traveller had covered half the distance, he had to wade through the waves on the sea-shore. To make up for these hardships, he had a fine view over Matsuhara in Miho as far as the Izu peninsula, regarded as one of the most beautiful regions in Japan. Looking at the picture, one might be deceived for a moment into thinking that Hokuju had forgotten Mount Fuji – he is renowned for having included it in all his pictures. But there it is in the distance beyond the pass.

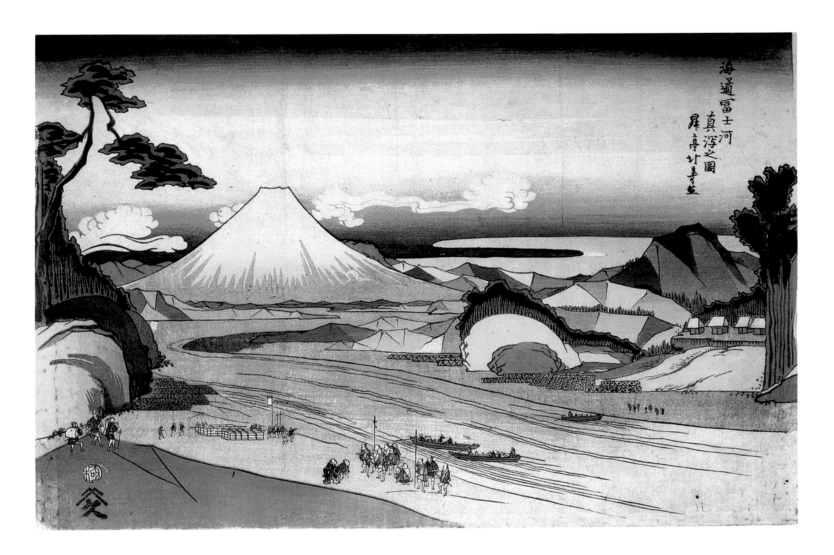

This picture depicts a travelling *daimyō* and his entourage about to cross the Fujigawa, one of three fast-flowing rivers along the *Tōkaidō*. The far side of the river has too few people on it in comparison with the near side, and the trees on the far side are strangely large. The perspective seems not to have been properly worked out. The clear colour composition of the juxtaposed mountain peaks is evidence of a certain idiosyncrasy; the large proportion of the picture occupied by the sky, along with the great depth of the horizon, are also characteristic of Hokuju's prints.

Shōtei Hokuju
12 Views of Famous Places near the Eastern Capital: The Fuji river on the Tōkaidō
Yoko-ōban 26.4 x 38.5
Nishiki-e
Published by Yamamotoya Heikichi
c. Bunka era (1804–1818) – Bunsei era (1818–1830)

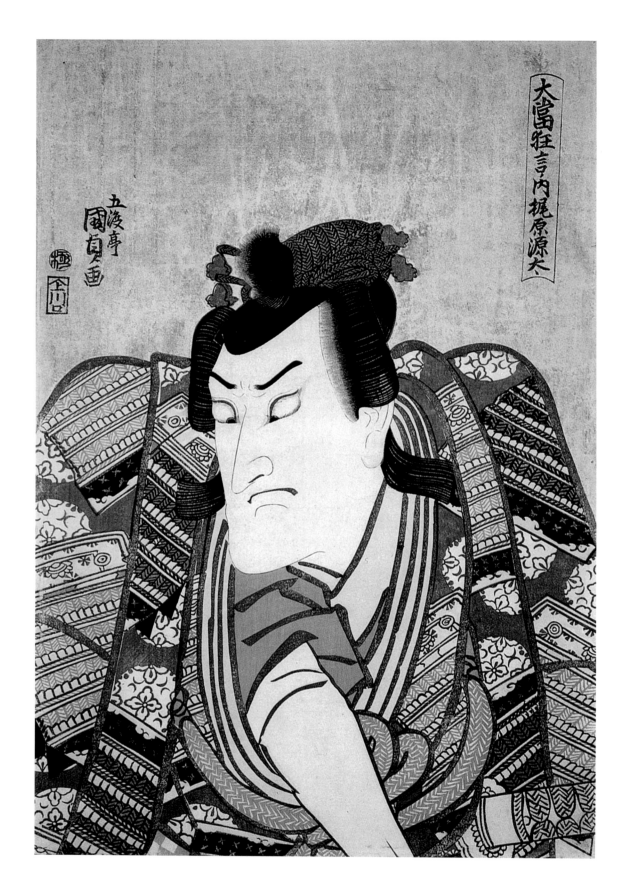

Utawaga Kunisada
Bandō Mitsugorō III as Kajiwara Genta
in a Popular Kyōgen
Oban 39.1 x 26.6
Nishiki-e
Published by Kawaguchiya Uhei
c. Bunka 11 (1814)

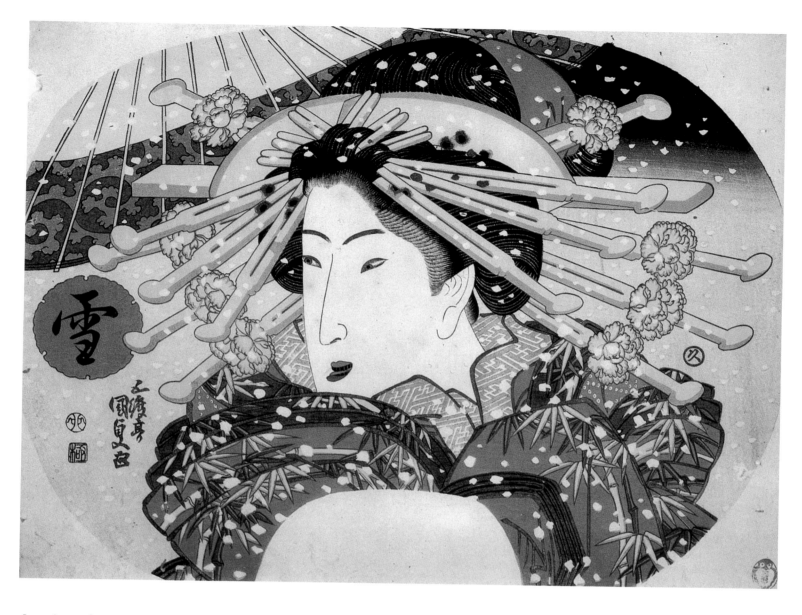

In a picture for a round fan, the piece intended for the fan is usually cut out; it is therefore rare to find complete pictures of this sort still preserved. One such is the masterpiece reproduced here. It depicts a courtesan whose hair is decorated with a comb and four ornate hair-pins. The coiffure is held in place by another four hair-pins. The "sasabeni" technique is used in this picture; i.e., the *beni* red has an admixture of green from bamboo grass. Here it can be seen in the lower lip, which has a green shimmer in place of the usual bright red. The courtesan, on her way to a brothel, has put up her umbrella; the heavy snow is settling on her sumptuous kimono, appearing to cover the bamboo pattern.

There are seven prints by Kunisada depicting actors. The one reproduced here is probably the most representative. Opinion differs as to the year in which Mitsugorō III became the most successful lead actor of his day, but it is safe to assume that it cannot have been any earlier than the 11th month of Bunka 11 (1814), as according to the signature and inscription, the print was produced in Bunka 11 or 12 (1814–1815).

This picture shows Bandō Mitsugorō III in the part of Kajiwara Genta, who is mentioned in the "Hiragana report". He is shown here wearing a garment whose design is based on that of a suit of armour. Historical sources mention a "dance of Genta", which he is said to have performed in a pleasure district. One of these sources, dating from the 3rd month of Bunka 8 (1811), bears the title "7 Pictures of Flowers", each picture depicting one of the seven roles performed in quick succession each with a different costume. Mitsugorō III was an outstanding dancer, and he rivalled Nakamura Utaemon III, whose star was already setting by this time, for acknowledgement as the best dancer of these seven roles.

Utagawa Kunisada
Snow
Uchiwa-eban 22.8 x 30.0
Nishiki-e
Published by Ibaya Kyūbei
Tenpō 2 (1831)

Utagawa Kunisada
Bandō Mitsugorō III as Kajiwara Genta
in a Popular Kyōgen *(p. 158)*

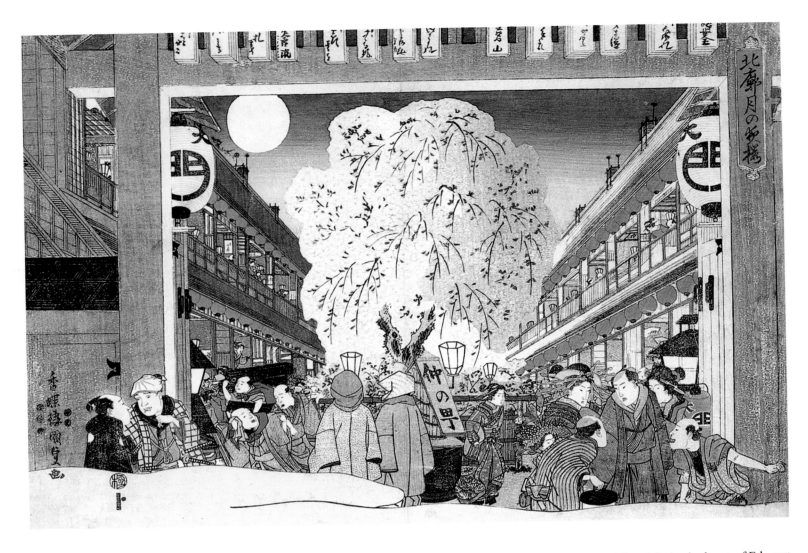

Utagawa Kunisada
Cherry Blossom beneath the Evening Moon
in the Northern Quarter
Yoko-ōban 25.7 x 37.5
Nishiki-e
Published by Yamaguchiya Chūsuke
Tenpō era (1830—1844)

The officially sanctioned pleasure quarter of Yoshiwara, which lay right in the heart of Edo not far from Nihonbashi, had been moved to Asakusa on moral grounds in the year Manji 2 (1659). To distinguish it from the earlier Yoshiwara, it was referred to as Shin-Yoshiwara (New Yoshiwara) or else as the "Northern Quarter", Asakusa being in the north of Edo. Visitors to the pleasure quarter would get there either by sedan clair along one of the side-streets, or else by boat along the river.

The great gate which formed the only means of entry to and exit from Yoshiwara was plain and simple, so as not to provoke the *Tokugawa* regime with any show of pomp and luxury. However it was precisely pomp, luxury and extravagance that awaited visitors as they passed through the gate. Inside, they were in a different world. Here Kunisada seeks to give full expression to the vitality of the quarter during the cherry-blossom season, presenting the cherry blossom in its full splendour in the main street, *Nakanomachi*. When darkness fell, the street was lit by the lanterns which lined the façades.

Yoshiwara was a "floating world", where people met who were intent on pleasure. Yet it was here that the culture of the Edo period came into full flower, with its arts of the wood-block print, literature, music and fashion.

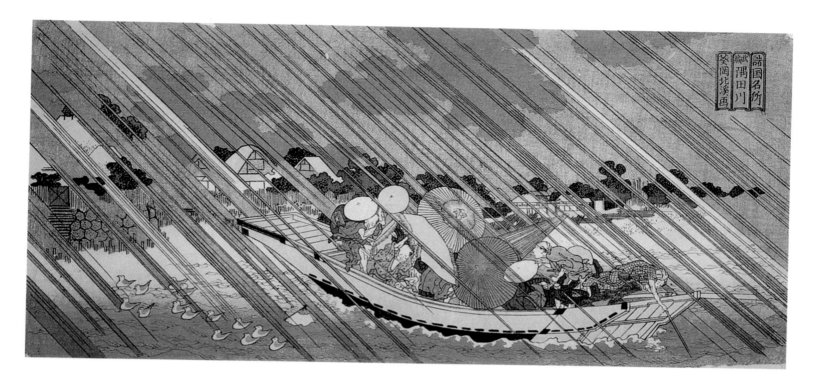

Hokkei's original name is said to have been Kyōsai Tatsuyuki. As he had been a fishmonger, however, he is generally known as "Uoya" (i.e. fishmonger) Hokkei, and this is the name used in the signature on the work reproduced here. After being apprenticed to Kanō Yosenin Tadanobu, he joined Hokusai's school. Many of Hokkei's works are reminiscent of the style of the Kanō school, in particular his landscapes in the Chinese manner. His illustrations to books of humorous verse are so numerous that one could be forgiven for thinking he was consciously trying to outdo Hokusai in this respect. But considering the volume of his total output, there are very few single sheets; among them, those comprising the series "Famous Places in All the Provinces" are among his most important works.

The print reproduced here depicts a boat caught in a sudden shower while crossing the Sumida river. The people in the boat are trying to keep the rain off with straw umbrellas and cloaks. The strong wind is blowing away a fan. Immediately alongside the boat, seagulls are sitting on the water, an allusion to an old song about the Sumida. The thick oblique strokes representing the rain may strike some viewers as disturbing. But the placing of the verse in the top right-hand corner skilfully provides an anchor, so to speak, for the rightward extension of the picture, and gives the whole print a polishing touch.

Uoya Hokkei
Famous Places in All the Provinces: The River Sumida in Musashi
Yoko-tanzaku-ban 20.8 x 30.7
Nishiki-e
Published by Nishimuraya Yohachi
Tenpō 5–6 (1834–35)

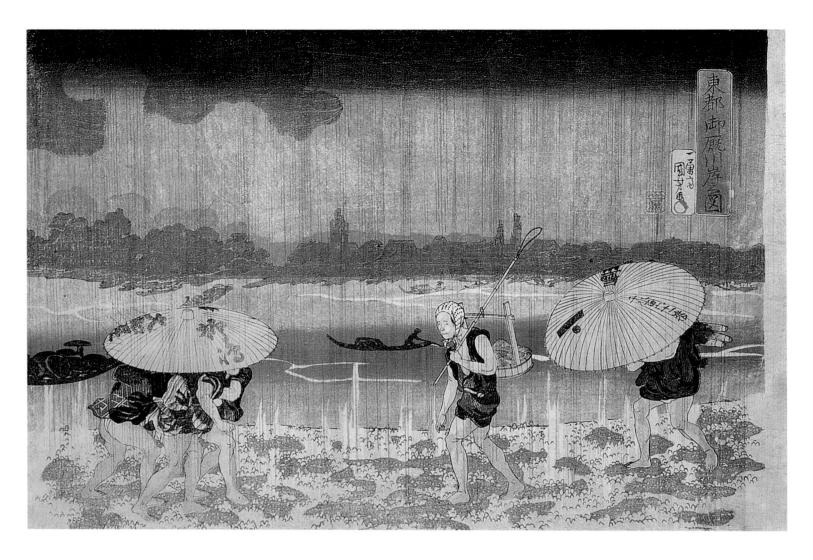

Utagawa Kuniyoshi
On the Banks of the Sumida in
Mimayagashi★
Yoko-ōban 26.7 x 38.8
Nishiki-e
Published by Yamaguchiya Tōbei
c. Tenpō 4 (1833)

Alongside Hiroshige, the painter of famous places, and Kunisada, the painter of *yakusha-e*, Kuniyoshi made a name for himself during the Tenpō era, as a painter of warrior pictures *(musha-e)*. He also left landscapes, however, which have an almost modern appearance quite typical of him. In fact, Kuniyoshi's landscapes enjoy particularly high esteem. They convey a quite different mood from those of Hokusai and Hiroshige. A further distinctive feature of Kuniyoshi's work is the portrayal of perfectly ordinary everyday scenes, where he uses Western techniques of light and shade, as well as smear techniques, to great effect. All this gives the work a modern appearance. The other woodblock prints in this series, "Shubi no Matsu", "Mitsumata", "Miyatogawa" and "Hashiba" all depict landscapes along the Sumida. As this was where Kuniyoshi actually lived, it is easy to understand how his life and work were dominated by the river.

From Mimayagashi, the boats from Asakusa go up the Sumida to Honjoishiwara, where today the river is spanned by the Mimaya bridge. The boat on the left of the picture, whose passengers have put up their umbrellas, is a ferry. On the shore, a group of men are battling their way barefoot through a violent downpour. The way three of them are crowding under a single umbrella is a humorous detail. The man with the headscarf is carrying eels in a basket attached to a stick over his shoulder by metal rings.

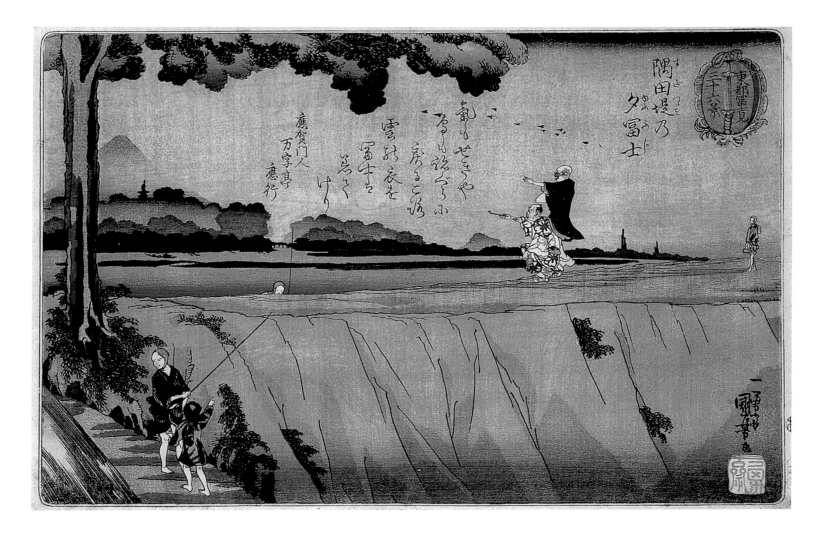

Of the woodblock prints depicting Mount Fuji, those by Hokusai's ("36 Views") and Hiroshige are the most famous. Kuniyoshi's landscapes, by contrast, have a very human touch, since they use Mount Fuji as a backdrop against which to depict scenes of the everyday lives of the citizens of Edo, such as here on the eastern bank of the Sumida, called Sumida Zutsumi, which runs north from Mukōjima.

This print shows the entrance to the Sani-*Inari* shrine. On the opposite bank, Sanyabori and the five-storey pagoda of the Asakusa temple can be made out. The young men with drums admiring the evening view of Mount Fuji are comical to behold. The verse in the top half of the picture reads: "Restlessness accompanies the return of the bird to its nest. Fuji wears a white mantle of snow."

Apart from this one, only four other views of Fuji by Kuniyoshi are known. Their titles are: "Distant View from Shōheizaka", "Fuji seen from Tsukudaoki in Clear Weather", "Fuji seen from Sannō-shinji during the Thaw" and "View of Fuji beneath the Shinōhashi Bridge".

Utagawa Kuniyoshi
36 Views of the Eastern Capital and
Mount Fuji: Fuji in the Evening, seen from
Sumida Zutsumi★
Yoko-ōban 23.8 x 25.9
Nishiki-e
Published by Murataya Jirōbei
Kōka era (1844–1848)

Utagawa Kuniyoshi
Ayus, Swimming Upstream, with Hagi
Branch
(p. 165 left)

Kuniyoshi was regarded as a master of the warrior picture; he was also a skilful exponent of *bijin-ga, yakusha-e* and caricatures. Far less well represented among his works are pictures of plants and animals. In addition to the two prints reproduced opposite, he also produced the following depictions of fauna in or beside the water: "Octopus", "Crab", "Crab and Turtle", "Black Carp", "Wistaria and Purple Carp", "Goldfish and Japanese Miniature Carp", "Crucian Carp", "Lobster and Small Fish" and "Globe Fish and Ray".

The ayu, depicted here, is an indigenous species of salmon which lives in clear water. The perspective has been chosen here so as to give the illusion of a ray of sunlight penetrating the water to illuminate the sea floor. Waves cast flickering shadows on the bed. Even the reflection of the light on the backs of the fish has been accurately noted. The delicate beauty of the water sparkling in the sunlight has been skilfully captured. The curving line of the hagi branch and the movement of the salmon bear witness to the strong feeling for rhythm which characterizes the composition.

During the mid-nineteenth century, as the Edo period was drawing to its close, Western stylistic devices were increasingly finding their way into *ukiyo-e* painting. In Kuniyoshi's work we find imitations of oil paintings and copperplate engravings, indications of his profound interest in Western art. He made use not only of the shading technique, but experimented with reflections too. The present work is one of the masterly results of intensive observation of light rays in water.

Utagawa Kuniyoshi
Catfish *(p. 165 right)*

Works depicting various kinds of fish are relatively numerous in Kuniyoshi's œuvre. The particular feature of the print reproduced here is its dynamic rendition of the fish swimming about in the water. It is not dissimilar to an underwater camera shot. The placing of the catfish vis-à-vis the smaller fish underlines the contrast already produced by the difference in their size. The indigo shading enhances the impression that the fish are swimming very rapidly. The sheet has a double signature.

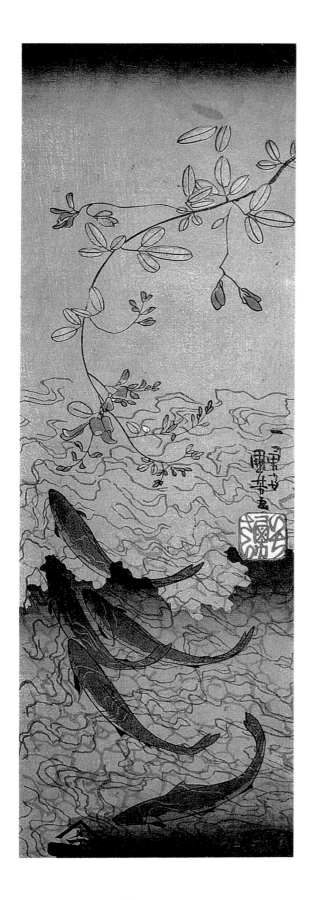

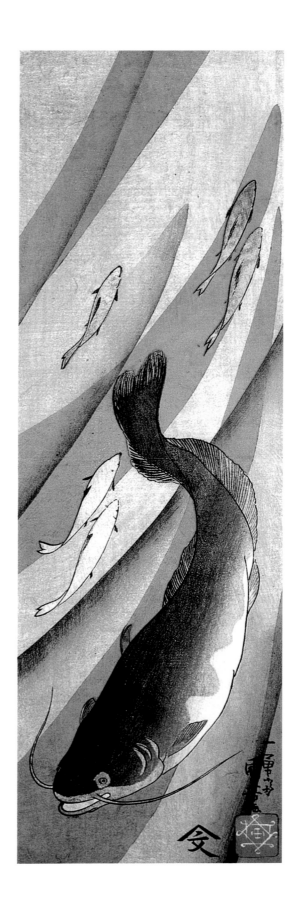

Utagawa Kuniyoshi
Ayus, Swimming Upstream, with Hagi Branch★
Chū-tanzaku-ban 36.8 x 12.2
Nishiki-e
Published by Tsujiokaya Bunsuke
mid Tenpō era (1830–1844)

Utagawa Kuniyoshi
Catfish★
Chū-tanzaku-ban 36.5 x 11.8
Nishiki-e
Published by Tsujiokaya Bunsuke
mid Tenpō era (1830–1844)

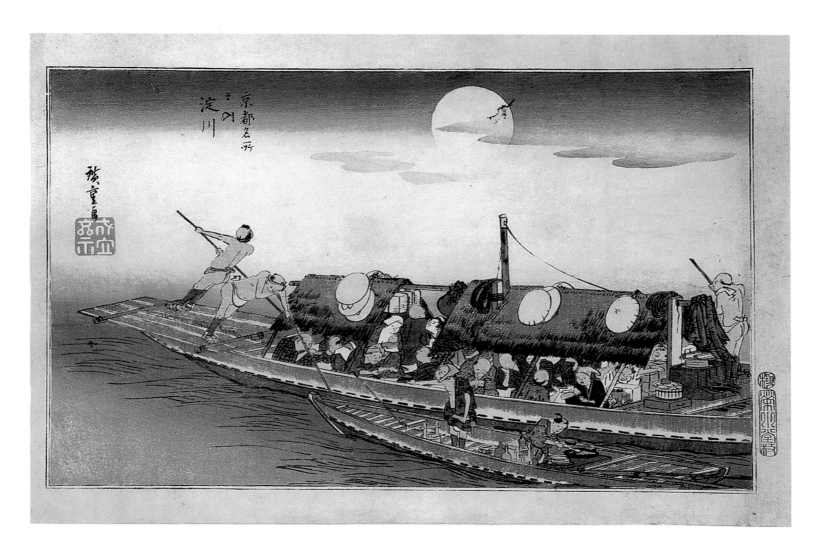

Utagawa Hiroshige
Views of Famous Places in the Capital
Kyoto: Yodogawa
Yoko-ōban 26.2 x 38.5
Nishiki-e
Published by Kawaguchiya Shōzō
c. Tenpō 5 (1834)

The series "Views of Famous Places in the Capital Kyoto" comprises ten works, some of which were based on the *yoko-ōban*-format series "Collection of Famous Sketches of Kyoto and its Surroundings". However it also includes works with new ideas and using individual formats.

The Yodogawa river, where the scene depicted here is located, starts life as the Setagawa river, flowing out of Lake Biwa and past the towns of Seta, Zensho and Ishiyama. It reaches the capital via the small town of Uji on its outskirts, and is then known as the Ujigawa. When it gets to Fujimi and Yodo it joins up with the rivers Katsuragawa and Kizugawa, after which it is known as the Yodogawa, the name under which it flows out into Osaka Bay. As an important artery for trade and communications, the Yodogawa has always been a much-used waterway, especially between Kyoto and Osaka. In the print reproduced here, we see a boat with passengers on board sailing by moonlight towards Osaka. With a crew of four and up to 28 passengers, boats like these would ply the river regularly every morning and evening between Osaka and Fujimi. The smaller boat is a kurawanka; these would frequently come down from Hirakata bringing snacks and sake to the passengers on the larger boat. Here we see the boatman hawking his wares, evidently in a loud voice.

Hiroshige was a much-travelled man. His series "53 Stations on the Tōkaidō" (pp. 173–178) made his reputation as a landscape painter. Around the year Kaei 4 (1851) he went to Hakone, and preserved his impressions in pictures in a diary entitled "Views of Famous Places in Musashi and Sagami", which is now in the Riccar Art Museum in Tokyo. The journey stimulated him to paint further pictures.

The work reproduced here arose after a trip to Kōshū (in the modern prefecture of Yamanashi) in the year Tenpō 12 (1841), when Hiroshige was 45 years old. "In the distance and nearby, there is row upon row of mountains. The mountains are high, and the valleys are deep, and the waters of the Katsuragawa are clear. One has to take but ten or twenty steps, and the landscape has changed before one's very eyes. With my poor imperfect brush, I cannot reproduce this at all." So reads the diary text to accompany the pictures. It goes on to say that he made the sketches of Saruhashi while eating his midday meal in an inn with a view of the bridge. The dynamic composition of deep gorge, high bridge and rising full moon arose while he was at the peak of his creative powers, and is typical of his painting style. Another collection, entitled "Views of Famous Places in more than 60 Provinces" includes a similar work with the title "Kai Saruhashi".

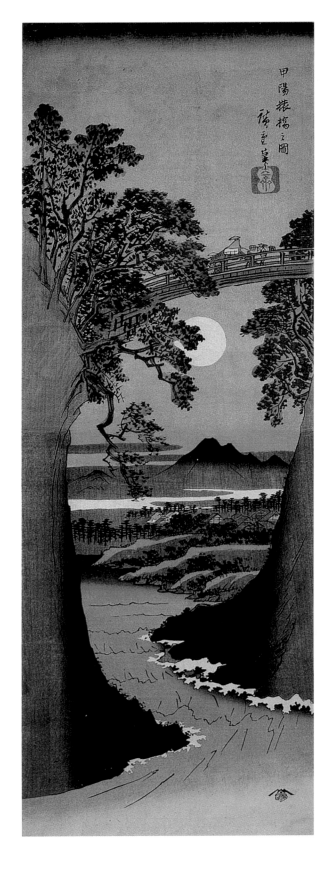

Utagawa Hiroshige
Saruhashi Bridge near Kōyō
Kakemono-eban 74.4 x 25.9
Nishiki-e
Published by Tsutaya Kichizō
c. Tenpō 13 (1842)

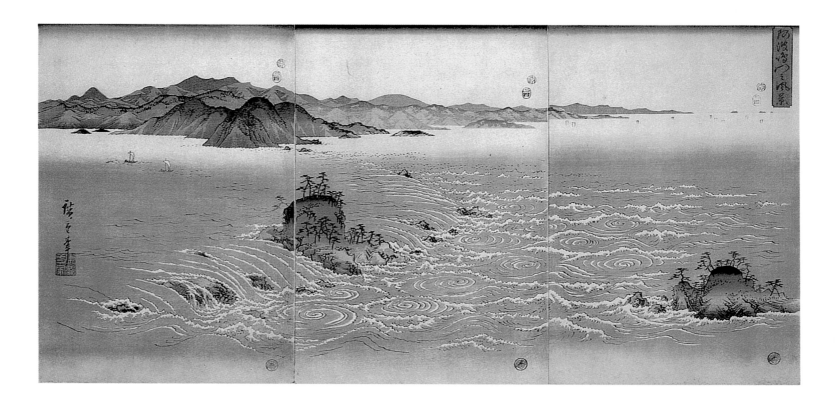

Utagawa Hiroshige
Snow, Moon and Flowers: View of Naruto in Awa
Oban, triptych, each sheet 37.9 x 26.0
Nishiki-e
Published by Okazawaya Taheiji
4th month of Ansei 4 (1857)

Together with "Snow in Kisoji" (p. 169, below), and "Moon over Kanazawa" (p. 169, above), this picture belongs to the series "Snow, Moon and Flowers", although no flowers are depicted here. Yet Hiroshige's imagination led him to see, in the foam of the sea, the "flowers of the waves". That is one explanation; another may be that the pictures were all published by Okazawaya Taheiji at the same time in Ansei 4 (1857) and simply given the same seal. The titles of the three pictures are written in three different scripts: Kisoji in semi-italic, Kanazawa in archaic Chinese characters dating from the Ching dynasty, and Naruto in a fully italic script, the differences in script reflecting the differences in the characters of the pictures: precise, fleeting, flowing.

The Naruto landscape is painted in light tones; the mountains in the mid and far distance along the Awajishima coast are reminiscent of pictures by Western painters. These pictures lack a realistic touch, making it doubtful whether the painter had actually been there personally. Certainly Hiroshige did not visit all the places he painted, but reconstructed many views with the help of geography books. This particular work resembles an illustration in the geography book "Views of Famous Places in Awanokuni", with the island of Hadakajima in the centre and the islands of Tobishima and Nakanose on the right-hand side, their cliffs being depicted from the same viewpoint.

Utagawa Hiroshige
Snow, Moon and Flowers: Moon over Kanazawa *(p. 169, above)*

The countryside around Kanazawa, today a suburb of Yokohama, was one of the favourite motifs of *ukiyo-e* artists. Using the technique of blurring the evening blue of the sky around the moon with white, and the haze above the horizon with pale violet, Hiroshige has even managed to capture the light of the moon. Like the "View of Naruto in Awa", this picture has similarities with Western landscape painting. An impression of depth is conveyed by the flock of wild geese flying in the direction of the moon. Kanazawa was not far from Edo, and had been famed for its natural beauty since time immemorial; it may safely be assumed that Hiroshige had often been there himself. In respect of its compositional technique, it resembles the diary illustrations "Views of Famous Places in Musashi and Sagami".

Utagawa Hiroshige
Snow, Moon and Flowers: Snow in Kisoji *(p. 169, below)*

This is the third masterpiece in the series "Snow, Moon and Flowers". The year Ansei 3 (1856) saw the appearance of Hiroshige's series "View of Famous Places in more than 60 Provinces", in which he portrayed almost all the sights of Japan. He died just two years later, in the 9th month of Ansei 5 (1858), but a year before his death he put all his talent into this indisputable masterpiece. Almost the whole of the triptych is taken up by the mountain scenery under its blanket of snow, its contours formed by the twilight of the sky and the course of the river below.

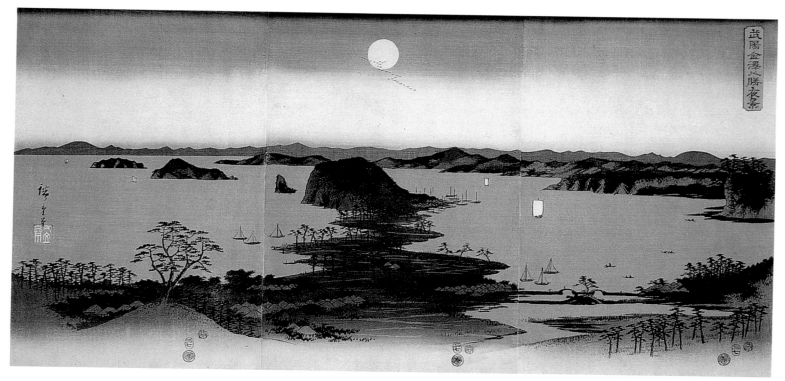

Utagawa Hiroshige
Snow, Moon and Flowers: Moon over Kanazawa★
Oban, triptych, each sheet 38.3 x 26.0
Nishiki-e
Published by Okazawaya Taheiji
7th month of Ansei 4 (1857)

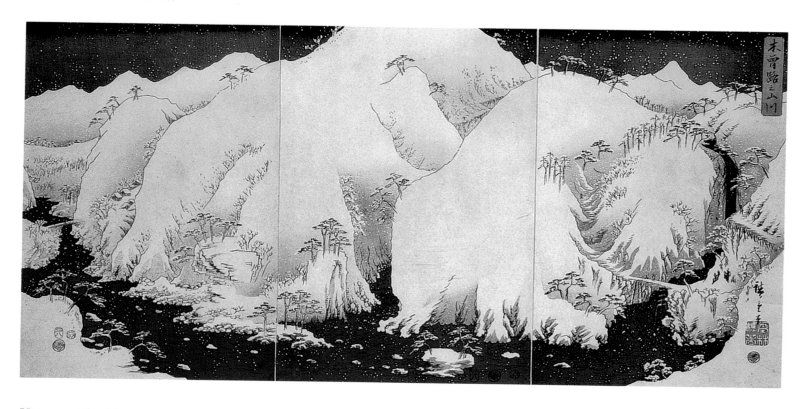

Utagawa Hiroshige
Snow, Moon and Flowers: Snow in Kisoji★
Oban, triptych, each sheet 37.9 x 25.9
Nishiki-e
Published by Okazawaya Taheiji
8th month of Ansei 4 (1857)

From the very earliest days of *ukiyo-e*, flower and bird motifs (*kachō-ga*) had been among the artists' themes; however, they were never very numerous. Only during the Tenpō era (1830–1844) did kachō-ga develop into a fully-fledged genre in its own right, alongside *bijin-ga* and *yakusha-e*, largely thanks to the efforts of Hiroshige and Hokusai. Unlike Hokusai, whose preference was more for realistic portrayals, Hiroshige integrated his birds and flowers into images of the four seasons, transporting them into a lyrical and transcendental world. In his *tanzaku-ban* in particular, their beauty finds its full expression; everything superfluous is abandoned, and as in a *haiku*, the work is reduced to its essentials. Many of these kachō-ga by Hiroshige date from around the year Tenpō 3 (1832).

The Chinese magpie as portrayed here was regarded as a lucky bird, and can also be found in Kitao Masayoshi's album "Pictures of Imported Birds". With its long tail and glossy blue feathers, it cuts a fine figure. The proportions within the picture are extremely well balanced, with the plum branch and its white blossom curving down from the top of the picture, and the magpie lowering its head.

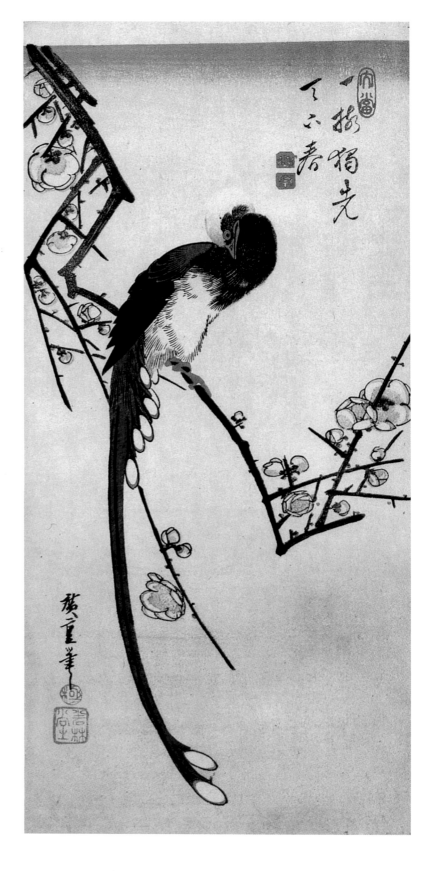

Utagawa Hiroshige
Chinese Magpie on a Plum Branch in Blossom★
O-tanzaku-ban 38.3 x 17.8
Nishiki-e
Published by Wakasaya Yoichi
early Tenpō era (1830–1844)

The poem on this picture reads: "The wild duck calls. When the wind blows, the surface of the water ripples." In many works depicting flowers and birds, Hiroshige quoted verses whose lines alluded to the subject of the picture and underlined its beauty. Many of the *haiku* he used were taken from the collection „Haiku by Old Masters on 500 Themes", as was this poem on the theme of "Winter". There are three other illustrations by Hiroshige of poems in which wild ducks are mentioned; each include their corresponding verses.

Between the dry, snow-covered reeds a wild duck appears. The colour of the water is taken up in the sky, lending the snowy landscape a feeling of crispness and biting cold. The duck stands out almost harshly against the reeds, which are rendered in the style of an ink drawing. The white areas of its plumage are uninked, the white being the white of the paper.

For a signature, instead of the two characters for good luck ("fuku") and ("kotobuki"), Hiroshige has used the characters for "horse" ("uma") and "stag" ("shika") – likewise regarded as lucky. Taken together, the two characters can also be read as "baka", which means "fool" or "idiot". Pictures with this signature are consequently known with gentle irony as "baka-in".

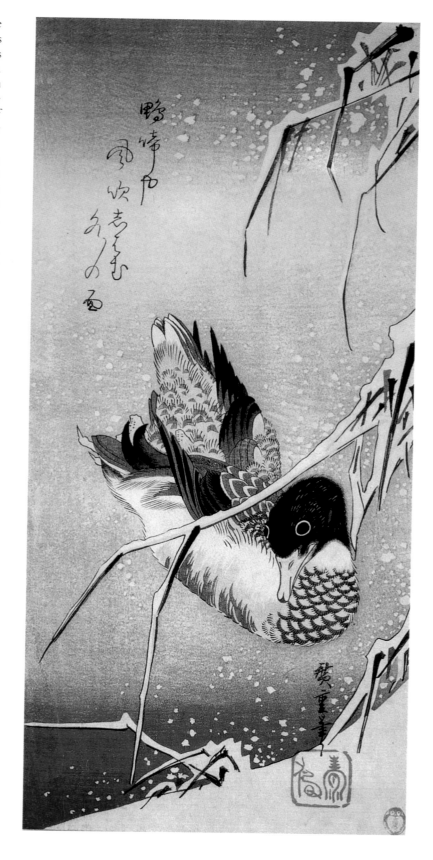

Utagawa Hiroshige
Reeds in Snow with Wild Duck★
O-tanzaku-ban 38.3 x 17.7
Nishiki-e
Publisher unknown
c. Tenpō 3–5 (1832–1834)

Utagawa Hiroshige
53 Stations on the Tōkaidō (p. 173–178)

In the year Tenpō 3 (1832), Hiroshige had his first opportunity to travel along the *Tōkaidō*. On the orders of the shōgun government, he accompanied one of their annual delegations to pay homage to the Emperor and present him with a horse. Hiroshige was to preserve the event in pictures. On his return to Edo, he assured himself of the support of a major publisher, Tsuruya Kieimon, and had the sketches of the journey brought out by the newly founded Hōeidō publishing house. Hiroshige's illustrations of his journey were so vivid that they increased the interest of many people to make the trip themselves. His book "Tōkaidō Chūhi-zakurige", published by Juppensha Ikku, along with other pictures of the *Tōkaidō*, sold like hot cakes.

This was a period of rapid development in Edo's trade and communications. There were more and more inns, and more and more means of transport such as horses and sedan chairs. Pilgrimages to Ise and Shikoku were becoming ever more popular, as were excursions made purely for pleasure. In particular, there was growing admiration for the imperial capital, Kyoto. Since the *Tōkaidō* represented the main traffic artery between Edo and Kyoto, the publication of the "53 Stations on the Tōkaidō" came at just the right time. The Hōeidō publishing house was soon occupied exclusively with the publication of Hiroshige's Tōkaidō, with the result that this series, to distinguish it from other sets of *Tōkaidō* illustrations, became known simply as the "Hōeidōban" (Hōeidō prints), and in this way the name of this small and otherwise insignificant publishing house has been handed down to posterity. The views themselves, which are a joy to the beholder and bestow on the journey a lyrical atmosphere all of its own, are not without their humorous moments. They achieved particular popularity through their portrayal of such favourite motifs as snow, moon, rain and mist, as well as the changing seasons and the forces of nature.

In addition, Hiroshige frequently employed the *fukibokashi* style, in which the paint for the background was blurred on the printing-block with a cloth; this gave outstanding expression not just to the Japanese feeling for nature, but also to the particular "colour mood" of Japanese landscapes, and in the succeeding period it inspired numerous artists to portray the countryside in regions throughout the country. Of the "53 Stations on the Tōkaidō" by Hiroshige – who from thenceforth was known simply as the "Tōkaidō painter" – the 30 or so that were published by Hōeidō are certainly among his masterpieces. In the whole history of *ukiyo-e*, these works, with editions in excess of 10,000, were unsurpassed bestsellers. Frequent reprints altered the character of the pictures, and some of the blocks had to be recut. The works illustrated here (pp. 173–178) form part of the very first edition, allowing us to appreciate the colours as Hiroshige intended them. It is primarily in respect of colour that later editions differ from the first.

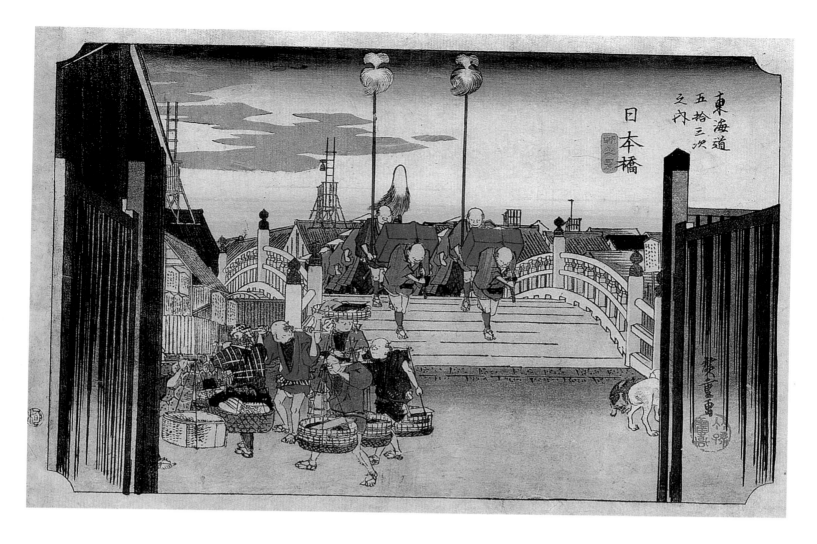

During the Edo period, the shōgun government would travel once a year, during the 8th month, to Kyoto, in order to pay homage to the Emperor and to ensure the continued legitimacy of its rule. In Tenpō 3 (1832) Hiroshige was a member of this delegation, commissioned to preserve the journey in pictures, and the occasion provided him with the first opportunity to travel the length of the *Tōkaidō* between Edo and Kyoto. At each stop he captured the everyday lives of the people in sketches. Once back in Edo, he immediately took up his paintbrush, and transformed these sketches into complete pictures. The result was this series of a total of 53 views, starting from Edo and ending with the bridge of Kyoto. To distinguish his prints from others illustrating the *Tōkaidō*, Hiroshige signed them both with his name and that of the publisher. The series made him famous almost overnight as a landscape painter.

The journey to Kyoto began in the heart of Nihonbashi. In the Muromachi district, close to Kitazume and Odawara, there were fishmarkets which were also known as the "citizens' kitchen". Here he depicted the rows of houses, first and foremost the House of Echizen, and the bustling lives of the local people. In the red glow of dawn, at about the 7th hour, the procession of a *daimyō* is seen setting off for the west, headed by servants bearing standards. In the foreground, fishermen are packing up their baskets, having sold their catch, and going on their way. One can almost feel the cool morning air, such is the tense mood of this first sheet of the series. It sold so well that the first printing block was soon worn out and had to be recut.

Utagawa Hiroshige
53 Stations on the Tōkaidō:
Morning View on the Nihonbashi Bridge
Yoko-ōban 24.8 x 37.2
Nishiki-e
Published by Takeuchi Magohachi, Tsuruya Kieimon
Tenpō 4–5 (1833–1834)

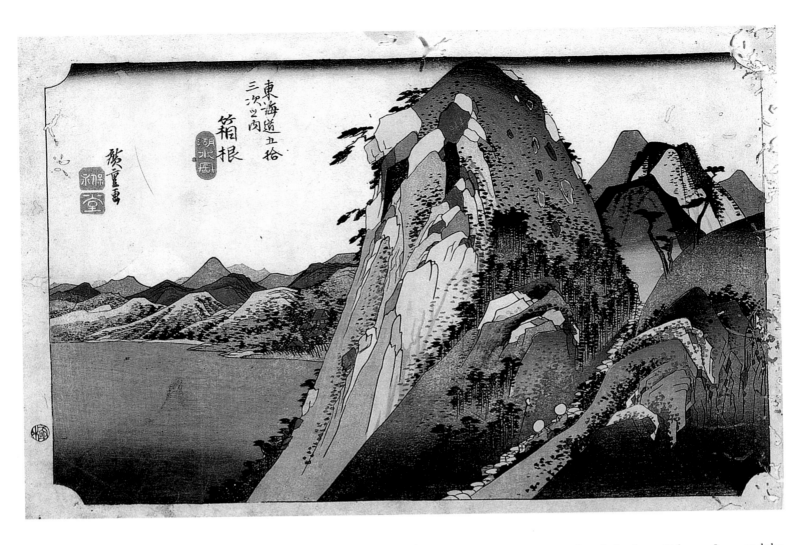

Utagawa Hiroshige
53 Stations on the Tōkaidō:
Lake by Hakone
Yoko-ōban 25.5 x 38.2
Nishiki-e
Published by Takeuchi Magohachi
c. Tenpō 4–5 (1833–1834)

The Hakone Road, the section of the *Tōkaidō* between the 9th Station – Odawara Inn – and the 11th Station – Mishima Inn – was not altogether safe. It led between looming cliffs through gorges of immeasurable depth, and constituted one of the most difficult stretches of the whole journey. People said that it was so steep in places that even monkeys broke their bones. And it was not just the natural hazards that posed a threat, but the road-blocks at the border posts too; responsible for Edo's security, the guards that manned them were armed to the teeth. Every traveller was meticulously and none too politely examined, adding a psychological dimension to the physical strain imposed by the journey itself.

The precipitous slopes of the Hakone region are mosaics of colour, and in terms of its palette this is the most striking work in the series. On the far left, Mount Fuji can just be made out in the distance, while the lake in the foreground presents a more friendly face. Even so, the icy gale that blows across it is almost tangible, as is the raw cold which froze the travellers as they made their way through the mountains. Hiroshige has given unambigous expression to the feelings he himself must have experienced as he passed through Hakone for the first time.

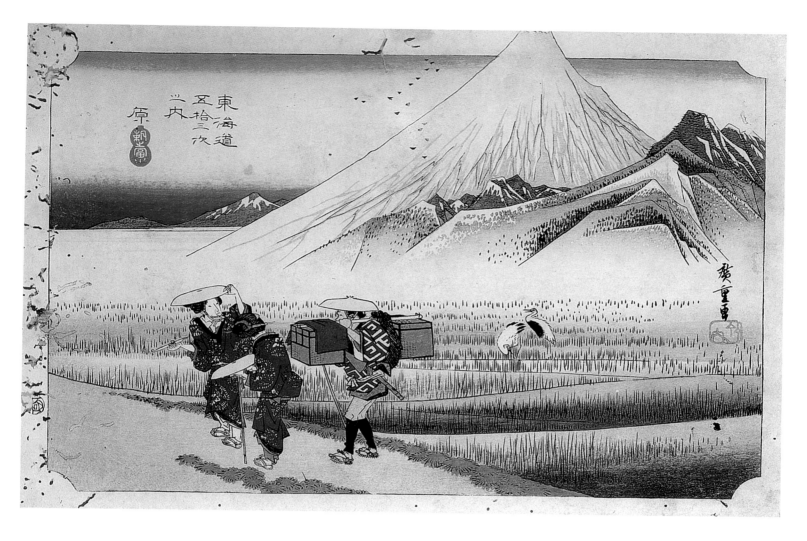

Hara is situated between the towns of Numazu and Yoshiwara. Mount Fuji rises majestically above the countryside. In this picture, Hiroshige has captured Japan's highest peak as seen from one of the best viewpoints. Fuji could be seen in the distance from Edo, but on his journey to Kyoto Hiroshige was able to get a close-up view. Those who see it never fail to be astonished by its actual height, and it was this aspect that Hiroshige liked to incorporate into his pictures, as here. In the right foreground can be seen Mounts Awata and Ashigara, along with one of the three peaks of the Aitaka range. Beside these broken, jagged mountains, the well-formed beauty of Mount Fuji stands out particularly well. On the low-lying land in the foreground stand a pair of cranes, but the tranquillity is distributed by the approach of two women and a man, the pattern on whose kimono is based on the first two characters of Hiroshige's name.

Utagawa Hiroshige
53 Stations on the Tōkaidō:
Mount Fuji seen from Hara at Dawn
Yoko-ōban 25.4 x 38.3
Nishiki-e
Published by Takeuchi Magohachi
c. Tenpō 4–5 (1833–1834)

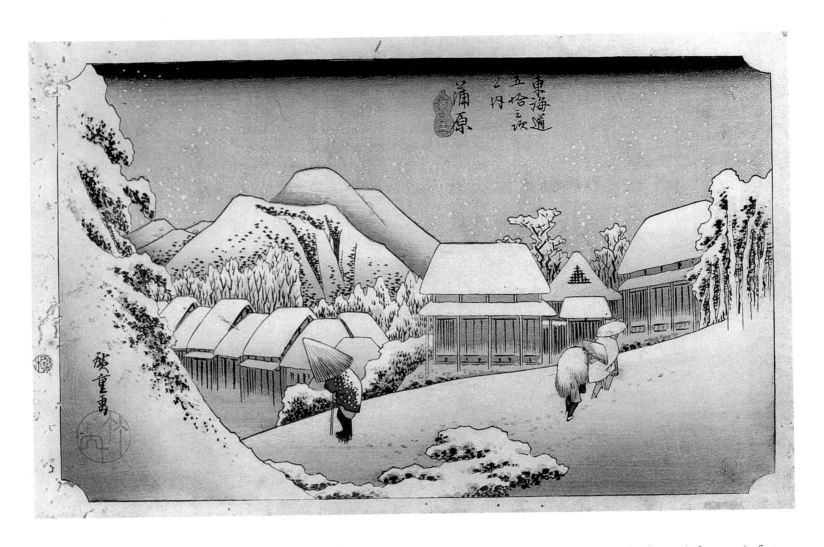

Utagawa Hiroshige
53 Stations on the Tōkaidō:
Nocturnal Snowfall in Kambara
Yoko-ōban 25.6 x 38.3
Nishiki-e
Published by Takeuchi Magohachi
c. Tenpō 4–5 (1833–1834)

Since the town of Kambara lies on a comparatively warm stretch of coast, it does not in fact see much snow, so this scene probably represents a figment of Hiroshige's imagination. It is evening, and the snow is falling in large flakes: mountains, houses and trees are all being buried under a thick white blanket. On their way through the dark, two travellers and a local inhabitant with bent back are trudging through the snow, leaving footprints as they go. Apart from the people, there is almost no colour in the picture, a sign of Hiroshige's sensitive virtuosity. He often used Prussian blue in his work, which earned him the nickname "Blue Hiroshige", and he also used it for colouring ink drawings. This particular picture shows another distinctive feature of his landscapes: the extremely skilful manner in which he depicts snow, and the almost lyrical cloak which he throws over Japan's countryside.

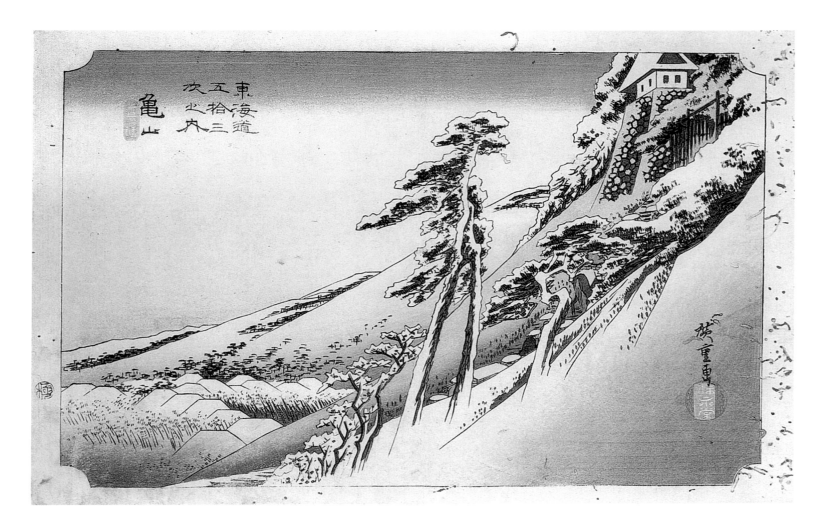

Beyond steep mountain slopes, further peaks rise up in the distance. The region lies under a thick blanket of snow. They sky is bright with the imminent sunrise of a new day. The world seems calm and peaceful. The snow swallows up every sound made by the group on their way to the summit. The wind-battered pines in the centre of the picture point all their branches in one direction. At the summit stands Kameyama Castle, which served both as an overnight stopping place for travellers and as a military base. Today, nothing remains of it but a park and a few ruins of the tower. It was in fact summer when Hiroshige was here, so that the idea for this picture must have taken shape in his mind's eye. In the Tōkaidō series snowscapes are very much the exception (but cf. p. 176).

Utagawa Hiroshige
53 Stations on the Tōkaidō:
Clear Winter Morning in Kameyama
Yoko-ōban 25.3 x 38.2
Nishiki-e
Published by Takeuchi Magohachi
c. Tenpō 4–5 (1833–1834)

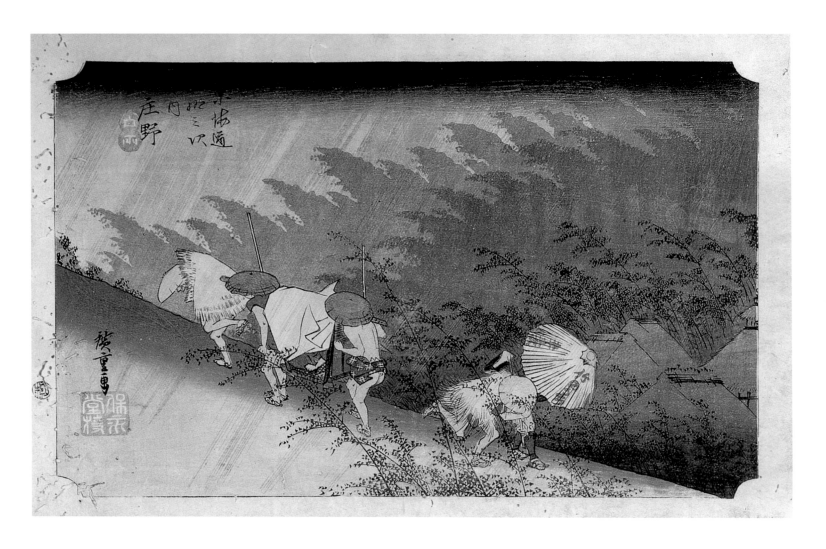

Utagawa Hiroshige
53 Stations on the Tōkaidō:
Sudden Shower over Shōno
Yoko-ōban 25.5 x 38.2
Nishiki-e
Published by Takeuchi Magohachi
c. Tenpō 4–5 (1833–1834)

The town of Shōno is about an hour's walk away from Ueno along the course of the River Suzuka. The stretch of the *Tōkaidō* between Yokkaichi and Kamemaya was almost uninhabited, and few travellers passed this way. However, in the Genna era (1615–1624) or thereabouts, Hakura Iganogami was ordered by officials in Kyoto to re-open the Post Station in Shōno, which lies deep in the mountains.

In this picture Hiroshige depicts a sudden downpour over Shōno. With hurried steps, the inhabitants run to take shelter. A basket-seller is running breathlessly up the steep mountain road, while a traveller helps to ensure that his baskets do not blow away, and a servant comes hurrying along with an umbrella.

Hiroshige attached great importance to the depiction of even the smallest details. The countryside, heavily veiled in rain, and the perspective depth of the bamboo forest in the background, are masterfully reproduced in a colour composition whose total effect is almost idyllic.

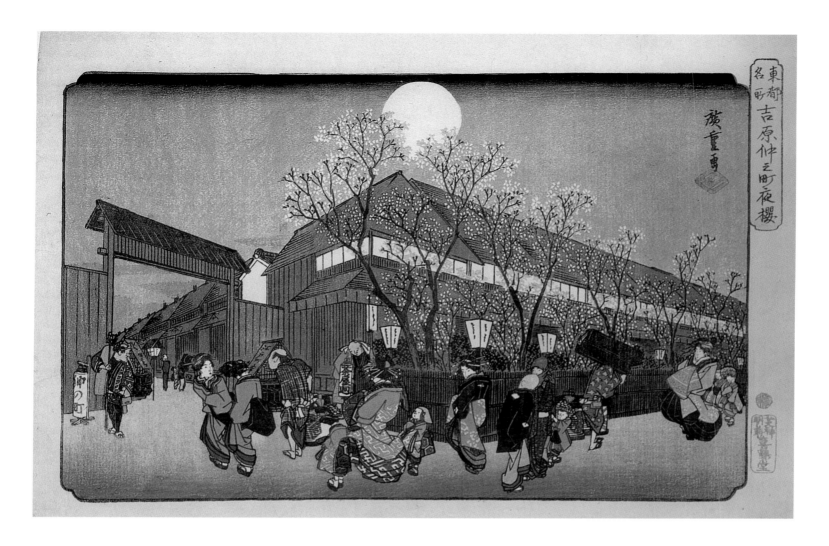

Hiroshige was honoured during his own lifetime with the epithet "meishoeshi", or "master of the depiction of famous places", in view of the abundance of such works emanating from his brush as "Famous Places in Edo" and "Famous Places in the Eastern Capital". He loved the city in which he had been born and bred, and scenes of the lives of its people were his most frequent motifs.

The picture reproduced here is taken from a particularly outstanding series, published by Sanoya Kihei. In allusion to the verse by the Han-dynasty Chinese poet Sobu, "A single moment on a spring evening is worth a thousand pieces of gold" (i.e. is beyond price), the atmosphere of the blossom and the hazy moon in the evening townscape of Yoshiwara is also something that money alone cannot buy. The cherry trees on Yoshiwara's main street, the *Nakanomachi*, had been planted during this period, and are shown here in full blossom. It is as though they were pouring down their scent upon the courtesans parading in their finery beneath them.

Hiroshige did not perhaps make such explicit use of perspective as Hokusai, but he integrated it more naturally into his landscapes and cityscapes. And yet this picture, with its two levels of perspective, shows that Hiroshige was thoroughly familiar with perspective painting.

Utagawa Hiroshige
Famous Sights in the Eastern Capital:
Cherry Blossom in the Evening on the
Nakanomachi in Yoshiwara
Yoko-ōban 26.4 x 39.2
Nishiki-e
Published by Sanoya Kihei
early Tenpō era (1830–1844)

Hiroshige's Tōkaidō series of the years Tenpō 4– 5 (1833–1834) (pp. 173–178) had brought him the reputation of being the best landscape artist in Japan. Moreover, he had depicted not only landscapes, but also the everyday lives of the people, and he had done so in his own, almost lyrical manner. Further series portraying the attractions of all the other regions followed. And yet most of his pictures focus on Edo, the city where he was born and where he lived. The most comprehensive collection dated from the final years of his life. It was entitled "Meisho Edo hyakkei" – "100 Views of Famous Places in and around Edo". The series was published by Uoya Eikichi between the 2nd month of Ansei 3 (1856) and the 10th month of Ansei 5 (1858). As these pictures proved extraordinarily popular, others followed, so that the figure of a 100 was soon exceeded. When Hiroshige died in the 9th month of Ansei 3 (1856), he had already painted 118 works for the series.

The index to the series lists the prints by season: 42 of spring, 30 of summer, 36 of autumn and 20 of winter. The best-known pictures in the collection are undoubtedly "Plum Orchard in Kameido", "Ōhashi Bridge, Sudden Shower near Atake" (p. 185), "Fireworks in Ryōgoku", "Will o'the Wisp on New Year's Eve" and "Temple Hall in Fukugawa". It must be said, though, that these works are simpler than those of his earlier years; his age was showing, his expressive skills declining. Even so, he took a great deal of trouble with coloration, and used all the techniques available to a master at that time: *karazuri, atenashi-bokashi, kimekomi, kirakake,* fumo-kuzuri etc. The works which most resemble his youthful style are those where subjects are depicted from above, as in "Ōhashi Bridge, Sudden Shower near Atake" and "Temple Hall in Fukugawa", along with those works in which he emphasized the foreground, behind which the background is allowed to spread out, as in "Plum Orchard in Kameido" and "Irises in Horikiri". It is the contrast that gives the landscape its depth. It should also be noted that some pictures, for example "Ōhashi Bridge, Sudden Shower near Atake" were influential not only in Japan, but also among Western painters such as van Gogh (cf. p. 32).

A peaceful New Year's scene in the district of Edo around what is now the Hibiya Park forms the motif of the print reproduced here. The gateway to the *samurai* house is decorated with a broad band of rice straw. On either side of the entrance stands a New Year pine tree, while in the left foreground, further pine decorations are to be seen. Behind these latter, and to the right, bats for playing shuttlecock intrude into the picture; the game was played by girls to welcome the New Year. The fronts of these bats were often decorated with *bijin-ga* or *yakusha-e*, the backs with bamboo patterns. The boys meanwhile would fly kites. In the top half of the picture, part of a Yakko kite can be seen; mostly, these were shaped like short kimonos.

In the background, the shape of Mount Fuji can be seen. The Tōkaidō series – produced almost 25 years earlier – already included masterly views of the mountain, and in the "100 Views of Famous Places in and around Edo", Hiroshige often included a view of it too. The people of Edo were proud that this highest and most beautiful peak in Japan was visible from their city. The morning and evening views of the sacred mountain never failed to fill them with emotion. Today, there are few days when Mount Fuji is visible from Tokyo.

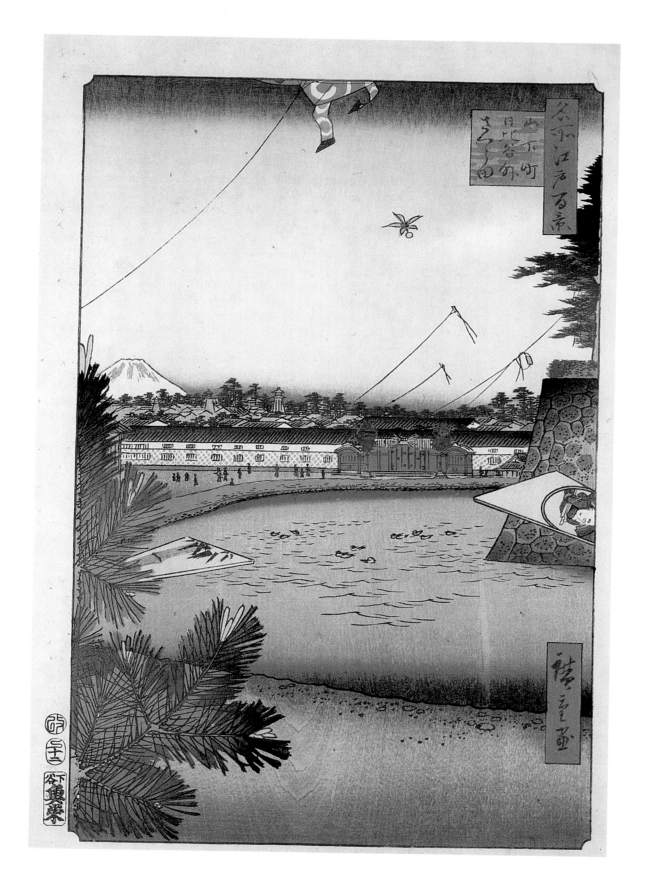

Utagawa Hiroshige
100 Views of Famous Places in and around Edo:
Sotosakurada in Hibiya
Oban 36.3 x 24.9
Nishiki-e
Published by Uoya Eikichi
12th month of Ansei 4 (1857)

Utagawa Hiroshige
100 Views of Famous Places in and around Edo: Motoyanagi Bridge by the Ekōin Temple in Ryōgoku
(p. 183)

On the opposite bank of the river, at the foot of the bridge, stands a weeping willow. This willow, or "yanagi", gave its name to the Motoyanagi bridge which stood a little way downstream from the modern Ryōgokubashi bridge, where a V-shaped canal flowed into the Sumida river. Today neither canal nor bridge exist. The modern Yanagibashi bridge is a little further upstream.

The precincts of the Ekōin Temple contained numerous statues of the gods of popular religion along Buddhist deities. It was often the venue for exhibitions of Buddhist statues imported from various countries. From the Tenmei era (i.e. from 1781) onwards, Sumō wrestling matches took place here twice a year, before large crowds of spectators. The beginning and end of the bouts would be signalled on a large drum outside the gate. The drummer is out of the picture, but part of the drum can be seen on the scaffolding in the foreground.

We are looking from a raised position down on the ferries plying the Sumida. This river with its boats was often used as a background in *ukiyo-e* painting. It was the most important artery for freight transport. The long vessel in the foreground is a raft used for carrying timber.

Utagawa Hiroshige
100 Views of Famous Places in and around Edo: Plum Orchard in Kameido
(p. 184)

The work reproduced here served, together with "Ōhashi Bridge, Sudden Shower near Atake" as a model for an oil painting by Vincent van Gogh (cf. p. 32). The foreground is taken up by a large plum-tree in close-up; behind it, plum blossom recedes into the distance. The figures of the visitors enjoying the magnificent sight appear almost toylike. The red of the sky and the green of the landscape represent the two major contrasting hues and enhance the impression of uniqueness conveyed by the picture.

The Plum Orchard lay to the rear of the Kameido-Tenjin shrine, which was famous for its wistarias. Here too stood Edo's most famous tree, the "garyū-ume", which was described by a poem in the "Report on Famous Places in Edo" in the following terms: "It really is as though dragons were lying here. Branches growing from branches seem to be one with the soil. The treetops extend to the left and the right. The scent of the blossoms puts that of orchids in the shade. The brilliant white of the dense growth of blossom dispels the dusk." Unfortunately the tree died after a flood disaster in Meiji 43 (1910), and the orchard fell into neglect. Today there are just a few stones to remind the visitor of the Plum Orchard villa which once stood here.

Utagawa Hiroshige
100 Views of Famous Places in and around Edo: Ōhashi Bridge, Sudden Shower near Atake *(p. 185)*

In respect of landscapes which lyrically portray not just the setting but the everyday lives of the local people, Hiroshige is unsurpassed. It is also only natural that most of his works depict contemporary Edo; after all, that was where he was born, where he lived and where he worked until shortly before his death. His "100 Views" formed the largest collection of such scenes, compiled, to judge by the signatures and inscriptions, posthumously in the year Ansei 5 (1858).

The work reproduced here, which along with "Plum Orchard in Kameido", inspired van Gogh (cf. p. 32), shows people caught in a sudden evening downpour. A woman who looks like the *geisha* Fukagawa — one can almost hear the clip-clap of her wooden sandals and her bright clear voice — is seen hurrying over the new bridge. A lonely raftsman on the Sumida is getting a drenching. The houses on the opposite bank are almost lost in the grey blur of the rain. Depicted from above, they lend depth to the picture. It was a new departure in the art of woodblock-print design to depict a bridge from the side, spanning a large area of the picture from left to right, giving the impression that the whole picture was expanding. The rain is depicted as long streaks, bursting suddenly from the black clouds in an expression of strength. Hiroshige has in masterly fashion captured the beauty of nature in rain on a summer evening.

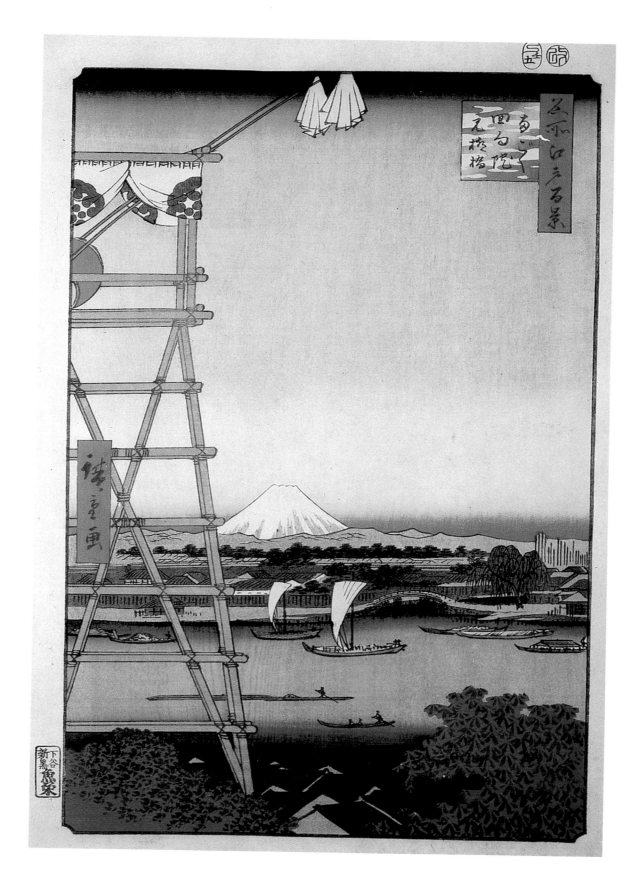

Utagawa Hiroshige
100 Views of Famous Places in and around Edo:
Motoyanagi Bridge by the Ekōin Temple in Ryōgoku
Oban 36.4 x 24.9
Nishiki-e
Published by Uoya Eikichi
5th month of Ansei 4 (1857)

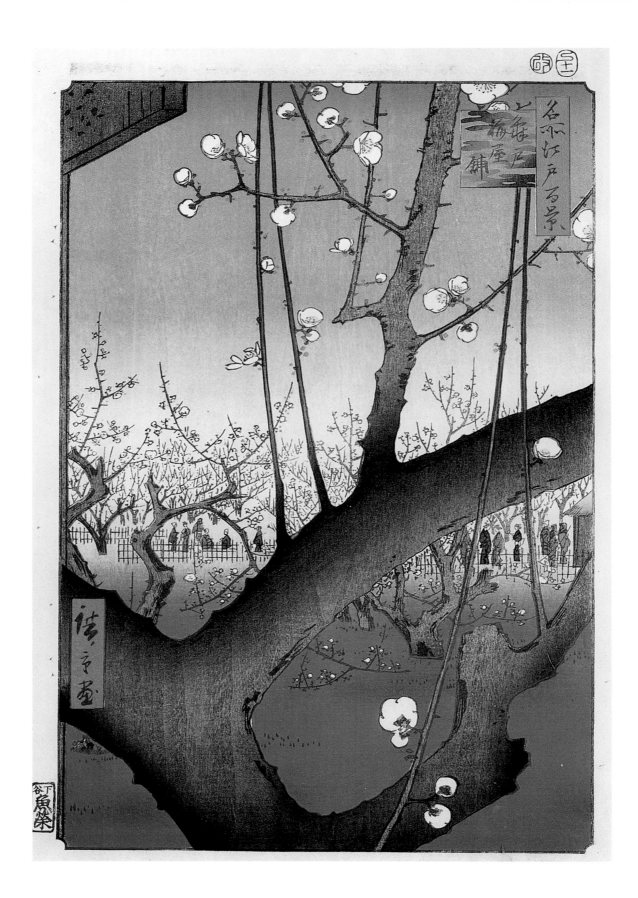

Utagawa Hiroshige
100 Views of Famous Places in and around Edo:
Plum Orchard in Kameido
Oban 36.3 x 24.6
Nishiki-e
Published by Uoya Eikichi
11th month of Ansei 4 (1857)

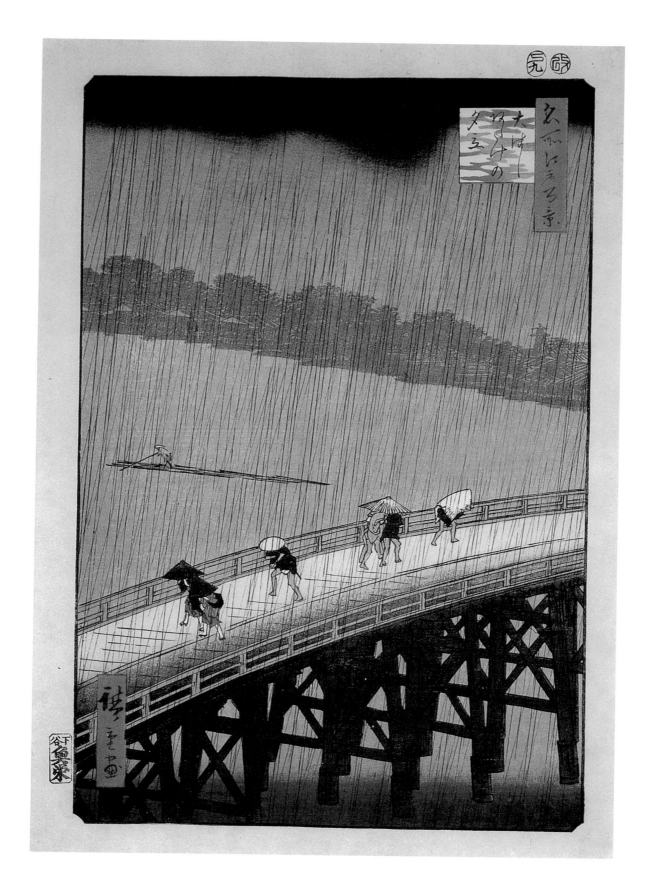

Utagawa Hiroshige
100 Views of Famous Places in and around Edo:
Ōhashi Bridge, Sudden Shower near Atake
Oban 37.4 x 25.6
Nishiki-e
Published by Uoya Eikichi
9th month of Ansei 4 (1857)

Utagawa Hiroshige
100 Views of Famous Places in and around Edo: Aoizaka Street near Toranomon
(p. 187)

Aoizaka at a late hour. The crescent moon and starry sky show that it is a cold night. The street, along which many *daimyō* had their villas, led to Toranomon Gate. The place where a pond, which served as a reservoir, flowed into a canal was also known as Aoigaoka. Nearby there was a temple dedicated to the patron god of seafarers, which was decorated on the 10th of every month by pilgrims. The two scantily clad men are on their way thither, the lanterns and handbells being signs of their pilgrim status. Such pilgrimages were often performed thus during the cold season.

By the roadside stand two soba kiosks. As they were often frequented at night by streetgirls, known as "alley whores", the kiosks were known as "alley-whore soba".

Utagawa Hiroshige
100 Views of Famous Places in and around Edo: In the Dyers' Quarter of Kanda
(p. 188)

Dyeing (konya) meant colouring cloth with indigo. During the Edo period, numerous dye-works had been set up in the district pictured here, and as a result it came to be known as "konyamachi". In the Kanda area, it was quite common to find accumulations of a particular trade in a particular district, and the trades often gave their name to the district.

Once dyed, the cloth had to be washed and dried. Konyamachi was dominated by tall drying frames of the kind depicted here. On the strips of cloth seen fluttering in the wind here, we can see the characters for "e" and "hiro" worked into a lozenge shape – an elegant monogram of the name "Hiroshige", which he also used on his seal. The master like to see his name on his pictures: it might appear on lanterns, or else on fabrics, such as kimonos (cf. p.175). In the background Edo Castle can be seen, and in the sky a large bird, while the horizon is dominated, as so often, by Mount Fuji.

Utagawa Hiroshige
100 Views of Famous Places in and around Edo: Nihon Dyke by Yoshiwara
(p. 189)

In order to reach the only pleasure quarter in Edo licensed by the shogunate, namely Yoshiwara, the visitor – whether he arrived on foot, by sedan chair, or by boat – had first to pass along the Nihon Dyke. Yoshiwara was laid out as a square, surrounded by a moat, and the only access to it was by means of the Nihon Dyke. On the right of the picture, next to the willow, was the gateway, Yoshiwara Daimon. Nailed to the willow was a notice proclaiming that any unauthorized entry to Yoshiwara was a punishable offence.

The surroundings of Yoshiwara are depicted in this print as rural, the capital being only just visible in the distance. At night, the quarter was sealed off, after which temporary tea-stalls were set up on both sides of the dyke. What with the coming and going of visitors to the pleasure quarter in their sedan chairs, and the activity of the tea-stall staff, the dyke was a busy place. In addition to the tea-stalls, there were also stands selling whatever fruit was in season. Not least because of this nocturnal business, Yoshiwara was known as a place where peace and quiet at night were unknown.

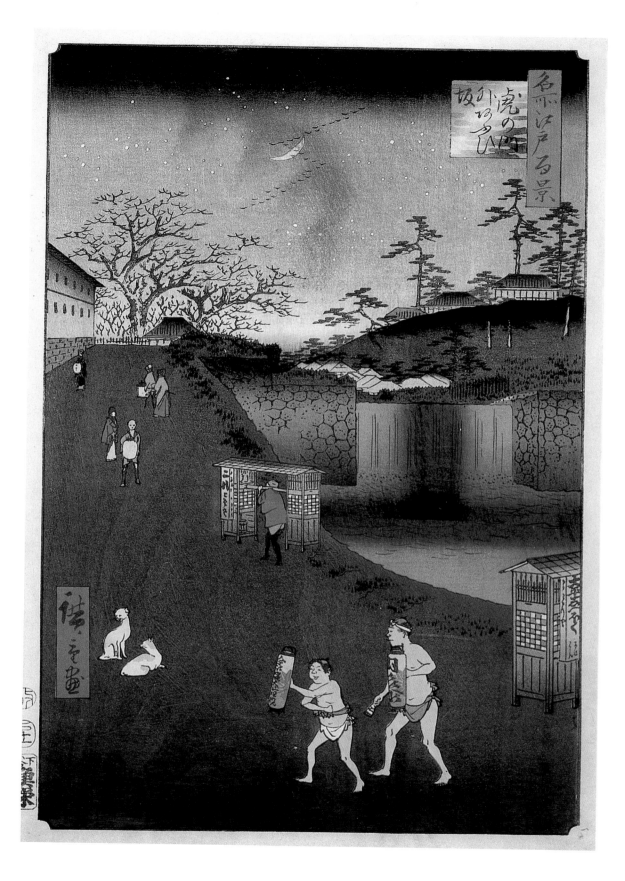

Utagawa Hiroshige
100 Views of Famous Places in and around Edo:
Aoizaka Street near Toranomon
Oban 35.2 x 23.8
Nishiki-e
Published by Uoya Eikichi
11th month of Ansei 4 (1857)

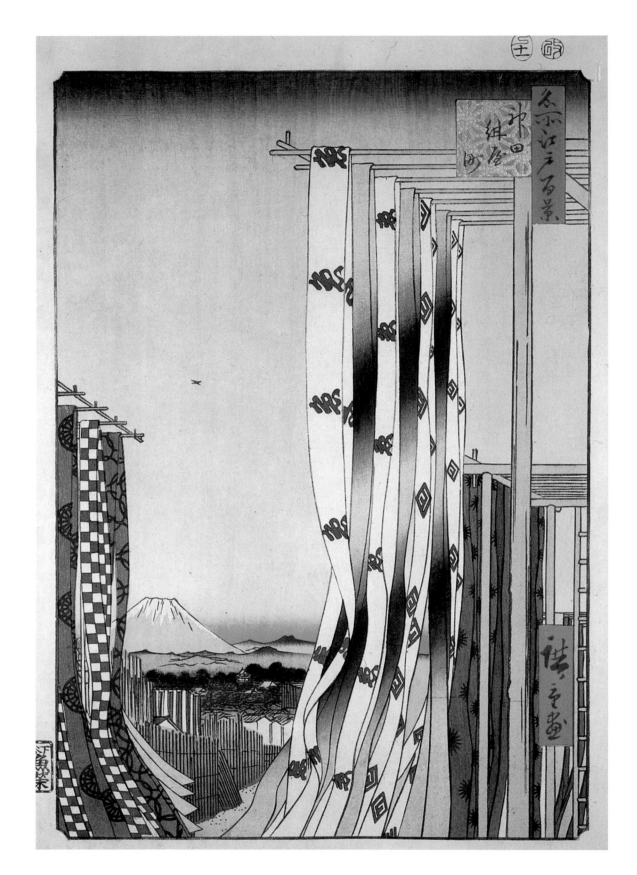

Utagawa Hiroshige
100 Views of Famous Places in and around Edo:
In the Dyers' Quarter of Kanda
Oban 36.3 x 24.8
Nishiki-e
Published by Uoya Eikichi
11th month of Ansei 4 (1857)

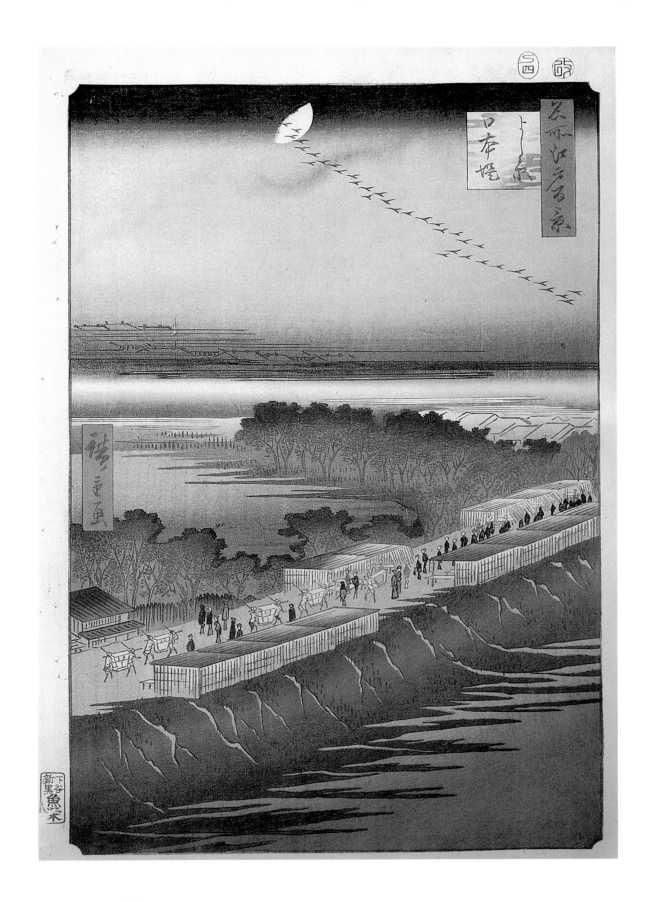

Utagawa Hiroshige
100 Views of Famous Places in and around Edo:
Nihon Dyke by Yoshiwara
Oban 36.3 x 24.9
Nishiki-e
Published by Uoya Eikichi
4th month of Ansei 4 (1857)

Glossary of Technical Terms

Abuna-e
Risqué picture. Erotic images and scenes of pairs of lovers.

Aizuri-e
Indigo print. Polychrome print with indigo or indigo shading as its chief colour. Used particularly towards the close of the *Tokugawa* period. Also known as "ai-e" (indigo picture).

Aragoto
Heroic strong-man role in *kabuki* theatre, introduced by the Ichikawa actor family.

Atenashi-bokashi
A technique used when no particular shading was required. Liquid was mixed with the ink and allowed to flow over the whole surface of the picture. The technique was frequently used for clouds and areas of water, for example in the first run-offs of Hiroshige's "100 Views of Famous Places in and around Edo".

Baren
Brayer used for pressing the paper on to the wood-block. A roller of bamboo-fibre cord wrapped in bamboo bark, with which pressure is applied to the back of the paper after it has been laid against the wood block.

Beni-e
Crimson picture. A further development of the *tan-e* in which crimson replaces vermilion as the chief colour. Other colours include indigo and yellow.

Benigirai-e
"Beni-no-like picture". A form of polychrome print in which red is not used. The chief colours are blue, grey and violet. It has its origins in a government decree of the Ansei era.

Benizuri-e
Crimson print. A simple polychrome print using different blocks for different colours, primarily *beni* and green. The technique of the multi-impression print was invented by Shisen,

a Chinese, and employed in Japan from the Enkyō era (1744–1748) onwards.

Beroai
Imported indigo, obtained from the indigo plant. *Beroai* was popular in the Bunsei era (1818–1830) and in the Tenpō era (1830–1844). A well-known example is Hokusai's series "36 Views of Mount Fuji" (pp. 148–150).

Bijin-ga
Pictures of beautiful women, usually courtesans, but occasionally girls from bourgeois households.

Bokashizuri
Shading. Gradation of colours and half-tones when printing a woodblock. See *fukibokashi*.

Bushi (or samurai)
Warrior. Member of the warrior class in the four-class system (shinōkōshō) of the *Tokugawa* period (1603–1867). They were dominant over the other classes and had corresponding privileges. They were followed in rank by the farmers (nō), artisans (kō) and merchants (shō).

Chūban
Medium format. Approx. 29.3 × 19 cm.

Chū-tanzaku-ban
Medium-format woodblock print with verse strips.

Daikagura
Temple dance in shintō shrines.

Daimyō
Feudal lord. The most powerful *daimyō* during the period from 1603 to 1867 were the *Tokugawa*.

Edo
"Eastern capital". The seat of the *Tokugawa* shogunate from 1603 to 1867. The old name for present-day Tokyo.

Ehon
Picture book. Books of pictures illustrating a wide variety of themes.

Fukibokashi
A printing technique. Part of the inked block is wiped with a damp cloth before the print is taken. The result is colour shading in strips, or without any pattern.

Furisode
Kimono with long sleeves reaching almost to the ankles. Usually worn by young unmarried girls.

Geisha
Girl trained in singing and dancing; she was employed to entertain guests, though her services were not necessarily of a sexual nature. Until the 16th century there were also male *geisha*.

Gohei
The cultic wand of a shintō priest, to which zig-zag-shaped pieces of paper are attached.

Haiku
Short poem in seventeen syllables of a lyrical nature. Often used on *tanzaku* in woodblock prints.

Hakama
Divided skirt.

Hanga
Print. The general term for a woodblock print.

Hangi
Printing block. Usually a plank of cherry-wood cut across the grain; for particularly fine prints, boxwood was also used. The design drawing – a mirror-image of the end result – was attached to this block.

Haori
Cape in the form of a short *kimono*, mostly worn by men.

Hashira-e
Post picture. A long narrow print, hung on posts. A special hard paper was used. The format was approx. 70 × 20 cm.

Hazama-ban
Portrait format. Approx. 33 × 23 cm.

Hosoban
Narrow format. Approx. 30–35.5 × 15.5 cm.

Ichimonji-bokashi
A technique whereby the top half of a picture is shaded in fine strips. Many of Hiroshige's skies are done this way. The technique is mostly used in the first print run.

Inari
Fox. God of Cereals, honoured along with his fox assistants in many shintō shrines.

Ita-bokashi
A printing technique whereby the part of the woodblock to be shaded is abraded and smoothed with spiky leaves. It was particularly popular for the shadows in the folds of garments or the shadows of mountains. Kiyonaga and Utamaro used the technique for clothes, while Hokusai and Kuniyoshi employed it in their Western-influenced scenes.

Jitsubushi
"Filling-colour" print. A technique whereby left-over white areas are inked in. The colours used may be yellow, indigo or crimson. An example in yellow is Utamaro's "Sewing" (p. 102).

Jōruri
Epic or narrative drama, which was sung with *shamisen* accompaniment. Originally written for puppet theatre, it was subsequently adopted into *kabuki*.

Kabuki
"Song-dance-art". Popular stage production, which developed into a specifically Japanese art form towards the end of the 17th century. All parts are played by male actors. More important than the personality of the actor was his stock portrayal of the character in question. For this reason, the actors' faces in the *kabuki* were made up in a manner specified for the particular role.

Kakemono
Hanging picture hung in the *tokonoma*. *Kakemono-eban* is the name given to woodblock prints in portrait format.

Kamuro
Pupil and maid of a courtesan, responsible for running light errands.

Karazuri
Blind printing. A technique whereby the paper was pressed against an uninked block,

creating a relief image. It was used especially for bean and hemp-leaf patterns on *kimonos*.

Kentō
Register mark. The register mark indicated exactly how the paper was to be placed in relation to the block in the second and subsequent colour printings of two-colour or polychrome prints to ensure perfect alignment of the different coloured areas. The register mark, in the form of two cuts at a right angle, was carved into the block at its corners.

Kimedashi or **kimekomi**
Printing technique whereby the block was pressed into the paper, leaving an impression of the lines and contours. Harunobu and Bunchō were particular exponents of the technique.

Kimono
"Wear-thing". Coat-like garment worn by both men and women, and kept together at the waist (in the case of women) or at the hips (in the case of men) by an *obi*.

Kira-e or **kirakake**
Mica print. A printing technique whereby two blocks are prepared for the background. One is inked with the basic colour, while the other is coated with bone-glue or paste. After the print has been taken, mica is scattered on the paper while it is still wet, and the surplus shaken off. This technique was popular with Utamaro and Sharaku.

Kisokaidō or **Nakasendō**
A road leading from Kyoto through the mountainous region of central Japan, the present-day provinces of Shiga, Gifu, Nagano and Gumma. In Kusatsu (Shiga prefecture) it forks off from the *Tōkaidō* and ends in central Tokyo near Nihonbashi.

Koto
Long, zither-like stringed instrument played with a plectrum.

Kyōgen
Farcical interlude during a *Nō* performance; also a term for a *kabuki* performance.

Maiko
Dancing girl. Young *geisha* whose training was not yet complete.

Motsukotsuhō
Unlined print. Technique in both monochrome and polychrome printing whereby no contour lines are drawn around the areas of colour.

Musha-e
Warrior picture. Portrayals of *bushi*.

Naga-ōban
Long format. Extra-long *ōban*.

Nishiki-e
Woodblock colour print. Brocade picture. Polychrome print. A further development of the *benizuri-e*. The impetus for its evolution came from the practice, which arose in the year Meiwa 2 (1765), of exchanging calendars, a practice indulged in by both high and low born individuals, by artists and art-lovers alike. It provided an opportunity for inventing and trying out new techniques. Harunobu made a major contribution to its further development.

Nakanomachi
The main street through the Yoshiwara red-light district. Every evening the highest-ranking courtesans would parade along it in their most magnificent costumes in order to receive their guests.

Nō
Classical dance and song drama, performed in masks and sumptuous costumes.

Nunome-zuri
Cloth print. A piece of paper-thin silk or gauze was stretched over the block, and then rubbed with a hard *baren*. As a result, the structure of the fabric was impressed on the block. This technique was very popular among woodblock cutters towards the end of the *Tokugawa* period (1603–1867).

Oban
Large format. Approx. 39.5 × 26.8 cm.

Obi
Sash for use with *kimono*. Men knot their narrow *obi* at the side. Women's *obi* are usually approx. 20 cm wide × 4 m long and are often made of brocade. The sash is tied in an elaborate bow at the back, or, in the case of courtesans, at the front.

Okubi-e
Portrayal of faces in profile or obliquely from the side. Typical are Utamaro's *bijin-ga* and Sharaku's *yakusha-e*.

Onnagata
Player of female parts. *Kabuki* actors specializing in women's roles. Since the 17th century, all roles in the *kabuki* theatre have been played by men.

Oōban
Extra-large format.

O-tanzaku-ban
Print with lines of verse in *oban* format.

Shamisen
Three-stringed guitar, played by courtesans and *geishas*. Also used as an accompaniment, for example to *kabuki* performances.

Shikishi-ban
Almost square format.

Shōji
Sliding doors composed of translucent paper within a wooden frame.

Shōmen-zuri
Glossy print. Also known as "tsuya-zuri". After a picture has been printed, this technique involves placing a mirror-image block against the underside and then rubbing the surface with a *baren* till it shines. This produces a glossy pattern on, for example, garments with a black ground.

Shozuri
First print run, by convention the first hundred prints taken from a block. Subsequent print runs are known as "atozuri". The first print run is characterized by the fact that the block shows no signs of wear. More care is given to the coloration and to the impression, so that *shozuri* prints are more valuable.

Shunga
Spring pictures. General term for erotic representations and illustrations.

Sumizuri-e
Ink print, or black-and-white print. Pictures dating from the early days of the woodblock print, which were produced in only one colour, namely blue-black ink. While simple, the technique has its own charm and importance.

Sumizuri-hissai
A *sumizuri* print subsequently coloured by hand.

Surimono
Lavishly produced prints commissioned by private customers for special occasions; not offered for sale.

Tan-e
Vermilion picture. It is a *sumizuri-e* which is hand-coloured in vermilion, green or yellow. As vermilion *(tan)* was the most frequently used pigment, it gave its name to the genre as a whole.

Tanzaku-ban
Sheet of verse and corresponding print format. Approx. 44 × 7.6 cm.

Tatami
Rice-straw mat of standard size, used to cover the floors of Japanese houses.

Tōkaidō
Eastern Sea Road. The traffic artery between the imperial capital Kyoto and the seat of government, Edo, present-day Tokyo.

Tokonoma
Alcoves. They are usually decorated with hanging pictures and ikebana flower arrangements.

Tokugawa
The name of the family which took over the government in the name of the Emperor in 1603 and transferred the seat of government to Edo. Kyoto with its imperial palace remained the official capital. As all the shōguns from 1603 to 1867 came from this family, the period is known as the Tokugawa period or Edo period.

Torii
Gate at the entrance to a shintō shrine.

Uchikake
Long overgarment, worn loose.

Uchiwa-eban
Fan picture. Woodblock print in which the outline of a fan forms a frame within the picture.

Uki-e
Perspective picture. Pictures emphasizing spatial depth in the Western manner. Masanobu was the first to use the technique, which was subsequently refined by Toyoharu. It is important as a forerunner of the woodblock landscape print.

Ukiyo-e
Pictures of the floating (fleeting) world. The fashionable genre painting of the *Tokugawa* period. For the most part, *bijin-ga* and *yakusha-e*. Today, virtually synonymous with the Japanese woodblock print, produced co-operatively by a painter, a block cutter and a printer. For polychrome prints, up to ten blocks were needed, sometimes even more. The pigments were applied with brushes or the ball of the thumb. The picture was printed on soft, absorbent paper – Japanese paper – rubbed against the block with a *baren* or brush.

Urushi-e
Lacquer picture. An early form of woodblock print. A coat of bone-glue was applied to the blue-black ink, giving a lacquered appearance. Sometimes copper filings were scattered on to the glue, producing a metallic glitter.

Waka
Short poem in 31 syllables.

Wakashūgata
An Actor specializing in the role of young samurai.

Yakusha-e
Portraits of *kabuki* actors.

Yamato-e
Pure Japanese painting. A style of painting which arose in the 10th century and which consciously sought to divest itself of Chinese influences. Its subject-matter was drawn from events in Japanese history.

Yoko-hazama-ban
Hazama-ban, but horizontal.

Yoko-naga-eban
Extra-wide horizontal-format picture.

Yoko-tanzaku-ban
Landscape-format version of *tanzaku-ban*.

Yoko-ōban
Landscape-format version of *oban*.

Za
Theatre.

Biographies of Artists

Technical terms in the following biographies are explained in the glossary on the preceding pages.

Ippitsusai BUNCHŌ

c. 1725– *c.* 1795, active around 1767–1778. Bunchō studied Kanō painting and was an exponent of *ukiyo-e*. The style of actor portrait pioneered by himself and Shunshō had a decisive influence on the future development of the woodblock print. Later, Bunchō was influenced above all by Harunobu, one of the great masters of *ukiyo-e*. Bunchō's own great masterpiece is generally considered to be his "Ehon butai ōgi", which he published jointly with Shunshō in 1770, and which contains the first realistic actor portraits. While these were his speciality, most of his works are in fact portraits of courtesans and pretty girls. Bunchō's particular flair consists in the way he combined the realism of Shunshō with the lyricism and exquisite colourfulness of Harunobu, thus creating a brilliance and quality all his own. Like many other *ukiyo-e* painters, Bunchō was also a talented poet.
ILLUSTRATIONS: pp. 77–79

Eishōsai CHŌKI

Active from around 1780 till after 1800. Chōki never achieved great popularity, but his achievement as an artist was nonetheless considerable. He was an *ukiyo-e* painter, an illustrator and a print artist, having studied under Sekien. Among a mass of very average prints and illustrations, he produced a small number of colour prints which are among the most beautiful *ukiyo-e* of all. It was his *bijin-ga* in particular, with their characteristically fine facial features, that brought him to public attention. While the influence of other artists is certainly apparent – Kiyonaga, Eishi, Sharaku, Utamaro and Harunobu among them – Chōki seems to surpass them all in poetic atmosphere and in the way he gave expression to idealized feminine beauty. Notable too is his compositional technique. From about 1790, half-length portraits came into fashion. Chōki, like Sharaku, would include a second figure in the picture, but he solves the compositional problem so

skilfully that an impression of photographic immediacy is created.
ILLUSTRATIONS: pp. 118–119

Kaigetsudō DOHAN

Active around 1710–1720. Dohan was one of six pupils of Kaigetsudō Ando, the founder of the Kaigetsudō school. Only twenty-two prints by members of this school are still extant, and of these, twelve are by Dohan. While his painting is little influenced by the Kaigetsudō school, his prints are among the best works of the period. They are frequently indistinguishable from those of Norishige. Characteristic of Dohan are his decorative *kimono* patterns, and the elegant shoulder-length hair of his sitters.
ILLUSTRATION: p. 6

Keisai EISEN

1791–1848. Eisen came from a *samurai* family belonging to the Fujiwara clan. At first he studied under Eizan. Alongside individual pictures, from 1811 his works include book illustrations, primarily of an erotic nature, for which he used the name Insai Hakusui. Under the names of Chiyoda Sai-ichi and Ippitsu-an Kako, he produced a number of humorous short stories. He is said to have lived a dissolute life as a heavy drinker, and for a time to have managed a brothel. While in Japan he owes his popularity to his erotic pictures and his voluminous female figures, in the West it is his landscapes which have attracted most attention. These were produced in conjunction with Hiroshige. The series "69 Stations on the Kiso Road" was begun by Eisen and completed by Hiroshige. In general, Eisen is probably to be assigned to the second rank of *ukiyo-e* landscape painters of the late Edo period.
ILLUSTRATIONS: pp. 2, 146

Chōbunsai EISHI

1756–1829. Eishi was the eldest son of a *samurai* family belonging to the Fujwara clan in Edo. Provided with a regular income, he first studied painting with the official teachers of the Kanō school, and then became a household official and court painter in the service of shōgun Tokugawa Ieharu (1737–1786). At the

age of thirty, he resigned this socially highly respectable position and turned to the popular *ukiyo-e* style, becoming a pupil of Bunryūsai and the Torii school. Like Utamaro, Eishi liked to paint women: either idealized girls in idyllic settings, or courtesans from Yoshiwara, which was developing its own distinctive culture as a pleasure quarter. Eishi's œuvre includes *shunga* – erotic pictures – as well as prints with themes taken from Japanese and Chinese mythology, and romantic scenes. He modelled himself first on Kiyonaga, then on Utamaro. He found his own artistic expression, however, in pictures full of elegance and aristocratic noblesse – pictures that were so highly regarded that they were even shown to the imperial family. One picture, entitled "Sumidagawa Landscape", was even owned by Empress Gosakuramachi.
ILLUSTRATIONS: pp. 111–113.

Chōensai EISHIN

Active around 1795 till about 1810. Eishin was an *ukiyo-e* painter and print artist, a pupil of Eishi. Two series of prints by him are known: "Ōgi-ya-uchi hanaōgi, oban" (*c.* 1796/97) and "Fūryū zashiki-gei jikkei" (*c.* 1800).
ILLUSTRATION: p. 131

Chōkōsai EISHŌ

Active around 1790–1799. An *ukiyo-e* painter and print artist, he was Eishi's most important pupil. In comparison with those of his master, his *bijin-ga* are less elegant, but they are more realistic, more robust and less elaborated. His works were underestimated for a long time.
ILLUSTRATIONS: pp. 114–116

Ichirakutei EISUI

Active between 1790 and 1823. Eisui was an *ukiyo-e* print artist and pupil of Eishi. Like Eishō and Eiri, he distinguished himself in the production of *okubi-e*; the pictures were in a sense pin-ups for Yoshiwara clients and visitors, rather than portraits in the usual sense.
ILLUSTRATION: p. 141

Kikukawa EIZAN

1787–1867. An *ukiyo-e* painter and print artist, he worked at first for his father, and then stud-

ied under Nanrei and Hokkei. He was influenced by Utamaro and Hokusai. During a period which was witnessing the manifest artistic decline of *ukiyo-e,* a period without first-rate artists or critics, Eizan, along with Toyokuni, was among the leading exponents of *bijin-ga.* His motifs were primarily standing female figures in a tranquil atmosphere.
ILLUSTRATIONS: pp. 22, 142–143.

Kabukidō ENKYŌ

1749–1803. An *ukiyo-e* print artist, Enkyō was also a playwright for the *kabuki* theatre. Only seven prints by him are known, owing much to Sharaku in style.
ILLUSTRATION: p. 136

Suzuki HARUNOBU

1725–1770, active 1760–1770. Born in Edo, where he also worked, Harunobu was one of the leading print artists of his time. He played a major role in the development of *nishiki-e,* the polychrome print. He is said to have studied under Shigenaga, but his early prints, mostly *bijin-ga* and *yakusha-e,* are more similar in style to those of the Torii masters Kiyomitsu and Kiyotsune. The strongest influence during his early years came from the Kyoto master Sukenobu, along with Kiyomitsu, Toyonobu and the *ukiyo-e* painters of the Kawamata school. His study of the principles and methods of the Kanō school and of such 16th-century Chinese genre painters as Ch'iu Ying and T'ang Yin is also reflected in his work.
In about 1762 Harunobu finally arrived at a style of his own, which from then on exercised a decisive influence on *ukiyo-e* painting generally. He is the archetypal painter of *bijinga* portraits. He presents ladies of the demimonde, middle-class women going about their everyday tasks, and women in mythological scenes, all executed in elegant colour and well-differentiated technique. In 1764 he was commissioned to design pictures for calendars, which were later brought out by the publisher Shokakudo. The impetus for the wider distribution of these early *nishiki-e* came from clubs of intellectuals, poets and artists in Edo. Harunobu, appointed the intellectual leader of one such club, was asked to design New Year's and other congratulatory cards, so-called *e-goyomi.* For club members, aesthetically demanding as they were, no price was too high. Costly materials were used, and by 1765 the polychrome print was in full flower. Instead of just two or three colours, the whole range of the artist's palette was now available.
Harunobu also painted erotic scenes, and he liked to have such celebrated beauties as O-Sen and O-Fuji sit for him.
ILLUSTRATIONS: pp. 16, 17, 57–65.

Suzuki HARUSHIGE

c. 1747–1818. Also known as Shiba Kōkan. In his youth, Harushige painted numerous *bijinga,* imitating the style of Harunobu. Later he developed an interest in Western art, and in 1783 produced Japan's first copperplate engraving. Thereafter he called himself Kōkan.
ILLUSTRATIONS: pp. 66, 69

Utagawa HIROSHIGE

1797–1858, active 1818–1858. Hiroshige, the last great master of *ukiyo-e,* was born in Edo in 1797, the son of a fireman. His mother died when he was only twelve, and he lost his father just a year after that. He inherited his father's position, but as early as 1811, in other words at the age of fourteen, he joined the school of the *ukiyo-e* master Toyohiro, having been rejected by Toyokuni, who was at that time extremely popular. After a year in Toyohiro's workshop, he was honoured with the artist's pseudonym of Utagawa Hiroshige. When Toyohiro died in 1828, he took over both his studio and his name, calling himself Toyohiro II.
His first publication, a book illustration, came out in 1818 and bore the signature Ichiryūsai Hiroshige. During this period he was also studying both the Kanō and the "impressionist" Shijō styles, which were to have such an influence on his later work. In the years up to 1830, he occupied himself, as his predecessors had done, with figural work, in particular prints of girls, actors and warriors. After Toyohiro's death, he transferred his attentions to another artistic theme, namely that of landscape and nature studies. This field had already been revolutionized by Hokusai, who had raised it to the status of an independent genre. Eisen and other portrait-painters had also taken up this new theme. Hiroshige began his own career as a landscape painter in 1830 with his "Famous Places in the Eastern Capital", but fame only came in 1833/34 with his "53 Stations on the Tōkaidō" – the great imperial road that linked Edo with Kyoto. These pictures represented the outcome of a journey in which he had participated as an official in a government mission to the imperial court in Kyoto. Hiroshige's orders were to produce sketches and drawings of various ceremonies. Further journeys followed, which inspired him to produce more landscape studies. From May to December 1841 he travelled through the province of Kai, in 1852 the provinces of Kazusa and Awa as far as the west coast, and in 1854 he made another official trip to Kyoto. The artistic yield of these travels came in the form of further series of woodblock prints: "Famous Places in Kyoto", "Eight Views of Lake Biwa", "Famous Places in Naniwa", "Eight Views of Kanazawa", "36 Views of Mount Fuji", and "69 Stations on the Kisokaidō" – the Kisokaidō being the mountain route from Edo to Kyoto. Hiroshige's landscapes are characterized by an atmospheric colour reflecting the changes in nature at different times of the day and year, and in rain, snow and storm. Nor should his tender pictures of flowers and birds be forgotten. Altogether, Hiroshige produced more than 5,400 woodblock prints. His success and his popularity are legendary. He also exerted an influence on Western art, and above all on the Impressionists, who were able to view his work at the Paris Expositions Universelles of 1855, 1867 and 1878. Vincent van Gogh acquired a number of his pictures.
ILLUSTRATIONS: pp. 166–189.

Uoya HOKKEI

1780–1850. A print artist, illustrator, writer and fishmonger, he studied first under Kanō Yosenin Masanobu, before becoming a pupil of Hokusai. In his own woodblock prints, he took over elements of the Chinese style favoured by Hokusai, in particular in his panoramic landscapes. He was also well-known for his illustrations to books of humorous poems, and for his *surimono.*
ILLUSTRATION: p. 161

Shōtei HOKUJU

1763–?, active from c. 1795 to c. 1825. Hokuju was one of Hokusai's most talented pupils, and perhaps the most original landscape artist among them. His pictures betray the influence of Western painting and a preoccupaton with perspective, something found in Hokusai's work from the early 1800s onwards. Conspicuous features of Hokuju's work are his "cubist" forms, as well as his skilful variations on traditional themes.
ILLUSTRATIONS: pp. 156, 157

Katsushika HOKUSAI

1760–1849, active from 1779–1849. Hokusai was born on 12 October 1760 in Honjo (also known as Katsushika), a suburb of Edo. An extraordinarily versatile artist, whose productivity seemed boundless, he is one of the greatest masters of the Japanese print. Nothing is known of his parents; at the age of three he was adopted by Nakajime Ise, a mirrormaker at the shōgun's court. He began to paint at the age of six. In 1772 he worked for a short time at a public library, and the following year embarked on an apprenticeship as an engraver and woodblock cutter. In 1777, at the age of eighteen, he was apprenticed to the *ukiyo-e* master Shunshō. Two years later he published his first pictures, actor-portraits, under the name of Shunrō. A little later he published some popular novels, and in 1782 his first self-illustrated book appeared. After eight years of collaboration with Shunshō, he left the latter's studio and joined the Kanō artist Yūsen Hironobu for a short while. In the following years he studied under various painters, including Tsusumi Tōrin, and Simiyoshi Hiroyuki; he also studied European painting under Harushige (alias Kōkan). From 1789 onwards he received numerous commissions for book illustrations; these included illustrations to works by the authors Bakin and Kyōden, which represent his first important works, published under the name of Kakō. From 1796 to 1805 he concentrated upon *surimono,* with which he

enjoyed considerable success. It was during this period, in 1797, that he assumed the name of Hokusai. The change of name marked an artistic climax in Hokusai's work. Between 1798 and 1805, he published a series of outstanding portraits of women, as well as colour illustrations for the books "Songs from Itako", "Famous Views of the Eastern Capital", "Views of the River Sumida", and "Mountains upon Mountains". His work hitherto had covered the whole spectrum of *ukiyo-e* art: individual prints, *surimono,* picture books, books of anecdotes, illustrations of verse and historical romances, erotic books, paintings and sketches. His creativity was destined to endure for a further twenty years. In 1805 he took up the study of Chinese painting and illustrating, and devoted his energies chiefly to the illustration of novels. After 1814 he started publishing his sketchbooks, or "manga", fifteen volumes in which he portrays in a realistic manner the lives and doings of the Japanese people, everyday life, mythological scenes, animals, plants and landscapes. The late 1820s ushered in the publication of numerous series of colour prints of landscapes, animals and spirits, including "Reflections of Poets", "100 Nurse's Tales", "A Round Trip Past the Waterfalls" (1827) and "Views of Famous Bridges in Various Provinces" (1827–1830). The most famous of these series are the "36 Views of Mount Fuji" and the three-volume "100 Views of Fuji" (1834 / 35). These are regarded as the highpoint of Japanese landscape art, and also as the summit of the artist's career. Hokusai's life was full of activity, but mostly spent in poverty; he changed his name 20 times, moved house 93 times, married twice, had several children and went on numerous journeys. But his life was also marked by his great artistic productivity: his work includes some 30,000 pictures in addition to the illustrations he supplied for some 500 books. In his later years, he acquired the nickname "Gakyō-rōjin" – "the painting-crazy old man". Not all his works are of the same quality, though, and his best work only dates from the seventh decade of his life. He brought a new greatness to *ukiyo-e*, and raised landscape, flower and bird painting to the status of independent genres. Hokusai's unusual effects are based on the boldness of his colour combinations, his perspectives, and the directness of his portrayal, which is sometimes drastically realistic. His work reflects the whole world of the imagination of the Far East. He handled a rich diversity of themes, from the brothel to the devotional Buddhist picture, from the plant to the heroic landscape, from the burlesque caricature to the ghost. He designed tobacco pipes, temples, miniature landscapes and panoramas, for which he used eggs, bottles and his fingers as painting implements. He was an improvisation artist, giving public performances of "live" art, and he painted temples using bundles of straw, brooms and rice sacks.
ILLUSTRATIONS: pp. 31, 147–155

Sugimura JIHEI

Active 1680–1698. Jihei was Moronobu's most successful follower. For a long time his works were attributed to Moronobu, and even today some can still be found exhibited under Moronobu's name in museums. His first book illustrations appeared in 1681, to be followed by further illustrations for novels and picture-books in the *ukiyo-e* style. During this period he even seems to have been a serious rival to Moronobu. Jihei's main interest lay in erotic pictures.
ILLUSTRATIONS: pp. 36, 37

Torii KIYOMASU

Active *c.* 1697–1722. Scholars are unclear as to Kiyomasu's family connections. He is said to have been the son or younger brother of Kiyonobu. Kiyomasu devoted himself to *bijin-ga* and *yakusha-e*; he developed Kiyonobu's style further and, together with Kiyonobu, founded the Torii school.
ILLUSTRATIONS: pp. 13, 42

Torii KIYOMITSU

1735–1785, active 1757–1778. Kiyomitsu is one of the leading exponents of *ukiyo-e.* He studied under his father, Kiyonobu II, and belonged to the third generation of the Torii school, its last great period. He is regarded as a pioneer of *benizuri-e* which he developed by employing blue, grey and yellow alongside the usual green and crimson. His preferred motifs were taken from the world of theatre, which he depicted in traditional Torii style as *yakusha-e.* His repertoire also included portraits of courtesans.
ILLUSTRATIONS: pp. 51, 52

Torii KIYONAGA

1752–1815. Kiyonaga was born in Uraga, the son of a bookseller, but moved at an early age to Edo. Accounts of his activities during the following years differ; what is certain is that he was a pupil of Kiyomitsu, the third Torii master. He did not confine his studies to the style of any one school, however, and was influenced by Harunobu, Koryūsai and Shigemasa. After Kiyomitsu's death in 1785, his son-in-law Matsuya Kameji attempted to recruit Kiyonaga as a painter of theatrical posters. After some hesitation, he took over the studio, as well as adopting the Torii name for the fourth generation. Between 1785 and 1811, he published some 120 illustrated books. In addition, he produced numerous individual prints, series of three or more *bijin-ga, musha-e* and *yakusha-e* – the traditional stock-in-trade of the Torii school – along with *surimono* and fan pictures. In spite of his obligations to the Torii school, Kiyonaga went far beyond what they attempted, in that he freed himself from stylized representations, creating portraits with realistic elements. In his theatre pictures, he incorporated the stage and the podium with its narrators and musicians, thus achieving a certain sense of depth.

The general trend in *ukiyo-e* art towards greater naturalism and larger figures culminated in Kiyonaga. Well-proportioned beauties integrated into realistically portrayed settings, elegance, and balance – these are the hallmarks of his work. During the twenty years in which Utamaro was the dominant figure on the woodblock-print scene, Kiyonaga confined his activities to painting and theatre-poster design.
ILLUSTRATIONS: pp. 18, 26, 27, 91–96

Torii KIYONOBU

1664–1729, active 1697–1729. Kiyonobu, the founder of the Torii school, studied under his father Kiyomoto, who was an actor, woodblock cutter and painter of posters for the *kabuki* theatre. He was born in Kyoto, but later went with his father to Edo. There he followed in his father's footsteps and began to paint colourful placards for the *kabuki* stage. He based his style on that of Moronobu. 1687 saw the appearance of his first illustrated book, and around 1700 he produced his first large-format hand-coloured prints with motifs taken from the *kabuki* stage in Edo. It was with him that individual portraits of actors became fashionable. Around 1710 there appeared a book of courtesan portraits illustrating the beauties of Yoshiwara. Like most *ukiyo-e* artists, he was also a master of *shunga.* Kiyonobu's hallmarks are his powerful, dynamic draughtsmanship and the pronounced strength of his lines. His later work is difficult to distinguish from that of Kiyonobu II.
ILLUSTRATIONS: pp. 14, 38–41

Torii KIYONOBU II

Active from *c.* 1725 to *c.* 1760. The work of Kiyonobu II, probably the son of Kiyonobu, does not match up to that of the first Torii generation. Even so, his few hand-coloured prints and illustrations bear witness to considerable individual skill.
ILLUSTRATION: p. 43

Torii KIYOSHIGE

Active post-1720 to *c.* 1760. Kiyoshige was a late pupil of Kiyonobu. His large prints in the style of Masanobu rank amongst the best works of the Torii school.
ILLUSTRATION: p. 48

Torii KIYOTSUNE

Active *c.* 1757–1779. An *ukiyo-e* artist and illustrator, he was the son of a publisher of theatre programmes. He studied under Kiyomitsu, but was equally influenced by Harunobu. There are very few individual prints by him extant; most, like that reproduced here, are in the style of *beni-e.*
ILLUSTRATION: p. 50

Isoda KORYŪSAI

Active *c.* 1765–1788. Koryūsai was a *samurai* in the service of the Tsuchiya lords. On losing his feudal masters, he moved to Edo, where he turned his hand to *ukiyo-e*. He may have been taught by Shigenaga. From 1768, while his friend and role-model Harunobu was still alive, he called himself Haruhiro; not until 1771 did he assume the name Koryūsai. In about 1780 the honorary title Hōkkyō – reserved for artists and scholars, though originally a rank in the priesthood – was bestowed upon him. Although his early works include many *bijin-ga,* where the influence of Harunobu is still marked, by the late 1770s he was creating *ōban*-size fashion prints in a style of his own, depicting an urbane, realistic feminine type. Characteristic of his work are an emphasis on clothes, elaborate coiffures and powerful figure-drawing without background. Of his 600 or so woodblock prints, most are portraits of courtesans and actors. Of all Japanese artists, it is probably he who created the most, and the most inventive, *hashira-e*; narrow, portrait-format pictures. Alongside these, he was responsible for numerous erotic pictures and series, as well as large-format studies of birds. In his later years he devoted himself almost entirely to the more highly regarded *ukiyo-e*.

ILLUSTRATIONS: pp. 18, 24, 25, 71–75

Utagawa KUNIMASA

1773–1810. Kunimasa served an apprenticeship as a dyer before becoming, or so it is thought, Toyokuni's favourite pupil. His first prints date from 1795. Outstanding among his works are his actor portraits, in which he attempted to combine the intensity of Sharaku with the decorative grace of his teacher Toyokuni.

ILLUSTRATIONS: pp. 138, 139

Utagawa KUNISADA

1786–1864, active 1807–1864. Kunisada became a pupil of Toyokuni at the age of 15, and would later, after the latter's death, assume his name. Kunisada's pictures reflect the culture of Japan in the years leading up to the country's opening to the West. His first book illustrations were published in 1807, his first actor portrait the following year; alongside theatrical scenes and courtesans, *yakusha-e* was his preferred genre amidst all his popular and extensive output. As he painted very many of these, continuing the stout realism of his teacher, he acquired the sobriquet "Yakusha-e no Kunisada" – Kunisada, the actor painter. In his numerous *bijin-ga* he clung to the ideal of beauty prevalent at the time. While his style must be described as powerful and realistic, even coarsely so, his draughtsmanship and coloration are if anything monotonous and lacking finesse. From 1830 he continued the development of the Utagawa school, and from 1844 onwards signed his works Toyokuni II.

ILLUSTRATIONS: pp. 158–160

Utagawa KUNIYOSHI

1797–1861. After serving an apprenticeship as a silk-dyer with his father, Kuniyoshi studied under Shūn'ei before becoming a pupil of Toyokuni in Edo in 1811. He is one of the leading representatives of the Utagawa school. As the prints, theatrical scenes and book illustrations which he started producing from 1814 onwards found few buyers, he lived at first by selling straw mats. It was not until 1827 that he achieved success with a series of heroes from the Chinese novel "Suikoden"; the pictures are marked by dramatic action and dynamic figures. He stuck with the theme of heroic episodes from history and legend, and in addition produced fantastical ghost scenes, charming pictures of girls, genre scenes, landscapes and pictures of animals. Twice his caricatures, in which alleged political allusions were detected, brought him into conflict with the authorities, who destroyed his printing blocks. In 1853 he triumphed in a contest with Edo's best-known painters, defeating his fellow competitors with an enormous work measuring some 50 m² in area. Whereas Kunisada was known for his *yakusha-e*, and Hiroshige for his *bijin-ga*, Kuniyoshi was recognized as the leading painter of *musha-e;* all three artists collaborated to publish series. Kuniyoshi is regarded as one of the most talented artists of the late Edo period; in his *musha-e, bijin-ga*, theatre pictures and atmospheric Western-style landscapes he introduced new stylistic forms which owed much to the techniques of European painting, and perspective in particular. Among his effects on his death are said to have been hundreds of cuttings from illustrated European magazines. His best-known series include "Mirror of the 24 Examples of Childish Love", "Picture Contest in the Genji Style" and "36 Glorious Battles". His later output, some of it presumed to be by his pupils, is of no particular note.

ILLUSTRATIONS: 21, 162–165

Kitao MASANOBU

1761–1816. Masanobu was a member of a *samurai* clan that had turned to trade. He himself worked as a merchant, but was above all an important poet and writer. A pupil of Shigemasa, he was active as a print artist primarily between 1778 and 1791. During this period he illustrated some 120 books written both by himself and others. His individual prints and series mostly depict beautiful women from the Yoshiwara district, where he was a daily visitor. In 1789 and 1790 the freedoms he took in his books and pictures brought him into conflict with the courts. In the years following 1792 he devoted himself almost entirely to literature. In 1806 a fire in his shop, where he sold books, tobacco products and medicines, forced him to take up art once more, but the commercial motivation of the albums and fan pictures dating from this period is unmistakable.

ILLUSTRATION: p. 85

Okumura MASANOBU

1686–1764. He was the son of a painter (who was probably responsible for the early erotic book illustrations that appeared under Masanobu's name in 1701). A book wholesaler and publisher, he was also a *haiku* poet. He is sometimes said to have been a pupil of Moronobu and Kiyonobu, but he was probably self-taught. During his lifetime, the woodblock print was developing from monochrome to polychrome, a process in which he was intimately involved for over fifty years. He is credited with the invention of the two and three-colour print *(beni-e)* as well as with the first *hashira-e*. He was also a master in the use of lacquer *(urushi-e)* and metallic and gold powders. The publishing house which he founded in Edo in 1724 encouraged the promotion of the colour print, and brought out many of his own works. As a painter, Masanobu interested himself in a very wide variety of themes. His motifs are taken from heroic legend, from the theatre and from life inside the brothels, in addition to landscapes and animals. His in some cases almost three-dimensional landscapes and pictures of architecture, probably designed for viewing in a peepshow, show the influence of European art in their emphasis on perspective. These pictures were extremely popular and fashionable, and were thus often imitated and pirated, a practice against which Masanobu tried in vain to defend himself by the use of long and detailed signatures. His pictures are of great charm in respect of colour, and are noteworthy also for the depth of their black and their strength of composition. Masanobu was the founder of the Okumura school, which takes its name from him, and he was of major importance in the history of the Japanese print. His immediate successor and perhaps his son was Toshinobu.

ILLUSTRATIONS: pp. 44, 45

Hishikawa MORONOBU

1618 (or 1625)–1694. The son of a dyer and embroiderer, he was born in Hoda in the province of Awa on Edo Bay. Even while still quite young, he probably designed costly garments on behalf of his father, which might well explain his predilection for details and decorative patterns. He was probably trained first by some unknown master in the art of the Kanō and Tosa schools. On his arrival in Edo in the 1660s, he soon concentrated exclusively on *ukiyo-e*. At this time, the woodblock print was still in its infancy. His first book illustrations appeared in 1672. His erotic illustrations with their scenes of courtesans and brothels were presumably based on anonymous erotic prints from Kyoto, to which, however, they were greatly superior, so that he can truly be called the father of the woodblock print as an independent genre, and its first great master. The delicate lines of his figures became the *ukiyo-e* ideal, and the stormy vigour of his compositions, while imitated by many, was only emulated by a very few later masters. He ist also the first artist of the genre about whose life anything is known, and was the founder of the

Hishikawa or Edo school, whose influence was still strong in the 19th century, and which set itself the task of portraying contemporary life. Some 150 woodblock albums survive from Moronobu's hand, employing the traditional monochrome technique; their motifs are chiefly historical and literary, but they also include *kimono* pattern books, *ukiyo-e* albums and collections of erotica. By contrast, there are very few individual sheets, most of them from dismantled albums, but they include some very beautiful female portraits. The print reproduced here was printed in black ink and then coloured by hand.
ILLUSTRATION: p. 35

Tōshūsai SHARAKU

c. 1770 – post-1825(?), active in Edo 1794/95. Sharaku's work is as brilliant as his life is mysterious. In fact we know as good as nothing about him. He appeared from the mists of history, worked for just nine months, left 144 pictures, and disappeared once more without trace. He may have been a *Nō* actor in the troupe of some feudal lord. Alongside a few wrestler portraits, his work consists entirely of *yakusha-e* for the *kabuki* theatre, busts or full-length scenes featuring one or two figures, all sponsored and printed by Tsutaya Jūzaburō, the most successful publisher of the day. His typical pictures are *okubi-e*, with caricature-like heads against a dark or occasionally gradated *kira* background, bearing a distant resemblance to the work of Shunshō and Toyokuni. The expressions on the grimacing faces, often exaggerated to the point of grotesqueness, together with the drama suggested by the economical gestures, bring out well not only the character of the part being played, but also the individual features of the actor himself. Sharaku's powerful draughtsmanship and his skilful use of colour-contrast exploit the whole gamut of technical possibilities available to the print artist. The idea that his super-realistic, often not exactly flattering portraits earned him the dislike of the public and the hatred of the actors is no more than a legend, though it does make his sudden disappearance more plausible. It is certainly true that the Japanese public were not prepared for Sharaku's incisive realism or his psychologically well-founded caricature, which were both revolutionary in *ukiyo-e* art and may well have been responsible for his extremely brief career.
ILLUSTRATIONS: p. 20, 121–30

Nishimura SHIGENAGA

c. 1695–1756. Shigenaga was a landowner, and worked as a bookseller in Edo. As a print artist he was self-taught, but he was a great teacher and innovator. He experimented with perspective, and was one of the first to interest himself in landscapes with figures. In addition he contributed towards the dissemination of the triptych, and developed the techniques of ishizuri-e and mizu-e. His own style owed much to Kiyonobu, Sukenobu and Masanobu.

His pupils Toyonobu and Harunobu became the leading artists of the next generation.
ILLUSTRATION: p. 49

Katsukawa SHŪN'EI

c. 1762–1819. Shūn'ei was Shunshō's most important pupil, giving a modern impetus to the Katsukawa school. By dint of particular emphasis on gesture and facial expression, he gave his *yakusha-e* enhanced individuality and dramatic power. His influence can be seen to particularly good effect in the work of Sharaku and Toyokuni. In private, Shūn'ei was an eccentric, but he had many friends, among them Shunchō, Utamaro and Toyokuni, with all of whom he occasionally collaborated.
ILLUSTRATIONS: pp. 86, 87

Katsukawa SHUNKŌ

1743–1812. Like all of Shunshō's pupils, Shunkō interested himself mainly in the theatre, in his best work matching up to the quality of his teacher. His first pictures appeared in the early 1770s. In the late 1780s he suffered a paralysis of the right hand, forcing him to work with his left. Typical of his work are heads of actors portrayed in close-up.
ILLUSTRATION: p. 83

Kubo SHUNMAN

1757–1820. Shunman was an intellectual who devoted his life primarily to literature. He was a pupil of Nahiko and Shigemasa, but was influenced above all by Kiyonaga. His own style was, if anything, simple, and his coloration, which was generally confined to grey, yellow and dark red tones, economical. He is best known for his *surimono* and *bijin-ga*.
ILLUSTRATION: p. 97

Katsukawa SHUNSHŌ

1726–1792. The scion of a *samurai* clan, Shunshō lived in Edo and studied under the painters Shunsui and Sūkoku. Until 1767 he worked primarily as a painter, but then took up the colour print before returning to painting again in 1785. In his handling of colour harmonies – he preferred warm brown, orange and ochre hues – he was influenced above all by Harunobu and Shigemasa. In his series on the world of the *kabuki* theatre he strove for portrait likenesses, unlike the conventional Torii school, whom he rapidly surpassed. Such likenesses only became possible with the advent of *nishiki-e*. Like Bunchō, he attached great importance to the depiction of facial expression and character, so that the public could recognize the actor without reading the accompanying inscription. After Sharaku and Kiyonobu, he is the leading master of the actor portrait. His *yaskusha-e* in the narrow *hosoban* format could often be combined into multi-sheet series, giving magnificent expression to the whole breadth of the stage. After 1770 he also produced numerous book illustrations, in part in collaboration with Bunchō and Shigemasa. Later still, he inter-

ested himself particularly in the portrayal of beautiful women from every social class going about their everyday activities; he did so in his own elegant and sometimes humorous way. Shunshō was the founder of the realistic Katsugawa school, and thereby gave a new impulse to its style. Among his pupils were Shunjō, Shunkō, Shūn'ei, Shunchō, and, not least, Hokusai.
ILLUSTRATIONS: pp. 80–82

Okumura TOSHINOBU

Active *c.* 1717– *c.* 1750, chiefly 1723–1728. Toshinobu was a pupil of Okumura Masanobu, who may possibly have adopted him as his son. Alongside book illustrations, his main output was of narrow one to three-figure hand-coloured lacquer pictures, portraying female beauties or actors in their stage roles. These pictures are both lively and harmonious and are distinguished by a rhythmic flow of line in the sitter's garments, doing full justice to Toshinobu's master.
ILLUSTRATIONS: pp. 46, 47

Utagawa TOYOHARU

1735–1814. Toyoharu studied in Kyoto under the Kanō painter Tsuruzawa Tangei. Around 1763 he moved to Edo, and studied under Shigenaga and Sekien, but was also influenced by Toyonobu. He came to public attention as the founder of the Utagawa school and as the teacher of Toyokuni and Toyohiro. His early prints, dating from 1768/69, are in the style of Harunobu, but reveal an almost fragile delicacy. Toyoharu's most important achievement was to develop the technique of perspective introduced in *uki-e* by Okumura Masanobu; this he did by studying Western painting, the influence of which is clearly apparent in his landscapes and townscapes. From him, a direct line runs all the way to Hokusai and Hiroshige, who were active towards the end of the Edo period. After 1799, he only painted posters for the theatre and for puppet shows.
ILLUSTRATIONS: pp. 88, 89

Utagawa TOYOHIRO

1773–1828. Toyohiro was originally a musician, but learned to paint in the Kanō style and from *c.* 1782 was a pupil of Toyoharu in Edo. Works by him are known dating from about 1790 on; from 1810 he worked mainly as a book illustrator. His speciality was *bijin-ga*. Among his numerous pupils were Toyokiyo, Toyokuma, Hironobu and above all Hiroshige, who adopted the style of his tranquil landscapes.
ILLUSTRATION: p. 145

Utagawa TOYOKUNI

1769–1825, active 1788–1824. The son of a puppet-maker, Toyokuni was a pupil of Toyoharu in Edo in 1782/83. From 1786 he was active as an illustrator of popular novels and short stories. His first published pictures were of female beauties, but later he concentrated on actor portraits. His famous series "Yakusha butai no sugata-e" (Pictures of Actors on the Stage), published between 1794 and 1796, was an immediate success with the public, thanks to its vigorous draughtsmanship and limpid coloration. Although Toyokuni was certainly one of the least original of the great masters, and borrowed from almost all of his famous contemporaries (for example Kiyonaga, Shigemasu, Eishi, Sharaku and Utamaro), he nevertheless assumed, after Sharaku's brief spell in the limelight, the leading role among the exponents of *yakusha-e*. At the same time he succeeded in displacing the Torii and Katsugawa schools from their predominant position in this genre and giving the Utagawa school a monopoly status which it enjoyed throughout the 19th century. His numerous pupils included Toyohiro, Kunimasa, Kunisada and Kuniyoshi.

ILLUSTRATIONS: pp. 21, 132–134

Ishikawa TOYONOBU

1711–1785. Active in Edo, Toyonobu is thought to have been a member of a vassal family of the Hojo clan. In 1744 he married into an innkeeping business, the management of which he assumed in 1757, thus bringing his career as an artist to an end. Toyonobu studied under Shigenaga, to whom he is no less indebted than to Masanobu. Before the advent of the polychrome print, he worked as a painter of *bijin-ga*. Publication of Toyonobu's prints started in 1731; they are characterized by an elegant line and technical perfection. Love scenes, courtesan portraits, actors and puppeteers constitute his motifs. His depiction of well-rounded female forms influenced Harunobu, while the ostentatious indifference of his sitters is reminiscent of the Kaigetsudō school. Like Shigenaga, he experimented with the depiction of the naked body, a thoroughly unerotic attempt to challenge the dominance of the *kimono* in the portrayal of feminine beauty.

ILLUSTRATIONS: pp. 16, 53–55

Kitagawa UTAMARO

1753–1806, active 1775–1806. Due not least to the sheer volume and versatility of his work, Utamaro is considered by many connoisseurs to be the most important master of the Japanese woodblock print, which he might well be said to have perfected. After his father's death, Utamaro moved from Musashi province to Edo, where in 1775 he joined the studio of the townscape painter Sekien, who may have been a relation. He remained there for seven years. At first he produced illustrations for plays and poems, before going on to actor portraits in the style of Shunshō. His brilliant talents were recognized by the leading publisher Tsutaya Jūzaburō, who in 1780 took him into his house, located at the entrance to Yoshiwara, which became a rendezvous for artists and poets. In 1782 Utamaro accepted a permanent contract from Jūzaburō, and adopted the name under which he would become famous. Of his contemporaries, he was influenced most of all by Kiyonaga, whose graceful and elegant female type he adopted and provided with a touch of eroticism and feminine psychology; other influences included Masanobu, Shunshō and Shigemasa. By the 1790s his style was fully formed, and with his *bijin-ga* he dominated the field of *ukiyo-e*. His special distinguishing features are his compositional skill and his easy command of technique, as can be seen, for example, in the combination of different printing processes, in relief printing and in the use of silver and gold powder, along with his subtle sense of colour with all its wealth of nuance. No other master of *ukiyo-e* devoted himself so consistently and with such success to the portrayal of beautiful women as did Utamaro. Outstanding examples of his work are his masterly portraits of the famous courtesans and demi-mondaines of Yoshiwara, who, through him, have become immortal. These pictures, which revere an ultra-slim, graceful and elegant female type, her garments wrapped carelessly about her, and yet which are also designed to convey the inner beauty of the sitter, were being exported even during his lifetime to China and, secretly, to Europe. Utamaro's predilection was for the use of bright, fresh colours, often on a mica-dust background, and strewn with gold dust or powdered mother-of-pearl. His favourite motifs were women at their everyday business, making themselves up, bathing, arranging their hair, walking in the garden, together with mothers with children, children's games, courtesans from the pleasure district, and pairs of lovers. In addition, he produced numerous albums, including magnificent biology books with plates of insects, shellfish, plants, birds and landscapes. His output also extended to mythology, genre scenes and numerous erotic prints, both single sheets and albums. His pillow-book "E-hon Utamakura", dating from 1788, is the most perfect and sophisticated work of erotic art ever produced in Japan. Shortly before his death Utamaro came into conflict with the censor as a result of a triptych published in 1804, whose historical motifs were suspected of satirizing life at the shōgun's court. For Utamaro the upshot was fifty day's house arrest in handcuffs. Alongside Hokusai, Utamaro was one of the first Japanese artists to become known in Europe. Toulouse-Lautrec was one of his admirers. In 1891, Edmond de Goncourt in Paris published the first biography of him.

ILLUSTRATIONS: pp. 19, 28, 99–109

Ingo F. Walther

Acknowledgements and Bibliography

The woodblock colour prints reproduced in this volume are all in the Riccar Art Museum in Tokyo. The editor and publisher wish to thank the museum and its curator, Mr Mitsunobu Satō, for their kind assistance. Since its recent move to a new building, the museum is now known as the Hirako Ukiyo-e Museum. The museum's collection includes works from the whole *ukiyo-e* period. Among its treasures are numerous prints bearing the appellation of "Japanese National Treasure" or "Major National Cultural Heritage Item", classifications reserved for only the rarest and most important works of art. The museum originally consisted of the Namiki Collection built up by Hiraki Shinji, which was later enlarged by the addition of the famous Matsukata, Mihara and Saiti Collections. The total collection was taken over by the Hiraki Ukiyo-e Foundation, which was set up in 1972, and merged with the Hiraki Collection to form a total of some 5000 items for Japan's first *ukiyo-e* museum.

BIBLIOGRAPHY

Bachofer, Ludwig: Die Kunst der japanischen Holzschnittmeister. Munich 1922

Beurdeley, Michel et al.: Le chant de l'oreiller. L'art d'aimer au Japon. Paris 1973

Binyon, Laurence and J. J. O'Brien Sexton: Japanese Colour-Prints. London 1923, 1954, 1960

Brown, L. N.: Block Printing and Book Illustration in Japan. London 1964

Chiba, Reiko: The Making of a Japanese Print. Tokyo 1972

Chibett, D. G.: The History of Japanese Printing and Book-Illustration. Tokyo and Palo Alto 1977

Clavery, Edouard: L'art des estampes japonais en couleurs. Paris 1935

Crighton, R. A. (ed.): The Floating World of Japanese Popular Prints: 1700–1900. Victoria and Albert Museum. London 1973 (catalogue)

Dawes, Leonhard G.: Japanese Illustrated Books. London 1972

Evans, Tom and Mary Anne: Shunga. The Art of Love in Japan. London 1975

Fenollosa, Ernest F.: Epochs of Chinese and Japanese Art. 2 vols. New York and London 1912, 1921

Fujikake, Shizuya: Japanese Wood-Block Prints. Tokyo 1928, 1959

Gentles, Margaret: Masters of the Japanese Print: Moronobu to Utamaro. New York 1964

Gookin, Frederick William: Japanese Color-Prints and Their Designers. New York 1913

Hájek, Lubor: Der frühe japanische Holzschnitt. Prague 1959

Halford, G. M. and A. S.: The Kabuki Handbook. Rutland (Vermont) and Tokyo 1956

Hempel, Rose: Japanische Holzschnitte. Stuttgart 1963

Hillier, Jack: Die Meister des japanischen Farbendruckes. Cologne 1954

Hillier, Jack: The Japanese Print. A New Approach. London and Tokyo 1960

Illing, R.: Japanese Prints. London 1977

Keyes, Roger S.: The Male Journey in Japanese Prints. The Fine Arts Museums of San Francisco. Berkeley, Los Angeles and London 1989 (catalogue)

Kurth, Julius: Der japanische Holzschnitt. Munich 1911, 1922

Kurt, Julius: Die Primitiven des Japanholzschnitts. Dresden 1922

Kurth, Julius: Die Geschichte des japanischen Holzschnitts. 3 vols. Leipzig 1925–1929

Lane, Richard: Japanische Holzschnitte. Munich and Zurich 1962

Lane, Richard: Images from the Floating World. The Japanese Print. London 1978

Masterworks of Ukiyoe-e. 11 vols. Tokyo 1968–1970

Michener, James A.: The Floating World: The Story of Japanese Prints. London, New York and Toronto 1954

Michener, James A. and Richard Lane: Japanische Holzschnitte. Fribourg and Munich 1961

Mogeon, Gaston: L'estampe japonais. 2 vols. Paris 1923

Mørrison, Arthur: The Painters of Japan. 2 vols. London 1911

Rumpf, Fritz: Meister des japanischen Farbenholzschnittes. Berlin and Leipzig 1924

Seidlitz, W. von: Geschichte des japanischen Farbenholzschnittes. Dresden 1897, 1928

Shibui, Kiyoshi: Estampes érotiques primitives du Japon. 2 vols. Tokyo 1928

Stern, Harold P.: Master Prints of Japan. New York 1968

Stern, Harold P.: Ukiyo-e Painting. Washington 1973

Stewart, B.: Subjects Portrayed in Japanese Colour Prints. London 1922

Turk, Frank A.: The Prints of Japan. London and New York 1966

Takahashi, S.: The Evolution of Ukiyo-e. Yokohama 1955

Winzinger, Franz: Die Kunst der japanischen Holzschnittmeister. Graphische Sammlung Albertina, Vienna, and Germanisches Nationalmuseum, Nuremberg. Nuremberg 1972 (catalogue)

Winzinger, Franz: Meisterwerke des japanischen Farbenholzschnitts, XI. (Publication of the Albertina, Vienna). Graz 1975

Winzinger Franz (ed.): Meisterwerke der erotischen Kunst Japans. Albrecht Dürer Gesellschaft. Nuremberg 1975 (catalogue)

Winzinger, Franz (ed.): Meisterwerke der erotischen Kunst Japans. Munich 1977

(Considerations of space prevent the extremely comprehensive literature on the subject in Japanese being listed in this select bibliography.)